MAINTENANCE MANUAL
AND INSTRUCTION BOOK

for

MATCHLESS
1955

SINGLE CYLINDER MOTOR CYCLES

Compiled and Issued by the Manufacturers:

MATCHLESS MOTOR CYCLES
(Proprietors: ASSOCIATED MOTOR CYCLES LIMITED)

Registered Offices:

PLUMSTEAD ROAD, PLUMSTEAD
LONDON, S.E.18 .. ENGLAND

Nearest Station:
WOOLWICH ARSENAL
(Southern Region Railway)

Factories:
BURRAGE GROVE and **MAXEY ROAD**
PLUMSTEAD, S.E.18

Telegrams and Cables: "MATCHLESS, WOL-LONDON"
Telephone: WOOlwich 1223 (7 Lines)
Codes: A.B.C. 5th and 6th Edition; Bentley's; and Private Codes

All correspondence to:
MATCHLESS MOTOR CYCLES, PLUMSTEAD ROAD, LONDON, S.E.18

Price: TWO SHILLINGS and SIXPENCE

PREFACE

TRADEMARKS & COPYRIGHT

A.J.S. & Matchless® are registered trademarks of AMC Ltd. (Associated Motor Cycles Ltd.). This publication is not sponsored by or endorsed by the trademark owner. We recognize that some words, model names and designations, for example, mentioned herein are the property of the trademark holder. We use them for identification purposes only. This is not an official publication however; it may include non-copyright works of the trademark holder.

INTRODUCTION

Welcome to the world of digital publishing ~ the book you now hold in your hand was printed using the latest state of the art digital technology. The advent of print-on-demand has forever changed the publishing process, never has information been so accessible and it is our hope that this book serves your informational needs for years to come. If this is your first exposure to digital publishing, we hope that you are pleased with the results. Many more titles of interest to the classic automobile and motorcycle enthusiast, collector and restorer are available via our website at www.VelocePress.com. We hope that you find this title as interesting as we do.

NOTE FROM THE PUBLISHER

The information presented is true and complete to the best of our knowledge. All recommendations are made without any guarantees on the part of the author or the publisher, who also disclaim all liability incurred with the use of this information.

INFORMATION ON THE USE OF THIS PUBLICATION

This manual is an invaluable resource for those interested in performing their own maintenance. However, in today's information age we are constantly subject to changes in common practice, new technology, availability of improved materials and increased awareness of chemical toxicity. As such, it is advised that the user consult with an experienced professional prior to undertaking any procedure described herein. While every care has been taken to ensure correctness of information, it is obviously not possible to guarantee complete freedom from errors or omissions or to accept liability arising from such errors or omissions. Therefore, any individual that uses the information contained within, or elects to perform or participate in do-it-yourself repairs or modifications acknowledges that there is a risk factor involved and that the publisher or its associates cannot be held responsible for personal injury or property damage resulting from the use of the information or the outcome of such procedures.

WARNING!

One final word of advice, this publication is intended to be used as a reference guide, and when in doubt the reader should consult with a qualified technician.

INDEX

	Page
Carburetter Service	38
Controls	7
Data	4 to 6
Driving	9
Electrical Service	75
Engine Service	25
Free Service	24
Fork and Frame Service	51
Guarantee	87
Introduction	3
Lubrication	14
Lubrication Chart	21
Maintenance	22
Service	85
Rear teledraulic legs	57
Repairs and Service	84
The Law	86
Tools and Special Equipment	88
Transmission Service	41
Useful Information	72
Wheels and Brakes	61
Tyres and Service	70

SPARES AND SERVICE DEPARTMENTS

HOURS OF BUSINESS FOR CALLERS

MONDAYS	8.30 a.m. to 12.55 p.m.
	2.0 p.m to 5.30 p.m.
TUESDAYS	Ditto
WEDNESDAYS	Ditto
THURSDAYS	Ditto
FRIDAYS	Ditto

NOT OPEN ON NATIONAL HOLIDAYS

1955 MATCHLESS MODELS

350 MODEL G3L RIGID FRAME (TOURING)
350 MODEL G3LS SPRING FRAME (TOURING)
350 MODEL G3LC RIGID FRAME (COMPETITION)
350 MODEL G3LCS SPRING FRAME (COMPETITION)

500 MODEL G80 RIGID FRAME (TOURING)
500 MODEL G80S SPRING FRAME (TOURING)
500 MODEL G80C RIGID FRAME (COMPETITION)
500 MODEL G80CS SPRING FRAME (COMPETITION)

G3L and G80 Rigid Frame

G3LS and G80S Spring Frame

INTRODUCTION

The modern motor cycle unquestionably provides one of the most healthy, economical and pleasant means of transport. In addition by reason of its superb braking, high power to weight ratio and ease of control it is, if used with due care one of the safest vehicles on the road.

It is our sincere desire that every owner should obtain from his mount the service, comfort and innumerable miles of low cost travel that we have earnestly endeavoured to build into it.

It must be borne in mind however, that although of simple design and construction, it is nevertheless a highly specialised piece of engineering and must in consequence be intelligently and efficiently maintained in order to provide unfailing reliability.

In this book we provide non-technical instructions for carrying out all the maintenance operations likely to be called for in normal service, together with assisting illustrations.

To owners of long experience we tender apologies for the elementary nature of some of the contents of this handbook, but owners whether novice or expert are advised to read the contents from beginning to end.

We are at all times pleased to give owners the full benefit of our wide experience in matters relating to motor cycles of our manufacture and elsewhere will be found details of the particulars required when making enquiries of our Service Department.

ASSOCIATED MOTOR CYCLES

Safety on the Road

In the interest of Safety on the Road a few words of warning are perhaps not out of place here.

The outstanding manœuverability of a motor cycle over all other vehicles on the road makes it necessary to exercise caution at all times.

There are unfortunately a few motor-cyclists whose reckless driving constitutes a menace not only to themselves but also to other road users resulting in the totally false impression in some quarters that motorcycling is a dangerous pastime.

Take a pride in your riding technique and never rely upon the other fellow doing the right thing.

Your example of careful, courteous and unobtrusive riding will materially contribute to road safety and to the reputation of a fine sporting pastime.

DATA

Identity

Engine Number	Stamped on left hand side of crankcase
Frame Number	Stamped on seat lug of main frame, on right hand side (below the saddle
Bore	350 c.c. Models—2·7187 in. ($2\frac{23}{32}$ in.
	500 c.c. Models—3·250 in. ($3\frac{1}{4}$ in.
Stroke	All Models—93 mm. (3·65625 in.)
Engine capacity, in cubic centimetres	350 Models—55/16M, 55/16MS, 55/16MC and 55/16MCS—347
	500 Models—55/18, 55/18S, 55/18C and 55/18CS—498

Capacities

Location		British	Metric
Engine	350 c.c.	21·170 cub. in.	347 c.c.
Engine	500 c.c.	30·380 cub. in.	498 c.c.
Gear box		1 pint	568·2 c.c.
Front fork (each side)		$6\frac{1}{2}$ fl. ozs.	184·6 c.c.
Rear leg (each leg)*		3 fl. ozs.	85 c.c.
Rear wheel fork hinge bearing*		$1\frac{1}{2}$ fl. ozs.	42·6 c.c.
Fuel Tank (all except Competition)		$3\frac{3}{4}$ gallons	17·04 litres
Fuel tank (Competition)		$2\frac{1}{4}$ gallons	10·2285 litres
Oil tank (to top level mark)		$4\frac{1}{2}$ pints	2·557 litres

*On Spring Frame Models only.

Carburetter (Touring and Rigid Frame Competition Models only)

	350 c.c.	500 c.c.
Type	Monobloc 376/5	Monobloc 389/1
Main jet	376/100 size 210	376/100 size 260
Pilot jet	376/076 size 30	376/076 size 30
Throttle valve	376/060 size 3	389/060 size 3
Choke size	1·1/16"	1·5/32"
Needle position	Central notch	Central notch
Needle jet	376/072 size ·1065	376/072 size ·1065

NOTE—
Early 1955 Models 500 c.c. up to Engine No. 27,000 are fitted with type Monobloc 376/14 carburetters with main jet size 240, throttle valve 376/060 size 3 and needle position 2nd notch from top.

All Spring Frame Competition Models are fitted with T.T. type carburetters.

Compression ratios

Model	Normal ratio	High ratio
350	6·53 to 1	According to piston.
500	6·26 to 1	See Spares List for ratios available.

Gear box ratios

Model	First gear	Second gear	Third gear	Fourth gear (top)
Touring	2·65 to 1	1·70 to 1	1·308 to 1	1 to 1
Competition (Rigid)	3·199 to 1	2·437 to 1	1·575 to 1	1 to 1
Competition (Spring)	2·65 to 1	1·70 to 1	1·308 to 1	1 to 1

Gear ratios, Touring (Rigid and Spring Frame) and Spring Frame Competition Models

Engine sprocket size	First gear	Second gear	Third gear	Fourth gear (top)
15 teeth	18·55 to 1	11·90 to 1	9·15 to 1	7 to 1
(c) 16 teeth	17·32 to 1	11·15 to 1	8·58 to 1	6·56 to 1
17 teeth	16·32 to 1	10·47 to 1	8·05 to 1	6·16 to 1
(a) 18 teeth	15·44 to 1	9·90 to 1	7·63 to 1	5·83 to 1
19 teeth	14·55 to 1	9·33 to 1	7·18 to 1	5·49 to 1
20 teeth	13·91 to 1	8·91 to 1	6·86 to 1	5·25 to 1
(b) 21 teeth	13·25 to 1	8·50 to 1	6·54 to 1	5·0 to 1

(a) Standard for 350 c.c. Touring Models and 500 c.c. Spring Frame Competition Models.
(b) Standard for 500 c.c. Touring Models.
(c) Standard for 350 c.c. Spring Frame Competition Models.

Gear ratios, Competition Rigid Frame Models

Engine sprocket size	First gear	Second gear	Third gear	Fourth gear (top)
15 teeth	22·4 to 1	17·25 to 1	11·03 to 1	7 to 1
(a) 16 teeth	21·0 to 1	15·98 to 1	10·33 to 1	6·56 to 1
17 teeth	19·7 to 1	15·0 to 1	9·7 to 1	6·16 to 1
(b) 18 teeth	18·68 to 1	14·2 to 1	9·2 to 1	5·83 to 1
19 teeth	17·57 to 1	13·38 to 1	8·65 to 1	5·49 to 1
20 teeth	16·8 to 1	12·8 to 1	8·37 to 1	5·25 to 1
21 teeth	16·0 to 1	12·18 to 1	7·81 to 1	5·0 to 1

(a) Standard for 350 c.c. Models.
(b) Standard for 500 c.c. Models.

Ignition (magneto)

Model	Make	Type	Rotation	Point gap	Ignition point before top dead centre (with control in fully advanced position)
Touring 350 c.c.	Lucas	SR-1	Anti-clock	·012 in.	Normal 39°—½"
Touring 500 c.c.	Lucas	SR-1	Anti-clock	·012 in.	Normal 39°—½"
All Competition	Lucas	NR-1	Anti-clock	·012 in.	Normal 39°—½"

Lighting (bulbs)

Location	Type	Voltage	Wattage	Part number
Head lamp (Pre-focus)	Double filament	6	30×24	312
Pilot lamps	Single contact	6	3	988
Rear lamp	Double filament	6	18 & 3	352
Speedometer	Single contact	6	1·8	53205

Oversize parts

The following are the only "oversize" variations provided for the 350 and 500 c.c. Single Cylinder machines.

Big-end rollers :
    ·001 in. oversize

Cylinder re-bore :
    ·020 in. and ·040 in. oversize

Pistons and rings :
    ·020 in. and ·040 in. oversize

Pistons (standard size)

Model	Top of skirt diameter	Front to rear clearance	Part number
350	2·7176 in.	·001 in.	013504
500	3·2490 in.	·001 in.	013505

All above measurements are subject to a toleration limit of + or − ·0005 in.

Piston rings

Piston ring gap—Normal	·006 in.
Permissible maximum	·030 in.
Piston ring clearance in groove	·002 in.

Sparking Plug

Model	Make	Type	Thread	Reach	Point gap
All	K.L.G.	FE80	14 mm.	$\frac{3}{4}$ in.	·020 to ·022 in.

Valve timing

All timing gears are marked for ease of setting. (See Illustration 10)

With Marks coinciding correct timing is assured.

Valve Guide Projection (Top of Guide to Boss)

Inlet—$\frac{1}{2}''$ Exhaust—$\frac{1}{2}''$

Valve timing pinion

Retained by nut, threaded $\frac{7}{16}$ in. by 26 threads per in. Left hand thread. Part number 000221.

Weight

Weight of machine with empty tanks

Model	Standard Rigid frame	Spring frame	Competition Rigid frame
350	344 lbs.	375 lbs.	300 lbs.
500	353 lbs.	386 lbs.	303 lbs.

Wheels (bearing end play)

Bearing end play   ·002 in. (just a perceptible rim rock).

CONTROLS

(1) **Throttle twist grip.** On right handlebar. Twist inwards to open. When fully closed engine should just idle when hot.

(2) **Air lever.** Small lever on right handlebar. Pull inwards to increase air supply to carburetter. Once set, when engine has warmed up, requires no alteration for different road speeds. Should be fully closed when starting engine from cold.

(3) **Ignition lever.** When fitted, Small lever on left handlebar. Advances and retards ignition point. Pull inwards to retard. Retard two-fifths of total movement for starting. (Only used on Competition Models).

(4) **Valve lifter lever.** Small lever close to clutch lever. Lifts exhaust valve from seat, releasing compression in combustion chamber, enabling engine to be easily rotated for starting. Also used for stopping engine if throttle stop is set as advised above.

(5) **Clutch lever.** Large lever on left handlebar. Grip to release clutch so that drive to rear wheel is disconnected.

(6) **Front brake lever.** Large lever on right handlebar. Grip to operate front wheel brake and, for normal braking, use in conjunction with rear brake application.

(7) **Rear brake lever.** Pedal close to left side foot rest. Depress with left foot to apply rear brake. Apply gently and use increasing pressure as the road speed decreases.

(8) **Gear change lever.** Pedal in horizontal position close to right foot rest. Controls selection of the four speeds, or ratios, between engine and rear wheel revolutions, with a " free," or neutral, position. See illustration 2.

(9) **Kick-starter lever.** Vertical pedal on right hand side of gear box.

(10) **Lighting switch.** In top of head lamp. Controls lamps by a rotating lever which has three positions :
    (1) " OFF " Lamps not on.
    (2) " L " Pilot lamps, rear lamp and speedometer lamp on.
    (3) " H " Main head lamp, rear lamp and speedometer lamp on.

(11) **Ammeter.** In top of head lamp. Indicates flow of electric current, in, or out, of battery. (" Charge " or " Discharge.")

(12) **Horn switch.** Press switch on right handlebar.

(13) **Gear box filler cap.** Located on top edge of kick-starter case cover. Allows insertion of lubricant and access to clutch inner wire and internal clutch operating lever.

(14) **Footrest for rider.**

(15) **Petrol tank filler cap.** Located in top of fuel tank. To release, slightly depress, turn fully to the left, and then lift away. There are two locking positions. The middle position, between the fully tightened down and " lift away " positions, is in the nature of a " safety " device to prevent loss that might be occasioned by unauthorised meddling.

(16) **Oil tank filler cap.** Located on top edge of oil tank. The construction and operation is exactly as the petrol tank filler cap.

(17) **Dipping switch.** Trigger switch on left handlebar. Used to select normal or " dipped " beam of head lamp when main lighting switch lever is in the " H " position. (The main head lamp bulb has two filaments.)

If any adjustment is made to the rear brake pedal make certain the brake does not bind and also see there is not excessive free pedal movement before the brake comes "on."

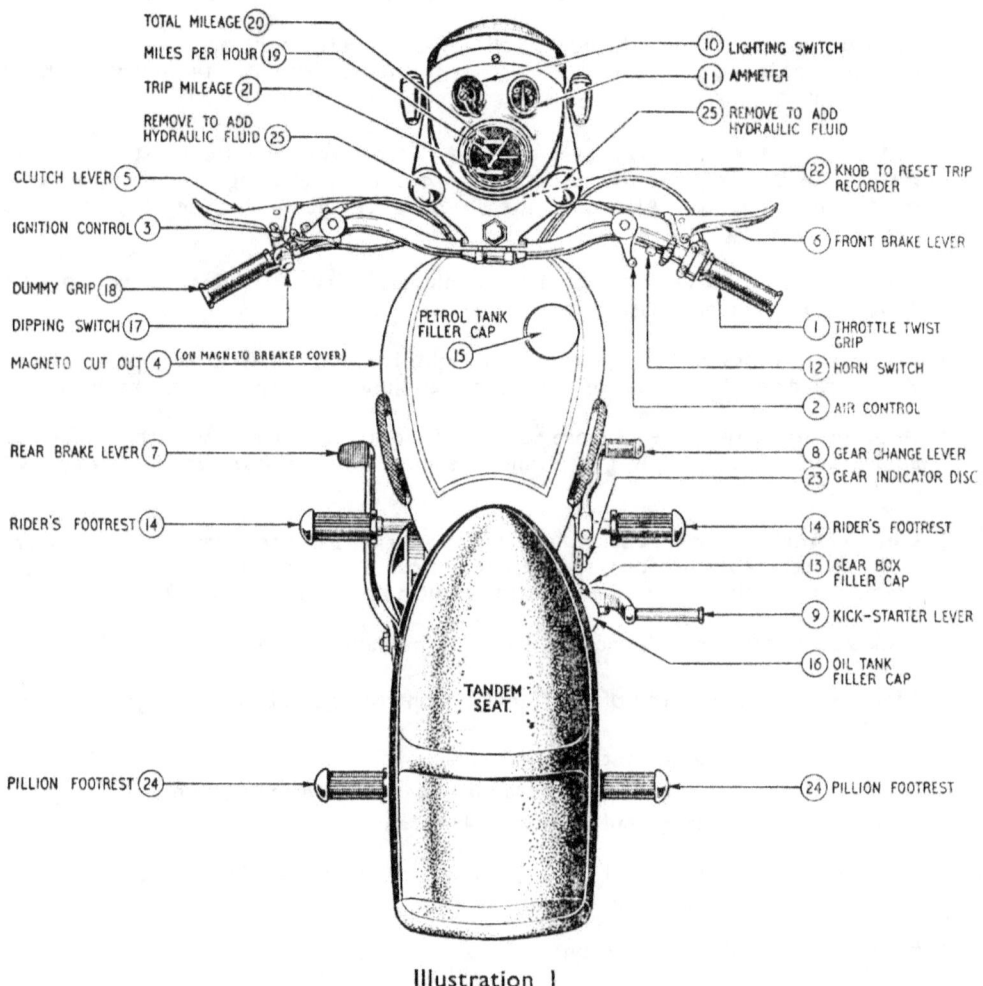

Illustration 1

Showing Controls

Before using the machine, sit on the saddle and become familiar with the position and operation of the various controls. Pay particular attention to the gear positions.

DRIVING

FUEL

Although various quality fuels are again available owners are advised to use only the best. The small economy that might be considered to accrue by using the cheaper grades is more than offset by the advantages obtained by using only Number One Grades.

FUEL SUPPLY

Two fuel feed taps are situated underneath the rear end of the petrol tank. (One each side.) Both must be shut off when the machine is left standing for more than a few minutes.

The tap plungers work horizontally. To open, pull plunger out. Push right in to close.

Normally, only use the tap on the right hand side of the machine and then the other side will act as a reserve supply. Always re-fuel as soon as possible after being forced to call upon the reserve (approx. $\frac{1}{2}$ gallon), and then, at once, close the " reserve " tap.

It will be noted that, by fitting two petrol feed taps, it is possible to remove the petrol tank from the machine without the necessity of first draining it of fuel.

STARTING THE ENGINE FROM COLD

(a) See that there is sufficient fuel in the petrol tank.

(b) See that there is sufficient oil in the oil tank.

(c) See that the gear pedal is in the neutral position.

(d) Pull outward the plunger of off-side petrol tap.

(e) See that the air control lever is in the fully closed position.

(f) Open the throttle not more than one-sixth of the total movement of the twist grip.

(g) Depress the plunger on the top of the carburetter float chamber until it can be felt the chamber is full of petrol.

(h) Raise the valve lifter lever and, while keeping it raised, turn over the engine several times by depressing the kick-starter pedal, three times, the object being to free the engine. (This only applies if the engine is cold.)

(i) Depress the kick-starter until compression is felt, then raise the valve lifter lever and ease the engine just over compression. Then, after allowing the kick-starter pedal to return nearly to its normal position, give it a long swinging kick with the valve closed. Flywheel momentum will carry over compression and the engine should fire immediately. If it fails to do so repeat exactly the same process.

Do not allow kick starter to return violently against its stop.

The kick-starter mechanism must be allowed to engage properly before putting heavy pressure on the kick-starter crank pedal pin. That means there are two definite and separate movements when operating the mechanism by depressing the crank.

The first is a slow and gentle movement which ends when it is felt the quadrant has engaged with the teeth on the ratchet pinion.

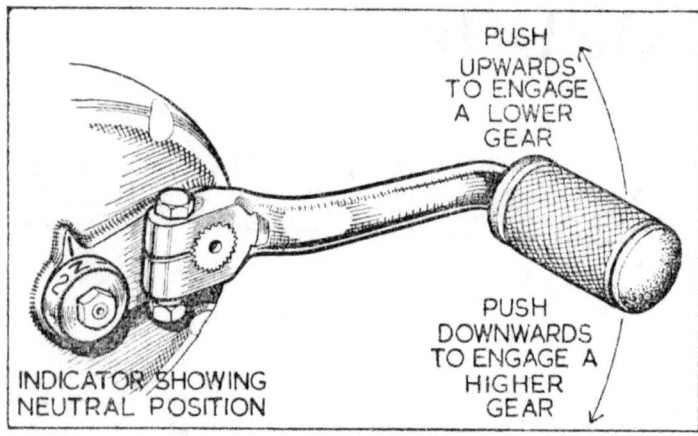

Illustration 2

Showing the gear indicator drum which upon assembly is set to record the various gears and neutral position, as the respective figure or letter N registers with index mark on the gear box shell.

Upon re-asembly, after dismantling for any purpose, the index disc should be correctly re-set for future reference.

The first slow and gentle movement is essential to avoid damage to the teeth of the kick-starter quadrant.

After the engine has started, slowly open the air lever until it runs evenly. Then set the throttle so that the engine is running at a moderate speed (neither racing nor ticking over) and allow to warm up. While doing this, check the oil circulation as detailed in page 13. The machine can then be taken on the road.

NOTE—Do not race up the engine from cold and do not flood the carburetter to such an extent that petrol is dripping because then, in the event of a backfire, there is a danger of such loose petrol igniting. This cannot possibly happen if the starting instructions are carefully followed, but, in the event of a fire, there is no cause for panic. Merely turn off the petrol tap to isolate the main supply, open wide the throttle and turn over the engine by operating the kick-starter pedal when suction will extinguish the fire.

STOPPING THE ENGINE

To stop the engine, close the throttle, raise the valve lifter lever and keep it raised until the engine has ceased to revolve.

ON THE ROAD

Having started and warmed up the engine, take the machine off the stand, sit astride it, free the clutch by pulling up the large lever on the left bar and engage the lowest gear. Next, slowly release the clutch lever and the machine will commence to move forward. As it does this, the engine speed will tend to drop as it picks up the load so it will be necessary to increase the throttle opening, gradually, to keep the engine speed gently rising.

When well under way, disengage the clutch, slightly close the throttle, engage second gear and release the clutch lever, then open up the throttle to increase the speed of the machine. Repeat these operations in order to engage third and top gears.

To engage a higher gear the pedal is pressed downward with the toe and a lower gear is obtained by raising the pedal with the instep. To engage first gear from the neutral position, the pedal is therefore raised. After each pedal movement, internal springs return the pedal to its normal horizontal position.

The pedal must be moved to the full extent of its travel when selecting a gear, either up or down. It must not be "stamped down" or jabbed, but firmly and decisively moved till it stops. A half-hearted movement may not give full engagement. Keep the foot off the pedal when driving and between each gear change because, unless the lever can freely return to its normal central position, the next gear cannot be engaged.

STOPPING THE MACHINE

To stop the machine, close the throttle, declutch by lifting the large lever on the left handlebar, and gently apply both brakes, increasing the pressure on them as the road speed of the machine decreases. Place the gear change foot pedal in the neutral position and stop the engine.

Before leaving the machine, turn off the fuel supply.

IMPORTANT NOTICE

NEVER DRIVE AWAY AT **HIGH SPEED** WHEN STARTING A RUN WITH A **COLD** ENGINE. **GIVE** THE OIL **A CHANCE** TO WARM UP AND THIN OUT, **PARTICULARLY** WHEN THE MACHINE IS **COLD.** UNTIL THE OIL REACHES ITS **NORMAL RUNNING TEMPERATURE** THE CIRCULATION IS RESTRICTED. **SEIZURES** CAN BE **AVOIDED** BY TAKING THIS SIMPLE ESSENTIAL PRECAUTION.

RUNNING IN

Although it is customary to quote permitted maximum speeds on the various gears during the period of running in, these are really no guide to overdriving, the only essential thing to avoid being the use of large throttle opening.

If the precaution is taken of limiting the use of the throttle to about one-third of its opening during the first 1,000 miles, irrespective of the road speed, and whether on the level or climbing, the necessary conditions for running in will have been observed.

Special attention must be given, during the running in period, to such details as valve rocker adjustment, chains, brakes, contact breaker points, and steering head bearings, all of which tend to bed down in the first hundred miles or so. Particular note must be made of the adjustment of steering head bearings, which, if run in a slack condition, will be quickly ruined. After this bedding down process has taken place, adjustments to such details will only be necessary at lengthy intervals.

After about 1,000 miles have been covered larger throttle openings may be gradually indulged in for short bursts only.

Until at least 2,000 miles have been covered the owner of a new machine is strongly advised to curb his natural desire to learn the mount's maximum capabilities. Restraint in this direction will be amply repaid later.

NOTES ON DRIVING

If, at first, the lowest gear will not engage, release the clutch lever and after a second or two, make another attempt. This condition may exist in a new machine, but it tends to disappear after a little use.

Always endeavour to make the movements of hand (on the clutch) and foot (on the gear pedal) as simultaneous as possible, and remember, in all gear changes, a steady pressure of the foot is desirable. This pressure should be maintained until the clutch is fully released. It is not sufficient just to jab the foot pedal and then release the clutch lever. When actually in motion, it will be found sufficient to merely free the clutch a trifle, to ease the drive when changing gear and, with reasonable care, changes of gear then can be made without a sound.

Do not unnecessarily race the engine or let in the clutch sufficiently suddenly to cause the rear wheel to spin. Take a pride in making a smooth, silent get-away.

When changing up to a higher gear, as the clutch is freed, the throttle should be slightly closed so that the engine speed is reduced to keep in step with the higher gear ratio. Conversely, when changing down to a lower gear, the throttle should be regulated so that the engine speed is increased to keep in step with the lower gear ratio.

Do not slip the clutch to control the road speed.

The clutch is intended to be used only when starting from a standstill and when changing gear. It must **NOT** be operated to ease the engine, instead of changing gear, or be held out, in order to "free-wheel."

The exhaust valve lifter is **NOT** used in normal driving on main and secondary roads.

When travelling slowly, such as may occur in traffic or on a hill, and the engine commences to labour, it is then necessary to change to a lower gear. Engine "knocking" or "pinking" and a harshness in the transmission are symptoms of such labour. A good driver is able to sense such conditions and will make the change before the engine has reached the stage of distress. The gear box is provided to be used and consequently full use should be made of the intermediate gears to obtain effortless running and smooth hill climbing.

Keep the feet clear of the brake and gear pedals when not actually using them and keep the hand off the clutch lever when not in use.

Drive as much as possible on the throttle, making the minimum use of the brakes.

When using the machine on wet or greasy roads, it is generally better to apply **BOTH** brakes together, because sudden or harsh application of either brake only, under such conditions, may result in a skid.

In all conditions, it is advisable to make a habit of always using both brakes together rather than habitually using the rear brake and reserving the front brake for emergency.

CHECKING OIL CIRCULATION

Provision is made to observe the oil in circulation and it is advisable to do this before each run.

If the filler cap on the oil tank is removed the bent over end of the oil return pipe will be noticed some two inches below the level of the filler cap orifice and the returning oil can be seen running from it. This check should be made immediately after starting the engine from cold. This is because while the engine is stationary, oil from all parts of the interior of the engine drains back into the crankcase sump, so that, until this surplus is cleared, the return flow is very positive and continuous. Therefore, if the oil circulation is deranged, the fact is apparent at once by the lack of a steady return flow.

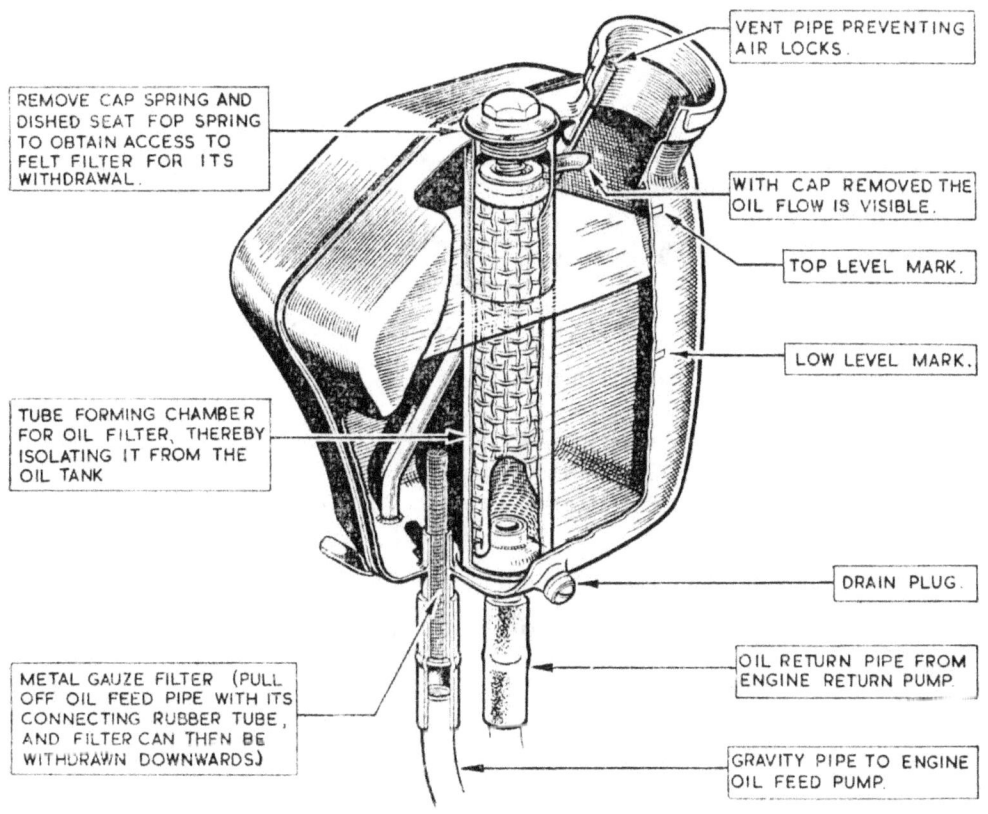

Illustration 3

Showing the oil tank with the felt filter in its cylindrical housing and the metal strainer mounted on the entry end of the feed pipe union. Also shows the direction of flow of oil from tank to engine and return flow from engine to tank via the small spout, located so that it can be inspected by removing the tank filler cap. An air vent pipe is provided to ensure freedom from air-locks.

LUBRICATION

LUBRICANTS TO USE

Efficient lubrication is of vital importance and it is false economy to use cheap oils and greases.

We recommend the following lubricants to use in machines of our make:

FOR ENGINE LUBRICATION

SUMMER		WINTER	
Mobiloil **D**	(SAE-50)	Mobiloil **A**	(SAE-30)
Castrol **Grand Prix**	(SAE-50)	Castrol **XL**	(SAE-30)
Energol 50	(SAE-50)	**Energol 30**	(SAE-30)
Essolube **50**	(SAE-50)	Essolube **30**	(SAE-30)
Shell Motor Oil X-100	(SAE-50)	Shell Motor Oil X-100	(SAE-40)

FOR GEAR BOX LUBRICATION

Mobiloil **D**	(SAE-50)
Castrol **Grand Prix**	(SAE-50)
Energol 50	(SAE-50)
Essolube **50**	(SAE-50)
Shell Motor Oil X-100	(SAE-50)

FOR HUB LUBRICATION AND ALL FRAME PARTS USING GREASE

Mobilgrease No. 4
Castrolease Heavy
Energrease C 3
Esso Pressure Gun Grease
Shell **Retinax** Grease **C.D.** or **A.**

FOR TELEDRAULIC FRONT FORKS AND TELEDRAULIC REAR LEGS

Mobiloil **Arctic**	(SAE-20)
Castrolite	(SAE-20)
Energol 20	(SAE-20)
Essolube **20**	(SAE-20)
Shell Motor Oil X-100	(SAE-20)

FOR REAR CHAINS

Mobilgrease No. 2
Esso Fluid Grease
Energol A.O.
Castrolease Grease Graphited

Heated Until Just Fluid

See Application Instructions, page 19

When buying oils and greases it is advisable to specify the **Brand** as well as the grade and, as an additional precaution, to buy only in sealed containers or from branded cabinets.

ENGINE LUBRICATION SYSTEM

This is by dry sump system. Oil feeds, by gravity, from the oil tank to the pump in the crankcase. The pump forces oil to various parts, which then drains to the bottom of crankcase sump. The pump then returns oil to the tank. This process is continuous while the engine is revolving. The pump is so designed that it has a greater capacity on the return side to that on the delivery side to ensure that all oil is extracted from the crankcase. A felt cartridge filter, in the oil tank, removes foreign matter collected by the oil in its passage through the engine. A metal gauze strainer is fitted to the oil feed pipe in the oil tank to prevent pieces of fluff, etc., which may find their way into the tank when replenishing, from entering the oil pump. (See Illustration 3.)

Felt filter and metal strainer should be cleaned in petrol each time the oil tank is drained.

ENGINE OIL PUMP

The pump has only one moving part. This is the plunger which revolves and reciprocates. Rotation is caused by the worm gear on the timing side flywheel axle. Reciprocation is caused by the guide pin which engages in the profiled groove cut on the plunger. Oil is fed to the pump through the lower of the two oil pipes between tank and crankcase and is returned through the upper pipe.

If, for any reason, the crankcase is dismantled **the oil pump plunger must be removed from its housing before attempting to separate the crankcase halves.** It is not necessary to remove the small timing pinion which will pass through in situ.

IMPORTANT

Under no circumstances should either the pump plunger or guide screw be disturbed in ordinary routine Maintenance.

ENGINE OIL CIRCULATION

The oil pump forces oil through :—

(a) Passages drilled through the timing side flywheel axle, timing side flywheel and crank pin to lubricate the timing side bearing and the big-end bearing. The splash passes to interior of cylinder, to lubricate the cylinder and piston, and then falls into the crankcase sump.

(b) A passage in crankcase, controlled by ball valve, direct to the cylinder, to assist in cylinder and piston lubrication and then falls into the crankcase sump.

(c) A passage in timing gear case where it " builds up " to a predetermined level to lubricate the timing gears and then overflows into the crankcase sump.

(d) Through a pipe from the front of oil pump housing to the rocker box by which all rocker gear and valve stems are lubricated and then falls through the push rod cover tubes and tappet guides to the timing gear case and, from there, drains into the crankcase sump, as detailed in Para. (c).

The oil pump extracts oil in the crankcase sump and returns it to oil tank. On its way it passes through the felt cartridge filter located in the oil tank.

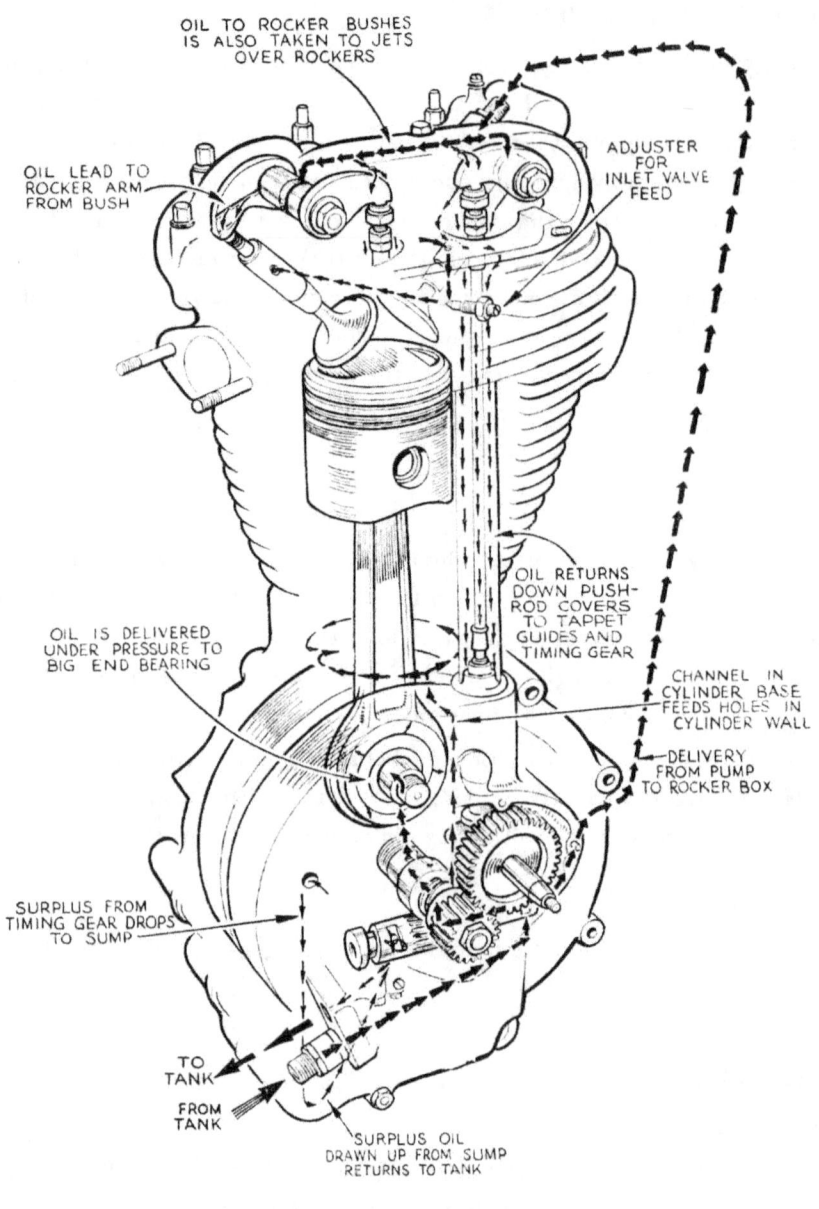

Illustration 4

Engine Oil Circulation

THE OIL TANK AND FILTERS

The level of oil in the supply tank should never be allowed to fall below the low level mark and, upon replenishment, should not be higher than the top level mark otherwise, when starting the engine, the bulk of oil in the crankcase sump may be greater than the space available in the tank.

The oil filter is made in cylindrical form of thick felt and is supported by a tubular wire cage. The felt is not detachable from the cage.

A metal gauze strainer is secured in the tank end of the feed pipe union.

After the first 500 miles, again at 1,000 miles, and subsequently at 5,000 mile intervals, it is recommended that the oil tank is drained, the oil filters cleaned in petrol and the tank replenished with new oil.

TO REMOVE THE FELT OIL FILTER

Unscrew the hexagonal headed cap on the top of oil tank and withdraw the dished washer and spring. Then insert a finger in the exposed open end of the felt filter and gently raise. As the filter emerges from the tank gently strain inward and backward on rigid frame model to clear the saddle frame or outward and forward on spring frame model to clear the twin seat. Care in this operation is necessary to avoid kinking the filter.

To re-fit filter :—
Reverse above instructions.

NOTE—If, after the filter has been removed from the tank, it is damaged, so that the felt is perforated, or the ends distorted, it is essential to discard it and to fit a new filter.
Be careful to avoid damaging the filter or the cork washer under the hexagonal cap.

To remove and clean the feed pipe metal filter :
First drain tank and then release the oil feed pipe from the rubber connecting sleeve on the metal feed pipe protruding from the bottom of the oil tank.

The metal filter may come away with the rubber sleeve, in which case there is no need to disturb it. On the other hand it may remain in the oil tank bottom pipe, in which case it may be withdrawn by grasping the ringed open end and pulling away.

After removal the filter should be cleaned in petrol and allowed to dry before re-fitting.

Reverse the above procedure to re-fit the filter and pipes.

ADJUSTMENT OF OIL FEED

The internal flow of oil is regulated by fixed restrictions. No adjustment is provided except for the oil feed to the inlet valve stem. This adjustment is made by a needle pointed screw located in the right side of cylinder head. (See Illustration 5.) It is locked in position by a nut. The approximate correct setting is one-sixth of a complete turn from the fully closed position. Once set it requires little, or no, adjustment.

Inlet valve squeak indicates the oil feed adjustment is not open enough. Excessive oil consumption, a smoky exhaust or an oiled sparking plug, generally indicates the oil feed adjustment is open too much.

EXHAUST VALVE STEM LUBRICATION

The exhaust valve stem is lubricated by oil flowing through a passage drilled in the cylinder head. No adjustment is provided.

LUBRICATION POINTS TO REMEMBER

A dirty, or choked, felt oil filter causes heavy oil consumption. This is because the return flow of oil to the oil tank is reduced, thereby allowing an excess of oil to "build up" in the crankcase sump, much of which passes to the piston.

A clogged metal strainer, in the gravity feed pipe, will also cause improper, or no, oil circulation. This can only occur as the result of adding dirty oil when replenishing the tank.

Both end caps on pump plunger housing must be air-tight

Check oil circulation before starting each run.

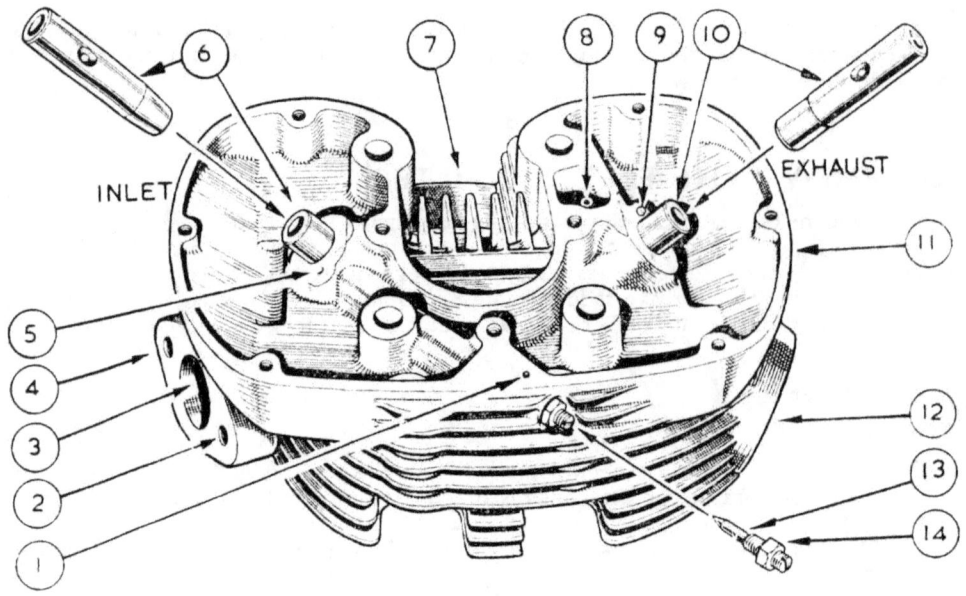

Illustration 5

The inlet valve guide is shown withdrawn as also is the inlet valve stem adjusting screw (with lock nut)

1 PLAIN HOLE, FOR OIL FEED TO INLET VALVE.

2 TAPPED HOLE, TO ACCOMMODATE CARBURETTER RETAINING STUD.

3 INLET PORT.

4 TAPPED HOLE, TO ACCOMMODATE CARBURETTER RETAINING STUD.

5 HOLE, TO ACCOMMODATE DOWEL LOCATING VALVE SPRING SEAT.

6 GUIDE, FOR INLET VALVE.

7 TAPPED HOLE, OR SPARKING PLUG.

8 PLAIN HOLE, FOR OIL FEED TO EXHAUST VALVE.

9 HOLE, TO ACCOMMODATE DOWEL PIN LOCATING VALVE SPRING SEAT.

10 GUIDE, FOR EXHAUST VALVE.

11 HEAD.

12 EXHAUST PORT.

13 NEEDLE SCREW, ADJUSTING OIL FEED TO INLET VALVE.

14 LOCK NUT, FOR NEEDLE ADJUSTING SCREW.

GEAR BOX LUBRICATION

Use one of the **grades of Oils specified**. **In** no circumstances must heavy grease be used.

Lubricant **is inserted through the** filler cap orifice mounted on **top edge of** kick-starter case cover.

The gear box must not be entirely filled with oil, and, under normal conditions, the addition of two fluid ounces of oil every 1,000 miles will be sufficient.

Excessive oil will **cause leakage.**

A screwed **drain plug in gear box shell, low down at rear, facilitates gear box** flushing and **change of lubricant.** An oil level plug, adjacent to K-S spindle, indicates maximum permissible oil level (content 1 pint).

HUB LUBRICATION

Keep hubs packed with grease. This prevents entry of water and dirt. Grease nipples accessible through hole in hub disc. Inject small quantity of grease. Excessive grease may impair efficiency of brakes.

BRAKE DRUM BEARING (SPRING FRAME MODELS ONLY)

The independent ball bearing upon which the rear brake drum is mounted on spring frame models is packed with grease upon assembly and requires no further attention for a considerable time.

During a general overhaul however it is recommended that the bearing is dismantled and re-packed with fresh hub grease.

CHAIN LUBRICATION

Front driving chain and dynamo chain run in oil bath. (Front chaincase.) Use engine oil. Maintain level to height of the inspection cap opening.

Oil in front chaincase also lubricates the engine shock absorber. Transmission harshness generally indicates level of oil in chaincase is too low.

Remove chaincase inspection cap each week, inspect level of oil, top-up as necessary.

To remove inspection cap :—

Unscrew knurled screw about four turns.

Slide cap sideways, till the back plate can be slipped through the opening, and take away the complete cap assembly.

When replacing inspection cap, centralise cork washer and then fully tighten knurled screw. Essential this is kept tight otherwise cap assembly will be lost.

Rear driving chain should be removed occasionally for lubrication particularly under winter conditions.

Clean chain in paraffin, allow to drain and wipe. Then immerse in one of the greases recommended, heated to just fluid state. Leave in soak for at least ten minutes while maintaining grease fluidity. Then hang to drain off surplus and replace.

Engine oil is a poor substitute for one of the recommended greases and if used the chain should be allowed to soak for several hours to ensure penetration to all joints, hanging to drain off surplus before refitting.

See chain removal and refitting instructions, page 49.

Magneto chain runs in case packed with grease.

BRAKE EXPANDER LUBRICATION

Grease nipple on each brake expander bush. (One on each brake cover plate.) Use grease sparingly. Excessive grease may impair efficiency of brakes.

BRAKE ROD JOINT LUBRICATION
A few drops of engine oil on each brake rod yoke end pin and on the threaded portion of brake rod. (One pin on yoke each end of brake rod and on bottom of front brake cable.)

BRAKE PEDAL LUBRICATION
Grease nipple in heel of foot brake pedal.

SPEEDOMETER LUBRICATION
One grease nipple on top of speedometer gear box attached to right side of rear wheel spindle. (No other part of the speedometer requires lubrication.)

STAND FIXING BOLT LUBRICATION
Several of the parts of a motor cycle that have a very small amount of movement, such as the hinge bolts of the stands, should be lubricated.

STEERING HEAD BEARING LUBRICATION
One grease nipple on Front Frame Head Lug and another on right hand side of Handlebar Lug.

CONTROL CABLE LUBRICATION
To ensure free smooth action the clutch and throttle cables are fitted with a conveniently situated grease nipple. Use engine oil and hold the grease gun as near verticle as possible (spout downward) to obtain efficient ejection of oil, the gun being primarily intended for grease. Lubricate at first sign of stiff or jerky action.

CONTROL LEVER LUBRICATION
Occasionally a drop of engine oil on all moving parts of the handlebar control levers.

If twist grip is too stiff : remove two screws binding the two halves of the clip. This releases the grip which may be pulled off the handlebar. Smear handlebar, the drum on which the inner wire is wound and the friction spring on the half clip with grease and replace.

REAR FORK HINGE (spring frame models)
Heavy Gear Oil. S.A.E. 140 (see page 57).

WHEN ORDERING SPARES
ALWAYS QUOTE
THE COMPLETE ENGINE NUMBER
(Including all the Letters in it).

THIS ENABLES THE MACHINE TO BE IDENTIFIED.

EACH SERIES OF FRAMES IS NUMBERED FROM ZERO UPWARDS. THEREFORE THE QUOTATION OF A FRAME NUMBER ONLY DOES NOT FACILITATE IDENTIFICATION.

LUBRICATION CHART

The figures in diamond frames refer to parts located on the left hand side of the machine and those in circles refer to parts located on the right hand side.

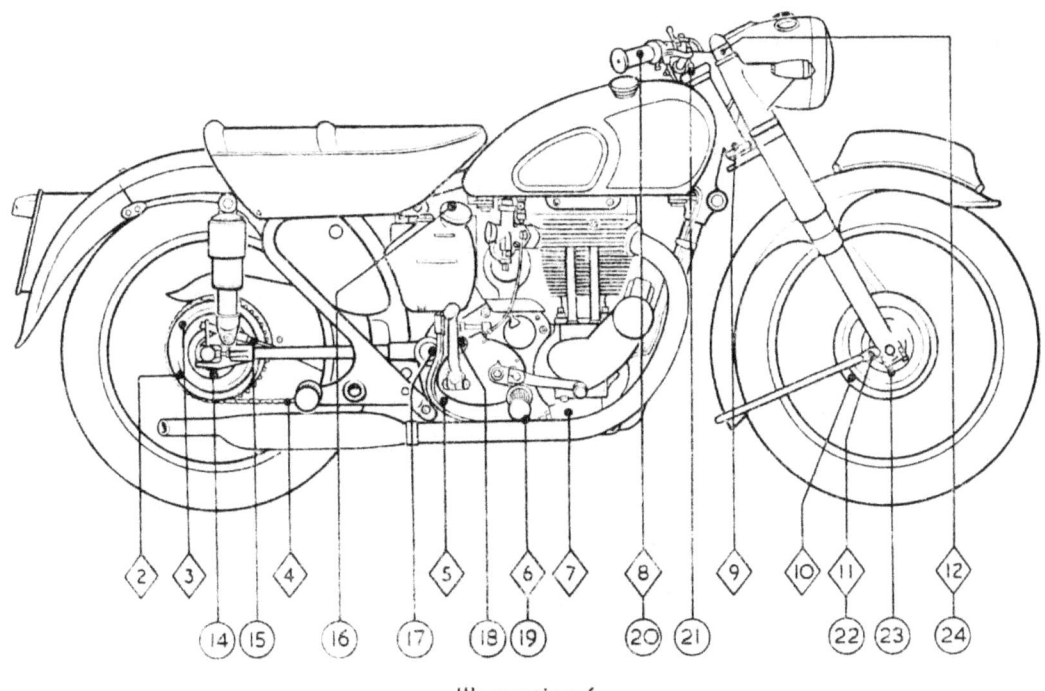

Illustration 6

Lubrication Chart

Engine Oil Locations

- 16 MAIN OIL TANK.
- 7 FRONT CHAINCASE.
- 8, 20 CONTROL LEVER MOVING PARTS.
- 2 BRAKE ROD JOINTS.
- 6, 11 FRONT, CENTRE AND PROP STAND
- 19, 22 HINGE PINS.

Hydraulic Fluid Locations

- 12, 24 FRONT TELEDRAULIC FORKS.

Heavy Engine Oil Location

- 18 GEAR BOX.

Grease Locations

- 23 FRONT HUB.
- 14 REAR HUB.
- 21 STEERING HEAD TOP BEARING.
- 9 STEERING HEAD BOTTOM BEARING.
- 15 SPEEDOMETER GEAR BOX.
- 10 FRONT BRAKE EXPANDER.
- 3 REAR BRAKE EXPANDER.
- 5 BRAKE PEDAL SPINDLE.

Heavy Gear Oil Location

- 17 REAR FORK HINGE. S.A.E.140

Molten Grease Location

- 4 REAR CHAIN.

When buying oils and greases it is advisable to specify the **Brand** as well as the grade and, as an additional precaution, to buy only in sealed containers or from branded cabinets.

MAINTENANCE

PERIODICAL MAINTENANCE

Regular maintenance, attention to lubrication, and certain adjustments must be made to ensure unfailing reliability and satisfactory service. This necessary attention is detailed below, and owners are strongly recommended to follow carefully these suggestions, and to make a regular practice of doing so from the first.

The reference numbers, in brackets, refer to the locations specified on the Lubrication Chart, Illustration 6.

DAILY

Oil tank — Inspect oil level (16.) and top-up if necessary. Check oil circulation.

Petrol tank — Check level and re-fill if necessary.

WEEKLY

Oil tank — Check level (16.) and re-fill if necessary.

Tyres — Check pressures and inflate if necessary.

EVERY 500 MILES

Oil tank — Drain at first 500 miles and re-fill with new oil, and clean felt filter. (16.)

Gear box — Drain at first 500 miles and re-fill (18.) 1 pint.

Chaincase — Check level of oil when machine is standing vertically on level ground, when level of oil should not be less than $\frac{3}{16}''$ below bottom edge of inspection orifice. (7.) Fill up to orifice if level is low.

Battery — Inspect each cell for level of electrolyte and top-up with distilled water if necessary. (See pages 79 and 80.) Level of electrolyte should just be over top of plates. Beware overfilling.

EVERY 1,000 MILES

Oil tank	Drain at first 1,000 miles and re-fill with new oil. (16.)
Rear chain	In wet weather, remove and soak in molten grease. (See page 14.) (4.)
Gear box	Add 2 fluid ounces of specified oil. (18.)
Hubs	Inject small amount of grease. (14 & 23.)
Expanders	Inject small amount of grease. (3 & 10.)
Steering head	Inject small amount of grease. (9 & 21.)
Small parts	Smear all moving parts with engine oil and wipe off surplus.
Air Filter	(If fitted) clean and re-oil filter element.

EVERY 3,000 MILES

Rear chain	In dry weather, remove and soak in molten grease. (See page 14.) (4.)
Brake pedal	Inject small amount of grease. (5.)
Speedometer	Inject small amount of grease into speedometer gear box. (15.)
Magneto	Clean contact breaker points and re-set if necessary.
Plug	Clean sparking plug and re-set points as necessary. (See page 76.)
Steering head	Test steering head for up and down movement and adjust if necessary.
Bolts and nuts	Check all nuts and bolts for tightness and tighten if necessary, but beware of over-tightening.
Rockers	Check O.H.V. rocker adjustment and correct if necessary.

EVERY 5,000 MILES

Oil tank	Drain and re-fill with new oil. (16.) If machine is only used for short runs renew oil every three months instead of mileage interval.
Filters	Clean metal mesh filter in oil tank. (Illustration 3.) Clean felt fabric filter in oil tank.
Dynamo	Clean as detailed in Electrical section.
Front fork	Check each side of front fork for hydraulic fluid content and, if necessary, top up. (12 & 24.) Insufficient oil content is indicated by abnormally lively action.
Rear legs	(If fitted) Check each leg for hydraulic fluid content and, if necessary, top-up. Insufficient oil content is indicated by abnormally lively action.
Carburetter	Remove carburetter float chamber cap and clean interior. Also detach petrol pipe banjo and clean gauze strainer. Extreme care required to avoid damage.

EVERY 10,000 MILES

Magneto and Dynamo	Get a **Lucas Service Station** to dismantle, clean, lubricate and generally service.
Air Filter	(If fitted) renew filter element.

FREE SERVICE SCHEME

FREE SERVICE SCHEME

All owners of **NEW MODELS** are entitled to one **FREE SERVICE AND INSPECTION** at 500 miles, or, at latest, three months after taking delivery.

This service is arranged by the supplying dealer to whom the **Free Service Voucher** must be handed. This voucher, together with the Instruction Manual, are supplied by us upon receipt of the signed application card to be found in the tool box upon taking delivery of a new motor cycle.

The **INSPECTION AND SERVICE** consists of:

(a) Check, and, if necessary, adjust:

    (1) Rocker clearances.
    (2) Contact breaker points.
    (3) Sparking plug.
    (4) Clutch.
    (5) Chains.
    (6) Wheel bearings.
    (7) Brakes.
    (8) Forks, legs, and steering head.
    (9) Alignment of wheels.
    (10) Tyre pressures.

(b) Tighten all external nuts and bolts, including cylinder bolts and fork crown pinch screws.

(c) Top-up battery and check all lighting equipment.

(d) Clean out carburetter and check for correct idling.

(e) Adjust and lubricate all cables.

(f) Grease all nipples.

(g) Drain oil system. Clean filter and replenish.

(h) Check oil level in front chaincase.

(i) Top-up gear box.

(j) Test machine on the road.

NOTE—Oils, greases and materials used are chargeable to the customer.

FOR THE CONVENIENCE OF OWNERS,

SPARES STOCKISTS

ARE APPOINTED FOR MOST DISTRICTS. TO SAVE DELAY, AND THE DELIVERY SURCHARGE, CUSTOMERS ARE RECOMMENDED TO ALWAYS APPLY TO THEIR NEAREST SPARES STOCKIST.

ENGINE SERVICE

ACCESS

For almost all service work to the upper parts of the engine, it is necessary, in order to obtain accessibility, first, to remove the petrol tank. The two petrol taps facilitate this operation by removing the need to first drain the tank of petrol.

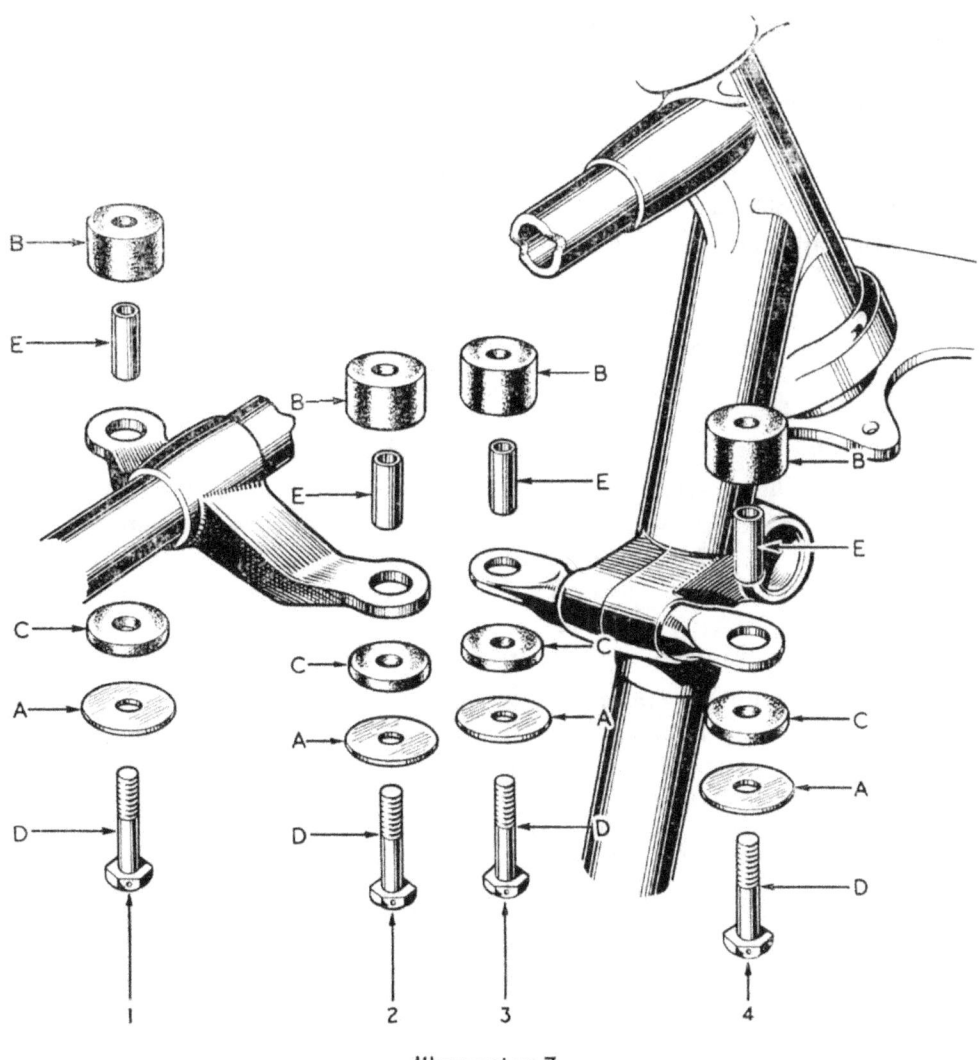

Illustration 7

Showing details and order of assembly, of the fuel tank fixing bolts and components

			Part Number	
A	...	METAL WASHER	014999	$1\frac{1}{4}''$ diameter.
B	...	THICK RUBBER PAD	014995	$\frac{5}{8}''$ high.
C	...	THIN RUBBER PAD	014996	$\frac{3}{16}''$ high.
D	...	TANK FIXING BOLT	014997	$1\frac{1}{4}'' \times \frac{5}{16}'' \times 26.$
E	...	SLEEVE FOR FIXING BOLT	014998	$\frac{13}{16}''$ long.

TO REMOVE THE PETROL TANK

Close both petrol taps and remove the cap nut securing each petrol pipe banjo connector. Use two spanners, one to hold the tap and the other to unscrew the cap nut.

Beware losing the fibre washers (4 in all) fitted one each side of each banjo connection. Cut the wires interlacing the four fixing bolts.

Remove the tank fixing bolts and the tank is then free to be taken away.

NOTE—The disposition of the various rubber and metal washers and tubular spacers should be specially observed so that they may be correctly replaced.

TO REPLACE THE PETROL TANK

Proceed in reverse order to removal. Screw firmly home the four fixing bolts and interlace them, in pairs, with 22 gauge copper wire.

TO REMOVE THE ROCKER BOX

Remove the petrol tank.

Remove the three nuts and fibre washers retaining the rocker box side cover and take away the cover.

Disconnect the oil pipe feeding oil to the rocker box.

Turn over engine until both valves are completely closed.

Remove engine steady bracket by removing bolt from frame clip and nuts and washers from the rocker box bolt extensions.

Remove the nine bolts retaining rocker box to cylinder head.

Disconnect valve lifter cable.

Tilt upward the right hand side of rocker box and extract the two long pushrods. Lay these aside so they may be identified and replaced in their original position.

The rocker box may then be lifted off.

TO REPLACE THE ROCKER BOX

Carefully clean the top of cylinder head and lower face of rocker box.

Revolve engine until both tappets are down, i.e., the top dead centre of firing stroke. Lay the composition jointing washer on cylinder head. This must be faultless. If necessary, renew.

Lay the rocker box in position then slightly raise the right hand side to allow the long push rods to be inserted into their original respective positions.

Insert all nine rocker box fixing bolts and note that the bolt with short head is in the centre right hand position and the bolts with threaded extensions are fitted one each side of the central short head bolt.

Tighten each bolt in turn bit by bit until all are fully home.

Replace the engine steady stay.

Turn engine over several times to ensure parts have bedded home.

Re-fix valve lifter cable.

Re-fix rocker box oil pipe union nut using two spanners to ensure that the union screwed into rocker box does not turn while the nut is being tightened.

Check tappet clearances and re-set if necessary.

Inspect rubber fillet on rocker box side cover and renew if not perfect.

Replace the side cover ensuring that a fibre washer is fitted under each of the three retaining nuts.

Beware of over tightening these nuts, the joint being made by the rubber fillet excessive pressure is not necessary

Replace the petrol tank.

DECARBONISATION

Instead of the usual stipulated mileage interval between periods of decarbonisation, it is recommended that this is undertaken only when the need for same becomes apparent because of excessive pinking, loss of power or generally reduced performance. When undertaken, unless it is thought necessary to inspect the piston and rings, the cylinder barrel is best left undisturbed. The various stages in decarbonisation are described below.

TO REMOVE THE CYLINDER HEAD

Remove

The petrol tank.
The sparking plug.—See note below.
The rocker box.

Remove the exhaust system by :

Remove nut, and washers, retaining exhaust pipe to its stay.

Remove nut, and washers, retaining silencer to its stay.

Remove complete exhaust system, by pulling away from stays and then downwards, from the exhaust port in cylinder head.

Remove carburetter by :

Unscrew two carburetter retaining nuts.

Take away carburetter and rest on saddle.

Remove

The four bolts retaining cylinder head to barrel, and head is free to be taken away. While doing this the push rod cover tubes will come away with the head.

Note

If the sparking plug resists removal, do not use force but brush paraffin round the body and leave for a time to soak before making further effort.

TO REMOVE AND REPLACE THE VALVES

Remove the cylinder head.

Remove the valve springs by inserting a finger in the spring coil and sharply pull upward.

The top spring collar and split collet can then be removed leaving the valve free to be withdrawn.

A sharp light tap on the valve collar may be necessary to free the taper split collet. It will be observed that the valve spring seat has a raised impression on its under side which registers with a hole drilled on the valve guide boss to ensure accurate positioning.

To remove a valve guide, thoroughly clean protruding end of guide to be removed. Apply gentle heat and press guide downwards. Re-heat when replacing and see that correct projection is obtained, viz. $\frac{1}{2}''$. Also see that oil hole in guide is in correct alignment.

TO REPLACE A VALVE

After cleaning valve guide bores, smear each valve stem with clean oil, insert, and apply top collar and split collet.

Then apply the valve springs which although possible to fit by hand are more easily manipulated with a special compressor tool Part No. 018276 illustration 8. To operate this tool apply the top end of the valve spring to its groove in the top cap, then insert a short rod (one of the rocker box fixing bolts suits admirably) through the holes in this tool and the valve spring coils and pull outward and upward until the ends of the prong of the spring can be rested on the seat, then press down with the fingers. Withdraw the bolt or rod when the compressor lies against the cylinder head, retaining pressure with the fingers until the bolt has been withdrawn and the tool removed, when the spring can be readily pushed down to its proper location with the prongs laying flat upon the seat.

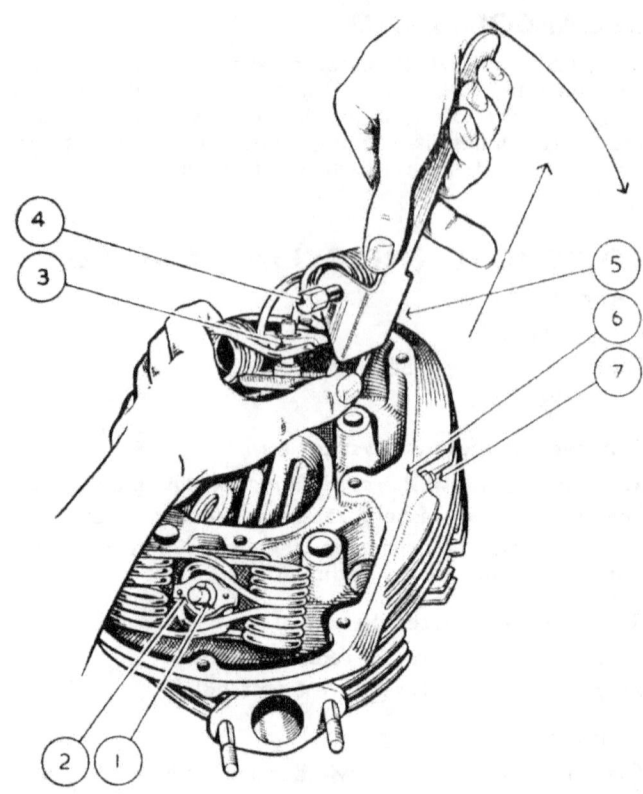

Illustration 8

Showing application of valve spring compressor

1 COLLET, FOR VALVE.
2 COLLAR, FOR VALVE SPRING.
3 COLLAR, FOR VALVE SPRING.
4 BOLT THROUGH TOOL AND COILS OF VALVE SPRING
5 VALVE SPRING COMPRESSOR TOOL.
6 OIL PASSAGE FROM ROCKER BOX TO INLET VALVE GUIDE.
7 SCREW WITH LOCK NUT ADJUSTING OIL FEED TO INLET VALVE.

NOTE—The special valve spring compressor tool is not part of the standard tool kit but can be obtained from any of our dealers (Part No. 018276.) Price 4/2.

It is essential that the collets are correctly located on the valve stems. It will be observed that the collet has two grooves machined in the bore and those two grooves must register with the two rings on the valve stem. If fitted so that only one of the grooves engages the ringed valve stem, damage will almost certainly result.

On 350 c.c. the inlet valve head is larger in diameter than the exhaust. Therefore unintended interchange is not possible.

On 500 c.c. both valve heads are identical in dimensions but are made of different materials. Therefore, upon removal, valves should be laid aside so that they may be identified for re-fitting. In case of doubt, see marking " In " or " Ex " on stem adjacent to collet grooves.

AN ILLUSTRATED SPARES LIST COVERING ALL MODELS DESCRIBED IN THIS MANUAL IS AVAILABLE UPON APPLICATION   PRICE: 2s. 6d.

REMOVING CARBON DEPOSIT

Do not use a sharp implement for removing carbon deposit from the interior of the cylinder head and the piston crown. A blunt piece of soft brass will be found quite suitable and the use of such will obviate the risk of making deep scratches. Care is necessary to avoid damaging the valve seatings and in no circumstances should any abrasive material, such as emery, or emery cloth, be used for cleaning and polishing.

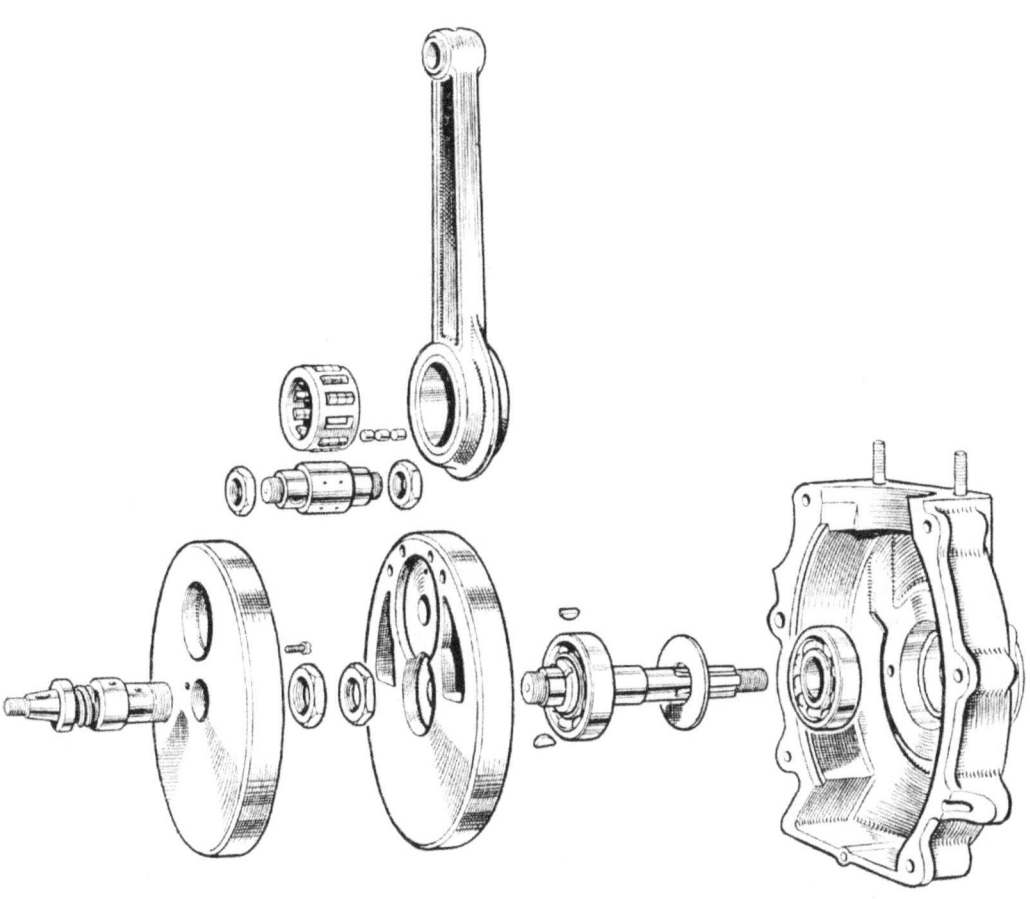

Illustration 9

Showing flywheel in exploded form

VALVE GRINDING

Before commencing valve grinding, carefully examine the face of each valve and, if found to be deeply pitted, have them refaced. (Most garages have suitable equipment for that purpose.) Any attempt to remove deep pit marks by grinding will inevitably cause undue and undesirable widening of the seats.

As a rule, inlet valves require very little attention and one light application of fine grinding paste should be sufficient to restore an even matt finish to both valve face and seat. The exhaust valves may require two, or even three, applications but, as already mentioned, excessive grinding is both unnecessary and harmful.

The grinding is accomplished by smearing a thin layer of fine grinding paste (obtainable ready for use at any garage) on the valve face and then, after inserting the valve in the head, partially revolve, forwards and backwards, while applying light finger pressure to the head, raising the valve off its seat and turning to another position after every few movements. (Never revolve the valve continuously in one direction.)

When the abrasive ceases to bite, remove the valve and examine its face.

The grinding may be considered to be satisfactorily completed when a continuous matt ring is observed on both valve face and seat.

After grinding, all traces of abrasive must be carefully washed off with petrol and a piece of rag, moistened in petrol, should be pulled through the bore of each valve guide to remove any abrasive that may have entered.

A holder for the valve, when grinding in the valve, can be supplied. The part number is 017482. Price 1/11.

TO REPLACE THE CYLINDER HEAD

A gasket is fitted between cylinder head and barrel. (*Touring models only*).

The top ends of the push rod cover tubes have rubber gaskets between tubes and head, they are a push fit and metal washers are located between the top edges of the gaskets and the cylinder head recesses. If the cover tubes are pulled away from the head, the gaskets will probably remain in position in the head.

A rubber gland is fitted at the bottom of each cover tube.

Replace the cylinder head by :

Carefully clean the top edge of the cylinder barrel and the under face of the cylinder head.

Fit the cover tubes, with their rubber gaskets and metal washers into the cylinder head.

Place the cylinder head gasket in position on the top edge of the cylinder barrel.

Place a rubber gland round each tappet guide

Place the cylinder head in position.

Ensure each cylinder head securing bolt has a plain steel washer on it and then replace the bolts and engage each a few turns.

Finally, screw down the cylinder head securing bolts, in turn, bit by bit, until all are fully home.

Replace

The sparking plug, but before doing so it is desirable to coat thread with "Oil Dag" or graphite paste to prevent seizure upon next removal.

The rocker box, carburetter, exhaust system, and the petrol tank.

NOTE—If old gaskets are re-fitted they must be in an undamaged state otherwise new must be used.

Whether new or re-used, the gasket should be annealed just prior to fitting. This is done by heating to "blood red heat" and plunging into clean cold water.

TO REMOVE THE CYLINDER BARREL AND PISTON

Remove

The cylinder head.

The four nuts retaining cylinder barrel to crankcase.

Take away

Cylinder barrel. (Ensure piston is not damaged in doing this. Steady piston with hand as barrel is withdrawn.)

Fill throat of crankcase with clean rag to prevent entry of foreign matter.

Remove

One gudgeon pin circlip. It is immaterial which circlip is removed. Use special pliers included in tool kit.

Gudgeon pin by pushing it out of piston.

Take away piston.

NOTE—The gudgeon pin is an easy sliding fit in both piston and connecting rod small-end bush.

Rings may be removed from a piston by " peeling off " with a knife, or by introducing behind the rings three pieces of thin steel spaced at 120° from each other and then sliding off the rings. (Do not scratch the piston.)

TO REPLACE THE PISTON AND CYLINDER BARREL

All parts must be clean.

Place rings on piston, scraper first then the two compression rings. On all models the top compression ring is chromium plated.

These chrome plated rings have a slightly tapered exterior and when new are clearly marked with the word TOP on one side to indicate assembly position. After use this word tends to become indiscernable, but over a large mileage the assembly position can be determined by brightness of the edge contacting cylinder wall. This bright edge is the lower one. When as the result of wear, contact with the cylinder wall appears uniform over the whole width of the ring, it is then immaterial which way round it is re-fitted.

Smear gudgeon pin with engine oil.

Refit piston by :

Introduce piston over connecting rod, so that slit in piston faces to the front of the machine.

Introduce gudgeon pin in piston and pass it through connecting rod small-end bush and centralise it.

Re-fit circlips. (Use special pliers). Use rotary action when bedding circlips in their grooves and make sure each circlip lies snugly in its groove. This is **essential** otherwise considerable damage will result.

Re-fit cylinder barrel by :

Take new cylinder base washer. Coat one side with liquid jointing compound and apply it to cylinder base. Ensure jointing does not choke any of the cylinder base oil holes.

Smear cylinder bore and piston with clean engine oil.

Space piston rings so that the gaps are evenly spaced at 120° to each other.

Gently fit barrel over piston and carefully compress each ring in turn, with the fingers, as it enters the chamfered mouth of the barrel.

Remove rag from crankcase throat.

Replace cylinder barrel holding down nuts, screwing each down, in turn, bit by bit, till all are fully home.

CAM CONTOUR

On the flanks of the cams are quietening curves which are very slight inclines from the base circles to the feet of the humps.

Therefore, it is necessary to ensure the tappet ends are on the base circles when checking valve clearances and valve timing.

It is for this reason valve clearances must be checked when the piston is at the top of its compression stroke, at which position both tappets are well clear of the quietening curves.

VALVE TIMING taken with valve ·001" off its seat

Inlet valve timing

Inlet valve opens 36° before top dead centre—350 c.c. models.
Inlet valve opens 18° before top dead centre—500 c.c. models.
Inlet valve closes 51° after bottom dead centre—350 c.c. models.
Inlet valve closes 69° after bottom dead centre—500 c.c. models.

Exhaust valve timing

Exhaust valve opens 50° before bottom dead centre—All models.
Exhaust valve closes 30° after top dead centre—All models.
(See page 89 for particulars of special timing disc graduated in degrees.)

Camshaft timing marks
**Use mark 2 for exhaust cam—all models.
Use mark 2 for inlet cam 500 c.c. touring models.
and also both 350 c.c. and 500 c.c. comp. springers.
Use mark 3 for inlet cam 350 c.c. touring models only.**

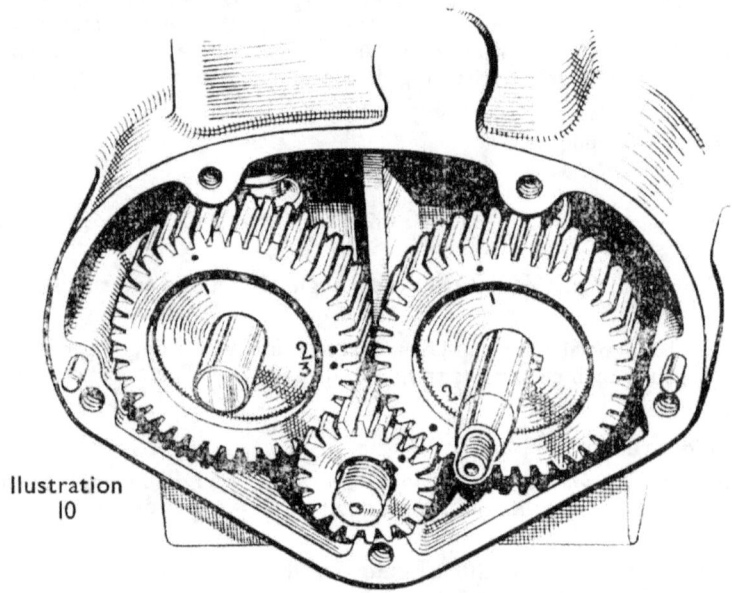

Illustration 10

When checking the valve timing the tappet clearances must be set to ·014 inch so that the tappets may be well clear of the quietening curves of the camshafts.

The timing gears are marked to facilitate their replacement.

To re-set the valve timing, by using the marks on the gears, proceed as follows :—

Turn over the engine till the mark on the small timing pinion is in line with the centre of the inlet (rear) camshaft bush. Insert the inlet camshaft so that the No. 2 or No. 3 mark on it is in mesh with the mark on the small timing pinion, according to model.

Rotate the engine in a **forward** direction till the mark on the small timing pinion is in line with the centre of the exhaust (front) camshaft bush. Insert the exhaust camshaft so that the No. 2 mark on it is in mesh with the mark on the small timing pinion.

TAPPET ADJUSTMENT

The top ends of the two long push rods have screwed extensions. These are locked in position by nuts, thereby providing tappet adjustment.

The correct tappet clearances, on all models, with valves closed and engine warm (not hot) is **NIL**. This means the push rods should be free enough to revolve and, at the same time, there should be no appreciable up and down play.

Prepare to adjust tappets by :

Set piston to T.D.C. (Both valves closed).

Remove the three nuts, and fibre washers under them, retaining tappet cover to rocker box.

Take away cover.

Adjust tappets on all 350 and 500 models by :

With spanners, hold the sleeve 5, either valve (Illustration 11) and slacken lock nut 2. Then screw, in or out, the head 3 until the clearance is nil.

Tighten lock nut 2 and re-check the clearance.

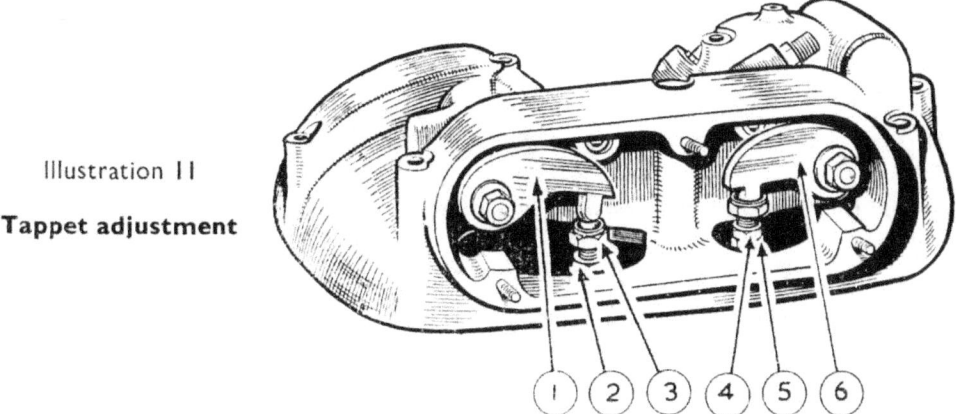

Illustration 11

Tappet adjustment

Finally

Check adjustments so that, with no up and down movement, the long push rods are free to revolve when the valves are closed.

1. INLET ROCKER ARM (TAPPET END).
2. NUT, LOCKING ADJUSTING CUPPED SCREW.
3. CUPPED ADJUSTING SCREW.
4. CUPPED ADJUSTING SCREW AND LOCK NUT.
5. SLEEVE, TO ACCOMMODATE ADJUSTING SCREW, ON TOP END OF PUSH ROD.
6. EXHAUST ROCKER ARM (TAPPET END).

Complete adjustment by :

Replace rocker tappet cover taking care to replace the fibre washer that is under each retaining nut.

As mentioned elsewhere do not over-tighten the nuts because the joint is made with a rubber fillet and undue pressure is not necessary.

NOTE—In normal conditions tappet adjustment should not be necessary more frequently than about every five thousand miles or after decarbonising and grinding valves. If adjustment is found necessary more frequently the cause should be investigated at once.

The tappet rods are made of Light Alloy, and in manufacture, the sleeve marked 5 in illustration 11 is fitted to the bare rod and then the push sleeve and the rod are threaded to take the adjusting screw marked 3.

It will consequently be seen that, contrary to the practice when steel rods are used, it is not possible to supply and fit sleeve 5 to an existing Light Alloy rod.

Consequently the " Push Rod, bare " will only be supplied for spares purposes complete with sleeve 5 already fitted and threaded.

TO RE-TIME THE IGNITION

The normal advance is 39° ($\frac{1}{2}$").

Have available a stout screwdriver, or an old type tyre lever with turned up end, also a small rod or stout wheel spoke 5$\frac{1}{2}$" long.

Before setting the ignition firing point it is essential the magneto contact breaker points are correctly adjusted. Therefore always check these first.

Check contact breaker points by :

Expose contact breaker by removing moulded end cover of magneto (secured by 3 captive screws).

Check setting of contact breaker points, and, if necessary, re-set same.

Set ignition firing point by :

Remove :—

The sparking plug high tension cable from plug.

The sparking plug.

The magneto chain case cover.

The rocker box side cover.

Unscrew, several turns, nut retaining magneto sprocket to camshaft. (No need to remove nut).

Lever off sprocket until it is loose on the taper of the shaft. (Use stout screw-driver or old type tyre lever.)

Turn over engine till both valves are closed.

Insert rod through sparking plug hole, feel piston, by rocking engine forwards or backwards till it is felt the piston is at the top of its stroke with both valves closed.

Mark rod flush with top face of sparking plug hole. Remove rod and measure $\frac{1}{2}$" above the flush mark and record position on rod.

Turn the front plate of the automatic unit with the fingers and thumb to its limit of movement and insert a wood wedge to hold the control in the fully advanced position.

Replace rod in sparking plug hole.

Slightly rotate engine **BACKWARDS** until upper mark on rod is flush with top face of sparking plug hole. (To rotate engine, engage top gear and turn back wheel by hand.) Rotate sprocket on magneto armature shaft, in anti-clockwise direction (as seen from sprocket end of magneto), till the contact breaker points are just about to separate. (To find the exact moment for the commencement of the point separation, place a piece of tissue paper between the points and turn the armature shaft (by the sprocket on it) until the paper is just released, and no more, upon a gentle pull.)

Tighten nut on camshaft and ensure engine, and/or magneto shaft, does not move in doing so.

Re-check the setting which must be $\frac{1}{2}$" before top dead centre. (With the ignition fully advanced.)

Do not omit to remove the wood wedge securing the automatic unit in the fully advanced position before refitting the chain cover.

See page 89 for particulars of special timing disc graduated in degrees.

Replace

Rocker box side cover, magneto side cover, magneto chain case cover, sparking plug (see note on page 36 re graphite on sparking plug thread), and sparking plug wire.

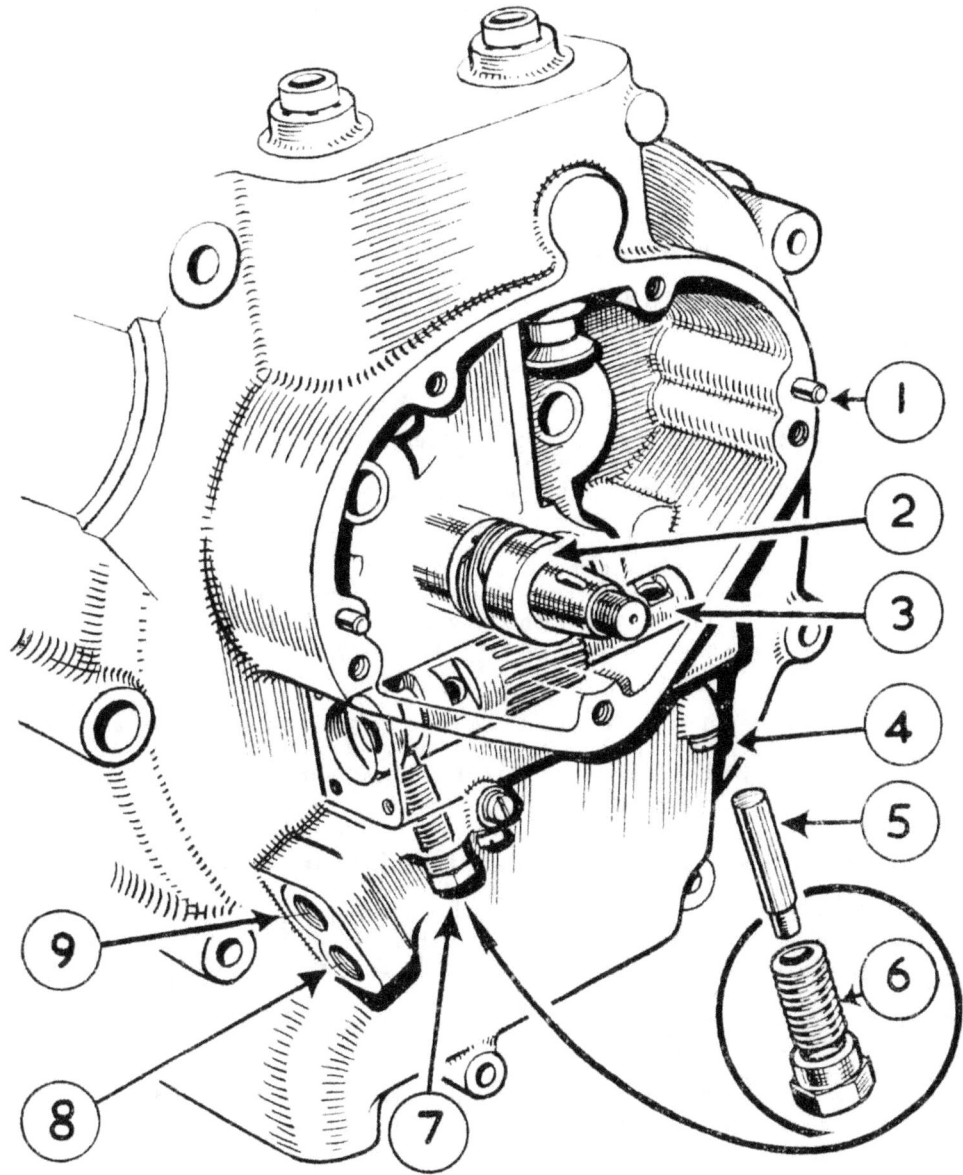

Illustration 12

The rotating oil pump plunger is here shown in situ, together with the guide screw which registers in the plunger profiled groove, thereby providing the reciprocating movement

1 DOWEL PEG, LOCATING TIMING GEAR COVER.

2 TIMING SIDE FLYWHEEL AXLE WITH INTEGRAL GEAR FOR DRIVING OIL PUMP PLUNGER.

3 OIL PUMP PLUNGER.

4 SCREW (ONE OF THREE) WITH FIBRE WASHER, PLUGGING OIL PASSAGES CAST IN CRANKCASE.

5 GUIDE PIN, FOR OIL PUMP PLUNGER. INSERTED RELIEVED TIP DOWNWARD AS SHOWN.

6 SCREWED BODY TO ACCOMMODATE THE OIL PUMP PLUNGER GUIDE PIN.

7 BODY, WITH GUIDE PIN IN POSITION ENGAGED IN PROFILED CAM GROOVE OF OIL PUMP PLUNGER.

8 TAPPED HOLE, FOR PIPE FEEDING OIL TO OIL PUMP.

9 TAPPED HOLE, FOR PIPE RETURNING OIL TO OIL TANK.

TO REMOVE AND REPLACE THE OIL PUMP PLUNGER IF AND WHEN NECESSARY ONLY

Remove

Lower end of rocker box oil feed pipe by unscrewing union nut.

Both oil pump end caps.

Oil pump plunger guide screw with pin. (See illustration 12.)

Oil pump plunger, by pushing at front and extracting from rear end of its housing.

Replace by :

Reversing above procedure.

NOTE—Remember there is a paper washer under each oil pump end cap and, when fitting a new paper washer to the front cap, ensure the oil passage in the front cap is not obstructed by the paper washer.

Important

Never attempt to insert the guide screw unless both oil pump end caps are removed, when by moving the pump plunger to and fro with the fingers it can be felt when the pin engages with the groove in the plunger. When correctly fitted the shoulder on the screw will abut against the boss into which it fits. (See illustration 12.)

Do not under any circumstances revolve the engine until quite certain that the pin is correctly positioned otherwise damage will inevitably result.
Securely tighten the screw to prevent any possibility of it unscrewing in use.

OVERSIZE PARTS AND RE-BORING CYLINDER BARREL

Pistons and rings, .020" and .040" larger than standard, are available. These degrees of oversize make it essential for the cylinder barrel to be re-bored to accommodate them. We can provide that service at prices quoted in the Spares List.

On the 350 c.c. the cylinder standard bore is 2.7187 ± .0005". The 500 c.c. cylinder standard bore is 3.250 ± .0005".

When the wear at the top of the barrel reaches .008" the barrel should be bored out .020" oversize and a new oversize piston and rings fitted.

Crankpin rollers .001" larger than standard can be supplied. We recommend only skilled mechanics should fit these because it is almost general that the big-end journals and sleeves require " lapping " to ensure a correct fit.

REMOVING SPARKING PLUG

Always exercise the greatest care to avoid thread seizure when removing a sparking plug. If any resistance is felt, apply paraffin. Before replacing plug, it is desirable to coat the thread with " Oil Dag " or Graphite paste. This will guard against seizure upon subsequent removal.

WHEN IN DOUBT REGARDING THE NAMES AND PART NUMBERS OF THE PARTS YOU REQUIRE, PLEASE SEND THE OLD PARTS TO SERVE AS PATTERNS.

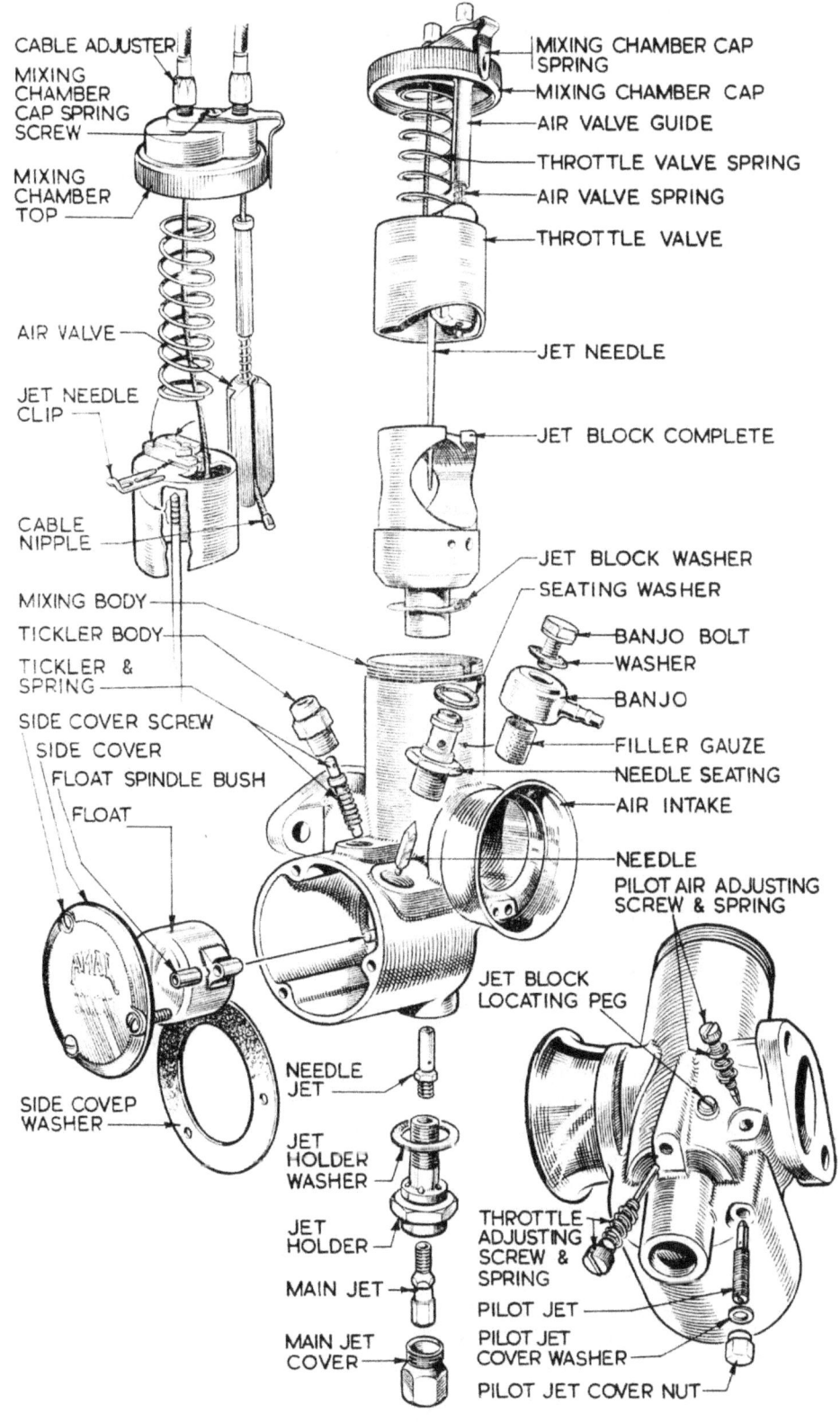

Illustration 13

Carburetter details in assembly order.

CARBURETTER SERVICE

The information given in this section includes all that will normally be required by the average rider. For further details, particularly those connected with racing and the use of special fuels, we refer the enquirer to the manufacturers of the carburetter, **Amal Ltd., Holford Road, Witton, Birmingham, 6.**

Our **Spare Parts Department** does not stock every part of the carburetter but confines its stock to those parts that, from time to time, may be required. Those parts include floats and float needles, jet taperneedles, needle jets, pilot jets, main jets and all washers.

CARBURETTER FUNCTION

The petrol level is maintained by a float and needle valve and, in no circumstances, should any alteration be made to these parts. In the event of a leaky float, or a worn needle valve, the part should be replaced with new. (Do not attempt to grind a needle to its seat.)

The petrol supply to the engine is controlled, firstly, by the main jet and, secondly, by means of a taper needle (see Illustration 13) which is attached to the throttle valve and operates in a tubular extension of the main jet.

The main jet controls the mixture from three-quarters to full throttle, the adjustable taper needle from three-quarters down to one-quarter throttle, the cut-away portion of the intake side of the throttle valve from one-quarter down to about one-eighth throttle, and a pilot jet, having an independently adjusted air supply, takes care of the idling from one-eighth throttle down to the almost closed position. These various stages of control must be kept in mind when any adjustment is contemplated. (See Illustration 13, for location of the pilot jet air adjustment screw.) The pilot jet, unlike on earlier models, is now detachable for cleaning purposes.

The size of the main jet should not be altered save for some very good reason. See " DATA " for details of standard sizes of jet, throttle valve, and jet taper needle. With the standard setting it is possible to use full air in all conditions, except, perhaps, when the engine is pulling hard up hill or is on full throttle, when some benefit may be obtained by slightly closing the air control.

Weak mixture is always indicated by popping, or spitting, at the air intake.

A rich mixture usually causes bumpy, or jerky, running and, in cases of extreme richness, is accompanied by the emission of black smoke from the exhaust.

CARBURETTER ADJUSTMENT

With the taper needle projection, main jet size, and type of throttle slide specified (see page 4) correct carburation except at idling speed is assured.

In the event of difficulty being experienced look for cause under heading Useful Information, pages 72 and 73.

To check for correct idling mixture, first run the engine until it is just warm but not hot when with the throttle nearly closed and air fully open it should fire evenly and slowly.

If it fails to do so, first of all make certain that the sparking plug is clean and the point setting correct. Having done this and idling is still uneven try resetting the pilot jet air screw.

Adjustment of this air screw is not unduly sensitive and it should be possible to obtain the correct setting for even firing in a few seconds.

In the event of even firing at idling speed being unobtainable by adjustment of the air screw look for obstruction in the pilot jet.

Having obtained even firing all that remains is to adjust if necessary the position of the throttle stop screw, until the desired idling speed is obtained.

TWIST GRIP ADJUSTMENT

A screw is provided in one of the halves of the twist grip body to regulate the spring tension on the grip rotating sleeve. This screw, which is locked by a nut, must be screwed into the body to increase the tension.

The most desirable state of adjustment is that when the grip is quite free and easy to operate but, at the same time, will stay in any position in which it is placed.

The complete twist grip can be moved on the handlebar by slackening the two screws that clamp together the two halves of the body. The most desirable position is that in which the throttle cable makes the cleanest and most straight path to the under-side of the petrol tank.

Smooth throttle operation is assured by the provision of a cable oil nipple. At the first signs of jerky action a little engine oil should be injected, applying the gun as near vertical as possible (nozzle downward).

AIR FILTER

In locations, such as the United Kingdom, where the roads and atmosphere are particularly free from dust, it is not considered necessary to have an air filter fitted to the carburetter, but in countries where the atmosphere contains a very heavy dust content, an air filter is essential in order to prevent abrasive wear.

The filter available (optional extra) for the conditions mentioned above is of the "Oil Wetted" type, and this requires periodical servicing.

When servicing the air filter, withdraw the filter element. Thoroughly wash this in petrol, paraffin or other suitable solvent and allow to dry. Then re-oil, using one of the light oils (SAE-20), enumerated in the final table on page 14, and allow to drain before replacing in the filter case. Clean regularly at intervals of 1,000 miles, and renew the element every 10,000 miles.

CARBURETTER TUNING INFORMATION

Poor idling may be due to :

Pilot jet not operating correctly (partially choked) or incorrect air supply.

Air leaks. Either at junction of carburetter and inlet port, or by reason of badly worn inlet valve stem or guide.

Faulty engine valve seatings.

Sparking plug faulty, or its points set too closely.

Ignition advanced too much.

Contact breaker points dirty, pitted, loose, or set too closely.

High-tension wire defective.

Rockers adjusted too closely.

Heavy petrol consumption may be due to :

Late ignition setting.

Bad air leaks. Probably at carburetter joint.

Weakened valve springs.

Leaky float. (Causing flooding.)

Taper needle extension insufficient.

Poor compression, due to worn piston rings or defective valve seatings. (Test compression with throttle wide open.)

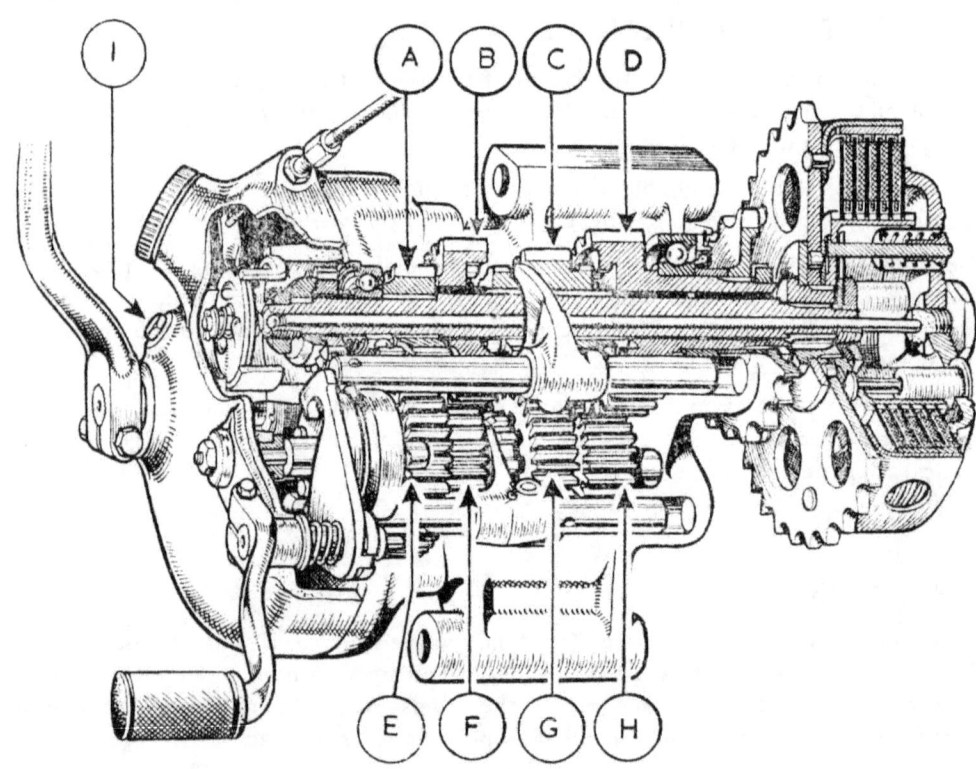

Illustration 14

A LOW GEAR ON MAINSHAFT
B THIRD GEAR ON MAINSHAFT
C SECOND GEAR ON MAINSHAFT
D MAIN DRIVING GEAR
E LOW GEAR ON LAYSHAFT
F THIRD GEAR ON LAYSHAFT
G SECOND GEAR ON LAYSHAFT
H SMALL PINION ON LAYSHAFT
I OIL LEVEL PLUG

Section through gearbox showing gears and clutch with actuating mechanism

TRANSMISSION SERVICE

THE GEAR BOX

The gear box provides four speeds and has a positive foot change, operated by the right foot and a kick-starter.

It is retained to the frame by being clamped between the two engine rear plates by two bolts. The bottom fixing bolt acts as a pivot. The top fixing bolt passes through the gear box top lug and the rear plates, which are slotted, thereby allowing a swinging fore and aft movement of the gear box to enable the front driving chain to be adjusted. That movement is controlled by a bolt that has an eye encircling the gear box top fixing bolt and which passes through an eye block secured to the right-hand side engine rear plate. Two nuts threaded on the eye bolt, one on each side of the eye block, provide means of accurately tensioning the front chain and, after that adjustment, locking the eye bolt in its required position.

Illustration 14 clearly shows the general internal gearbox layout, the simple gear selection and kickstarter mechanism. It will be seen that movement of the foot change lever causes movement of the cam barrel through the medium of an ingenious trip fork to which the lever is attached.

This cam movement actuates the sliding gear striker forks causing movement of the sliding gears which engage the stationary gears by dogs. As each gear is selected it is held in engagement by means of a spring loaded conical ended plunger operating in depressions on the end of the cam barrel.

The trip mechanism referred to allows the foot change lever to return to its normal position, upon foot pressure being released, in readiness for the next change of gear. Downward direction of movement causes engagement of higher gears and upward movement with the toes causes a lower gear to become engaged.

As mentioned elsewhere an external marked disc shows at a glance which gear (or neutral), is engaged.

The unusual method of clutch operation should be noted, the necessary thrust rod movement to free being obtained through the medium of three balls operating on inclined planes (see illustration 15).

Operation of the clutch handlebar lever moves clutch operating lever B causing inward movement of the thrust rod by reason of the three balls mounting the inclined planes in which they are located. The resulting inward movement of the clutch thrust rod forces out the pressure plate, normally maintained in contact with the friction plates by the springs E, thereby allowing the engine to drive the clutch sprocket D without imparting drive to the mainshaft C.

Consequently no power is transmitted to the rear wheel, the clutch is said to be "out" or "free." Upon releasing the clutch handlebar lever the clutch operating lever returns to its normal position by the pressure of the spring forcing the balls down these inclined planes thereby allowing the spring pressure through the medium of the pressure plate to be transferred to the friction plates which causes the gear box mainshaft to revolve and impart driving power to the rear wheel.

TO REMOVE KICK-STARTER CASE COVER FOR EXPOSURE OF K.S., GEAR CHANGE AND INTERNAL CLUTCH ACTUATING MECHANISM

Remove oil drain plug and drain off oil contents of the gear box.

Remove the large oil filler plug and slack off the clutch cable adjuster sufficiently to permit the cable end to be detached from the slotted end of the internal clutch operating lever which is exposed by the removal of filler cap.

Unscrew the clutch cable adjuster until it is free from the K.S. case cover and withdraw the cable nipple through the adjuster hole.

Remove the nut and small spiral spring securing small gear indicator disc from the cam barrel spindle.

Next remove the five cheese head screws by which the K.S. case cover is secured to the gear box end plate.

Withdraw the cover about $\frac{1}{2}$ inch, holding the K.S. pedal firmly while doing so.

Now swing the K.S. crank round until it can be tied to the foot change lever. This prevents the K.S. return spring unwinding and facilitates re-assembly.

The entire cover can now be removed.

Re-assemble in exactly reverse order, taking care to avoid damage to the paper joint gasket.

NOTE—The position of the various cheese head screws securing the K.S. case cover are as follows :—

In the top position, screw measuring $3\frac{1}{8}$ inches under head.
In the bottom position, screw measuring $2\frac{7}{8}$ inches under head.
In the rear position, screw measuring $\frac{7}{8}$ inch under head.
In the front position, top screw measuring $1\frac{1}{8}$ inches under head.
In the front position, bottom screw measuring $1\frac{3}{8}$ inches uuder head.

TO REMOVE GEAR BOX END PLATE FOR EXAMINATION OF GEARS

Remove K.S. case cover as already described.

Remove split pin securing both gear striker shaft pins and withdraw the pins and also the cam barrel in which they operate together, with the spring loaded conical ended plunger which engages depressions on the underside of the cam barrel.

Remove the mainshaft end nut and draw off the K.S. ratchet driver, pinion, spring and bush upon which the pinion is mounted.

Remove the three cheese head screws by which the end plate is secured to the gear box shell and the end plate is then free to be withdrawn leaving the gears and gear striker shafts in situ.

Take care to avoid losing the steel ball fitted in the end of the mainshaft and interposed between the clutch actuating lever and the clutch thrust rod.

TO RE-ASSEMBLE

If gears have been disturbed insert them in their proper order with slider shafts in correct location and apply end plate with paper joint gasket in position.

Re-fit the three cheese head screws and firmly tighten down with a stout screwdriver.

Then insert conical ended plunger and spring and apply the gear selection cam barrel with any one of the depressions on its underside engaging with the conical end of the spring loaded plunger.

Next insert the selector shaft pins and secure each in position with its split pin.

Complete the assembly in reverse order of dismantling ascertaining, before applying the K.S. case cover, that the ball is inserted in the end of the mainshaft.

Fill to correct level with one of the recommended oils and lastly re-fit the gear indicator disc and adjust its position to give correct indication of gears.

TO REMOVE FRONT CHAINCASE AND CLUTCH ASSEMBLY

To remove outer half of front chaincase

Place tray under chaincase to catch oil.

Remove left side footrest arm.

Remove screw binding chaincase metal band at its rear.

Remove metal band.

Remove endless rubber band.

Remove nut and washer, in centre of chaincase front.

Take away outer half of chaincase.

TO REMOVE FRONT DRIVING CHAIN AND CLUTCH ASSEMBLY COMPLETE

Unscrew the nuts retaining the clutch springs, using end of spanner Part No. 017254.

Take away the clutch spring pressure plate with the clutch springs and clutch spring cups and flatten the turned up part of the lock plate that is under the large central nut.

Remove front chain connecting link and take away chain.

Engage top gear, apply rear brake, and unscrew nut retaining the clutch centre to the gear box mainshaft sleeve.

Remove the lockplate and plain washer from gear box mainshaft.

Remove complete clutch assembly by pulling it away, as one unit from gear box mainshaft. Take care not to lose any of the twenty-four clutch sprocket bearing rollers which may be displaced when the clutch centre and sprocket assembly is withdrawn from the mainshaft. The clutch centre is a sliding fit on the mainshaft sleeve and an extractor should not be required.

TO REMOVE DYNAMO CHAIN AND BACK HALF OF CHAINCASE

Remove engine sprocket nut and withdraw shock absorber spring, cupped washer and cam.

Remove the spring lock ring on dynamo sprocket retaining nut.

Take away lock washer surrounding dynamo sprocket nut.

Apply spanner (017254, included in tool kit) to the two flats on the back of the dynamo sprocket and, holding same, unscrew the nut retaining the dynamo sprocket. Holding sprocket thus relieves the dynamo shaft of bending strain.

Release dynamo sprocket with suitable extractor.

Take away, as one assembly, the dynamo sprocket, dynamo chain and engine sprocket assembly. (The dynamo chain is "endless.")

Straighten tabs on lock washers under the three bolts retaining the back half of chaincase to the boss on the crankcase and remove the three bolts.

Remove the long headed bolt (under battery carrier) fixing rear chain guard to front chaincase.

Remove wide nut and washer on centre fixing bolt, when back half of chaincase can be taken away.

TO RE-FIT THE FRONT CHAINCASE AND CLUTCH

Fit back half of front chaincase by :

Place on face of crankcase boss and back face of chaincase some liquid jointing compound, "Wellseal" recommended.

Ensure the spacer is in position on the centre fixing bolt. This is located between the engine plate and the chaincase. (It is 1-13/32" long.)

Place in position rear half of front chaincase.

Fit long headed bolt, holding rear chain guard to front chaincase, but do not fully tighten.

Fit to crankcase boss the three lock washers and bolts retaining case to boss.

Fully tighten the three bolts and turn up the tabs of the three lock washers.

Fit spacer nut (inside chaincase, $\frac{7}{8}$" long) and washer to the centre fixing bolt and fully tighten.

Fully tighten long headed bolt holding rear chain guard to front chaincase.

Fit dynamo sprocket and chain and engine sprocket by :

Ensure dynamo sprocket key is in position (in dynamo armature shaft.)

Ensure the spacing collar, which fits between crankcase ball bearing and the back of the engine sprocket, is in position on the driving side flywheel axle.

Take dynamo driving chain and place it round the small sprocket of the engine sprocket assembly and the sprocket that fits on the dynamo shaft and fit these three parts, in one movement, to the driving side flywheel axle and the dynamo shaft.

Fit the dynamo shaft plain washer and sprocket retaining nut, screwing nut with fingers only.

Hold the dynamo sprocket by applying spanner 017254 to the flats on the back of the sprocket and fully tighten the sprocket retaining nut. (This holding relieves the dynamo shaft of all bending and twisting strains while the sprocket retaining nut is being securely tightened.)

Fit the dynamo sprocket retaining nut lock washer and lock ring. Ensure the lock ring lies snugly in the groove cut in the nut.

Fit engine shock absorber cam, spring, cap washer and retaining nut but do not fully tighten nut.

Fit the clutch centre and sprocket by :

Place on the gear box main shaft splined sleeve the thicker of the two clutch sprocket roller bearing retaining washers.

Place on the gear box main shaft splined sleeve the clutch sprocket roller bearing ring.

With grease, stick in place on the bearing ring the twenty-four clutch sprocket bearing rollers.

Introduce clutch sprocket over the rollers.

Place on the gear box main shaft splined sleeve the thin clutch bearing retaining washer.

Push on the splined sleeve the clutch centre hub.

Fit the plain washer, lock plate and nut that retains the clutch centre but do not fully tighten the nut.

Fit the front chain and lock the clutch centre nut by

Replace the front driving chain. Ensure the spring connecting link is fitted so that the closed end of the spring clip faces the direction of rotation.

Engage top gear, apply the rear brake and then fully tighten the nut that retains the clutch centre to the gear box mainshaft.

Turn up the edge of the lock plate so that it tightly abuts against a flat of the nut.

Fit the clutch plates and springs by

Slide into position, in the clutch case attached to the clutch sprocket, a steel plain clutch plate.

Slide into place a clutch friction plate (plate with fabric inserts) and follow with a steel plain plate, then another friction plate and so on, alternatively, till all plates are fitted. (Five plain plates and four friction plates on 350 c.c. ; six plain, and five friction on 500 c.c. and all competition models.)

Drop into the spring pressure plate the clutch spring cups.

Show up the spring pressure plate and insert over the studs the clutch springs, retaining each one a few turns, as fitted, with a clutch spring adjusting nut.

Fully tighten the clutch spring adjusting nuts, using end of spanner Part No. 017254.

Slacken back, four complete turns, each clutch spring adjusting nut.

Engage top gear, apply rear brake and then fully tighten the engine shock absorber retaining nut.

Check front driving chain for adjustment

Check dynamo driving chain for adjustment.

Check clutch operarating lever for correct free movement as detailed elsewhere.

Fit outer half of front chaincase by

Ensure faces of both halves of chaincase are clean.

Ensure the rubber and metal bands are clean and undamaged.

After carefully positioning the outer half so that its exterior edge exactly coincides with that of the inner half, apply the endless rubber band.

Fit the metal band, starting at the front end of the chaincase and drawing together the two free ends with the fingers of one hand while with the other hand insert the binding screw.

Whilst slowly tightening this binding screw apply at the same time light taps all round the band exterior using a small rubber mallet.

These light taps will cause the metal band to creep on the rubber to ensure an even all round pressure.

Remove the inspection cap from the chaincase and pour in engine oil to the level of the bottom edge of the inspection cap orifice and then replace the cap.

NOTE—If, after replacing a front chaincase, it is found not to be oil tight, the general reason is distortion of the two joint faces or incorrect position of rubber band. These faces must be undamaged and, on test, should closely fit to a surface plate. They must also be absolutely clean before replacement and the edges must be in exact register, one with the other. Any distortion caused by accidental impact must remedied before refitting.

If any doubt exists, **CHECK** for **DISTORTION BEFORE ASSEMBLY**

CLUTCH SPRING ADJUSTMENT

If clutch slip occurs the most probable cause is either incorrect cable adjustment or absence of free movement of the internal clutch lever. If both are found to be correct the clutch spring adjusting nuts may require adjustment.

To obtain access to clutch spring adjusting nuts, remove the domed clutch cover (secured by eight screws.)

With the slotted driver provided on one of the thin spanners in the tool kit, screw each nut, in turn, fully home, then unscrew exactly four complete turns.

Before replacing the domed clutch cover, test for slip by starting up the engine, engaging top gear, and applying the rear brake when it should be possible to pull up the engine on full throttle without slip occurring.

If to cure slip it is found neccessary to further tighten the adjusting nuts this is a clear Indication that either the clutch springs have lost their tension, the inserts are so worn that they require renewal or that they have become impregnated with oil.

In the two former instances renewals are necessary, but if oil is the cause of slip this may be rectified by soaking the plates in petrol and allowing to dry off. If inserts are glazed roughen with sand paper.

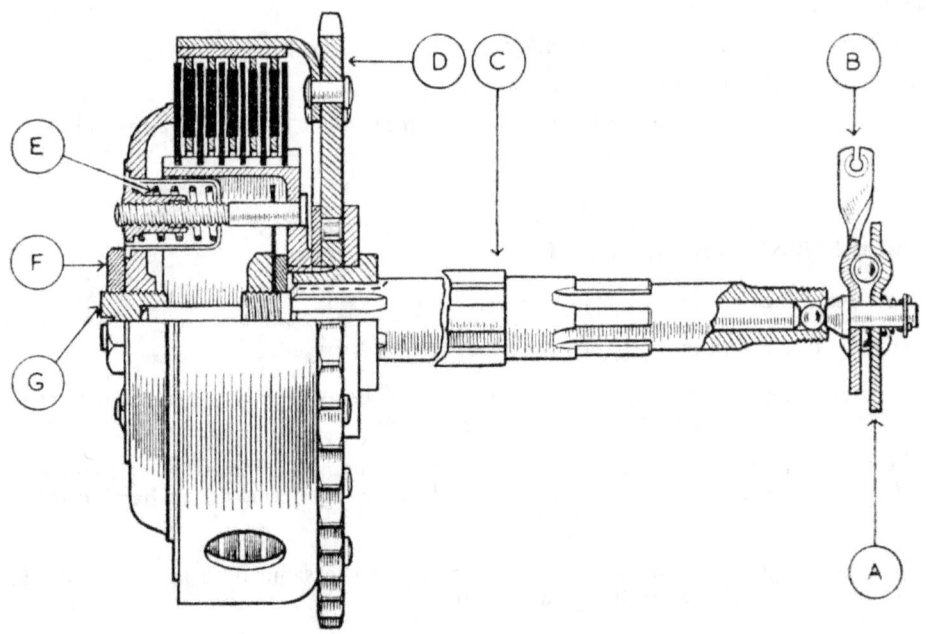

Illustration 15

A   FIXED CLUTCH INTERNAL ACTUATING PLATE
B   CLUTCH INTERNAL OPERATING LEVER
C   GEAR BOX MAINSHAFT
D   CLUTCH SPROCKET
E   CLUTCH SPRING
F   LOCK NUT FOR CLUTCH ROD THRUST CUP
G   THRUST CUP (in clutch pressure plate) FOR CLUTCH ROD

Showing clutch, gear box main shaft and clutch operating mechanism

CLUTCH OPERATING MECHANISM ADJUSTMENT

Correct adjustment of the clutch operating mechanism is of the utmost importance and the following instructions must be carefully observed.

In order to understand the method of clutch withdrawal a study of illustrations 14 and 15 should be made. See also paragraphs 7 and 8, page 41 (Transmission Service).

To enable the clutch to function satisfactorily 1/8" to 3/16" free movement of the operating cable is essential. This is checked by lifting the outer casing of the clutch cable at the position where it enters the screwed adjuster on the kick starter case cover. If the adjustment is correct it should be possible to freely move the casing up and down with the fingers 1/8" to 3/16".

If the free movement is excessive causing clutch drag or noisy gear changing, adjustment should be made as follows.

Release the clutch cable adjuster lock nut and then screw in the adjuster as far as it will go to ensure that the operating lever B (illustration 15) is in its normal position.

Now turn to the opposite side of the cycle and remove the domed clutch cover secured by eight screws.

Then using the sparking plug box key supplied in tool kit, loosen lock nut F.

Then with a screw driver gently screw in the thrust cup G until contact with the thrust rod can be felt after which unscrew exactly one half turn and then securely retighten the lock nut F taking care to observe that the screwed thrust cup does not also turn while doing so.

Replace the clutch cover and then make the final adjustment by unscrewing the cable adjuster until the recommended free movement of the casing is obtained after which retighten the cable adjuster lock nut.

As a result of wear of the clutch friction plate inserts after prolonged use, the plates tend to close up towards each other. This will have the effect of reducing the free movement in the operating mechanism referred to above.

Clutch slip resulting from lack of free movement will rapidly ruin the inserts and may generate sufficient heat to soften the clutch springs. Therefore should clutch slip develop an immediate check of free movement must be made.

In this case after slacking off the cable adjuster, unscrew the cup G a turn or two and then gently screw in until contact with the thrust rod is felt after which as already detailed it should be unscrewed exactly one half turn before retightening the lock nut F.

Lastly adjust the cable for the specified free movement.

To remove a clutch control cable

Remove the oil filler cap from the kick-starter case cover.

Screw right home the clutch cable adjuster that is located in the top of the kick-starter case cover.

Disengage, from the operating lever, the clutch cable inner wire by operating through the oil filler cap opening.

Completely unscrew the clutch cable adjuster.

Disengage, from the handlebar operating control lever, the clutch inner wire.

Pull cable, by its lower end, till removed from the machine, easing it through the frame cable clips while doing so.

To replace a clutch control cable

reverse the above instructions and, finally, adjust as detailed earlier.

FRONT CHAIN ADJUSTMENT

Tighten the front chain by :

Slacken : Nut on right-hand side of gear box top fixing bolt.

Forward nut on the adjusting eye-bolt. (Two or three turns.)

Remove inspection cap from front chaincase.

Screw up the rear nut on adjusting eye-bolt until, with the finger through the inspection cap orifice, it can be felt that the chain is dead tight. Then slack off the rear nut and carefully tighten the forward nut until the correct chain tension is obtained, after which securely tighten the rear nut to lock the assembly. (The correct chain whip is $\frac{3}{8}$ inch.) Check the adjustment in more than one position and adjust, as above, at tightest place.

It is important that these instructions to over-tighten and then slack back are carefully followed.

Tighten nut on gear box top fixing bolt.

Replace chaincase inspection cap.

REAR CHAIN ADJUSTMENT

To obtain rear chain adjustment the rear wheel is bodily moved in the rear frame fork ends which are slotted for the purpose. Adjusting screws with lock nuts are provided on the forward side of each slotted end.

To adjust the chain place cycle on stand and slightly slacken wheel spindle end nut (both ends on rigid frame models). On spring frame models also slightly slacken the brake drum dummy spindle locknut, the hexagon of which is adjacent to the spindle end nut. Then slacken back the adjuster screw lock nut on each side and screw each adjuster bolt in turn further in on rigid frame models and further out on spring frame models until the correct chain tension is obtained, taking care to move each side adjusting screw exactly the same amount.

While on the stand the chain whip should be $\frac{1}{2}$" in the case of rigid frame models and $1\frac{1}{8}$" for spring frame models (see notes below). Then retighten spindle end nut or nuts and also the adjuster screw lock nuts. Chain whip must always be checked midway between the two sprockets and the rear wheel should always be turned to obtain the position of least slackness. This is because rear chains rarely wear evenly and there is usually one position at which the chain is tighter than at any other. It is at this tightest position that the adjustment check should be made.

> NOTE—On spring frame models the chain adjustment specified while cycle is on the stand is reduced to $\frac{1}{2}$" when the wheel is on the ground and rider seated. This is due to chain sprocket centres varying slightly as the result of movement of the rear swinging arm.

NOTES ON REAR CHAIN ADJUSTMENT

Before tightening the rear chain always first check front chain adjustment and if attention is necessary adjust the front chain first. This is because adjustment of the front chain disturbs that of the rear chain.

Therefore, after making adjustment to the tension of the front chain, always afterwards check that of the rear chain.

It should also be noted that adjusting the rear chain will disturb rear brake adjustment, which should therefore always be checked subsequently.

REMOVING AND REFITTING REAR CHAIN

To protect the rear chain from mud and water it is very closely shrouded by the chain guard and removing the chain without first detaching the chain guard can present considerable difficulty. A simple procedure however is as follows.

First obtain a piece of thin string about ten feet long.

With cycle on the stand turn the rear wheel until the chain connecting link is at a position near the rear sprocket and remove the connecting link.

Now pass the string through the centre hole of the end link of the top run, draw the two ends of the string level and tie together.

Then pull the bottom run of the chain backwards with one hand while keeping the string taut at the rear end with the other hand.

As the end of the top run of the chain disengages with the gear box sprocket it will leave the string attached lying one strand each side of the sprocket teeth.

When the chain is well clear cut the string one side only at a point about one foot from where it is looped through the chain link.

Leave the string then *in situ* awaiting chain refitting.

To refit the chain.

Pass the longer cut end of the string through the centre hole of the end chain link and then tie the two loose ends of the string together.

Then pull the string from the rear end, at the same time guiding the chain up to engage with the gear box sprocket.

Continue pulling until the chain encircles the rear wheel sprocket, then remove the string and refit the connecting link, taking care while doing so to attach the spring clip with its closed end facing the direction of rotation.

DYNAMO CHAIN ADJUSTMENT

The dynamo armature shaft is eccentric to the body of the dynamo. Therefore, by partially revolving the dynamo in its housing the distance between the two dynamo driving sprockets can be varied, thereby allowing latitude for chain adjustment.

Tighten dynamo chain by :

Remove inspection cap from front chaincase.

Slacken dynamo clamping strap bolt.

With the fingers turn dynamo bodily in an anti-clockwise direction till, by passing a finger through the inspection cap opening, it can be felt the chain tension is correct.

The chain whip should be about $\frac{1}{4}$". Ensure, when feeling tension, the front driving chain is not confused with the dynamo chain which lies behind the front driving chain.

Tighten dynamo clamping strap bolt.

Re-check chain tension.

Replace chaincase inspection cap.

MAGNETO CHAIN ADJUSTMENT

The magneto platform hinges on one of its fixing bolts. This provides sufficient movement for adjustment to the magneto driving chain.

Tighten magneto chain by :

Remove magneto chain case cover.

Slacken nut on rear bolt supporting magneto platform.

Insert a screwdriver under that end of the magneto platform and lever upwards until the chain tension is correct.

The chain whip should be about $\frac{1}{4}''$.

Tighten nut on platform supporting bolt.

Re-check chain tension.

Place a supply of grease on magneto driving chain and using a broad pen knife blade or thin strip of metal work well into the interior of the auto ignition advance unit a generous quantity of either Mobilgrease No. 2 or Esso Fluid Grease.

Replace magneto chain cover.

ENGINE SHOCK ABSORBER

The engine shock absorber is a spring device for smoothing out the engine impulses.

The engine sprocket is a free fit on the driving side flywheel axle. It has, integral with it, a face cam that engages with a similar face cam ("shock absorber cam") which is keyed to the driving side flywheel axle by splines. A spring keeps the shock absorber cam in close engagement with the cam on the sprocket, and, the shock absorber cam being driven by the engine, over-rides the sprocket cam under the influence of the engine impulses. The shock absorber spring is compressed by the over-riding of the cams, thereby absorbing the shocks.

It is essential the faces of the cams are adequately lubricated otherwise the shock absorbing action will be nullified and this is automatically taken care of, providing the level of the oil in the front chaincase is maintained according to the instructions given in the "Lubrication Section."

The shock absorber spring is retained by a cap washer and a retaining bolt which must be fully tightened.

The dynamo sprocket is integral with the engine sprocket.

Behind the engine sprocket (between the sprocket and the crankshaft ball bearing) is a spacing collar which is a sliding fit on the driving side flywheel axle and in no circumstances must this be omitted.

NOTE—At the first sign of transmission harshness examine front chaincase for correct oil level, and dismantle and lubricate the shock absorber parts if the harshness continues. For access to the shock absorber parts it is necessary to remove the outer half of the front chaincase.

The order of assembly of the engine shock absorber is

1. The spacing collar between the crankshaft bearing and the engine sprocket.
2. The engine sprocket.
3. The shock absorber cam.
4. The shock absorber spring.
5. The cap washer.
6. The retaining nut.

FORK & FRAME SERVICE

STEERING HEAD ADJUSTMENT

The steering head frame races are of the floating self-aligning type and have spherical seats. Therefore they do not fit tightly in the head lug.

Occasionally test the steering head for correct adjustment by exerting pressure upwards from the extreme ends of the handlebars.

It is particularly important that the adjustment is tested after the first one hundred miles because of the initial settling down that always occurs in that period.

Should any shake be apparent, adjust the steering head bearings.

Adjust steering head bearings by :

Jack up the front of the machine so that all weight is taken off the front wheel. (A box under each footrest serves that purpose.)

Slacken the two fork crown pinch screws.

Slacken the domed nut at top of the steering column.

Screw down the nut underneath the domed nut a little at a time (using adjustable spanner 017249) and, while doing so, test the head assembly for slackness by placing the fingers over the gap between handlebar lug and frame top lug, at the same time exerting upward pressure by lifting from the front edge of the front mudguard. Tested in this manner the slightest slackness is discernible.

Continue to tighten the lower adjusting nut until no perceptible movement can be felt and yet the steering head is perfectly free to turn, then tighten down the domed nut in order to lock the adjustment.

Securely tighten the two fork crown pinch screws. (This is very important.)

Remove packing from under footrest.

FRONT FORKS (TELEDRAULIC)

Owing to the unusual construction of the " **TELEDRAULIC** " fork it is desirable to understand what happens in use and, in order to follow clearly the descriptions and subsequent assembly and adjustment instructions, reference to Illustrations 16 and 17 will be necessary.

As will be seen from the general arrangement drawing, Illustration 17, the main members of the forks are two long tubes. These are of heavy gauge and are externally ground to very fine limits. These fork main, inner, tubes are firmly fixed to the handlebar clip lug by the top bolts 021830 and are clamped to the fork crown by the clamping screws. Upon the external of these tubes are mounted the springs and sliding members, to which latter the front wheel, mudguards and front stand are fixed.

The telescopic action of the sliders, combined with the hydraulic dampers, described later, explain the word " **Teledraulic**," coined for the description of the fork.

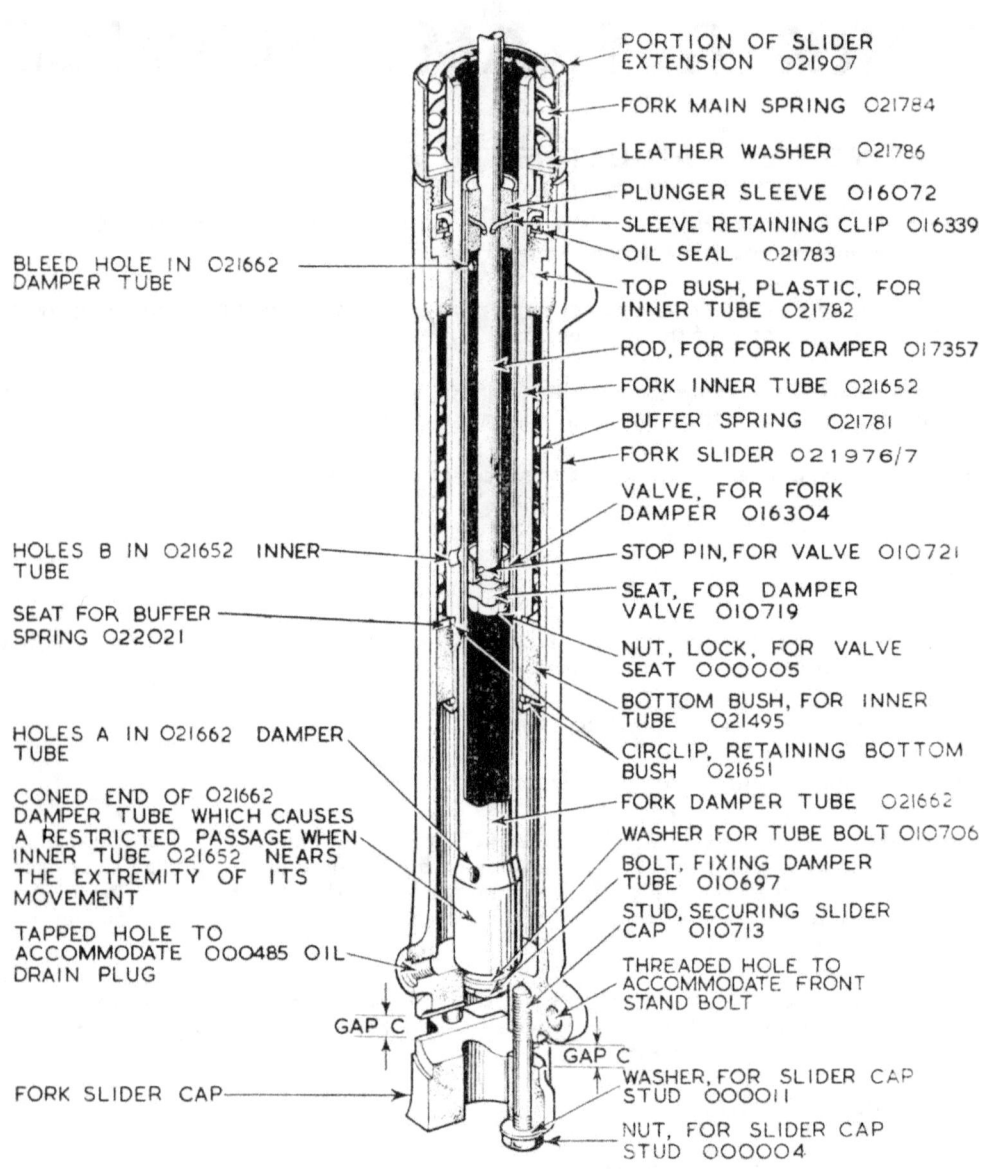

Illustration 16

Introduced in early 1941 for use under strenuous war conditions by all the allied armies, it remains unaltered, except in detail, to this day, and copied practically universally. The hydraulic dampers operate in tubular members located inside the main tubes. As will be seen the aluminium sliding members operate upon steel bushes attached to the bottom ends of the main tubes and also upon bakelite bushes, secured to the top end of the sliders themselves. Above these bushes, an oil seal is fitted, the object of which is to prevent leakage of oil from below into the main spring chamber. The normal level of oil is well above the bottom extremity of the main inner tubes and bearing this in mind, it is at once clear that upward movement of the sliders resulting from impact with road bumps in addition to meeting resistance from the main springs also causes oil to be ejected by the close fitting steel bushes. This oil is forced upward through the open ends of the main inner tubes and also through the holes A (Illustration 16) in the bottom of the damper tubes, then past the damper disc valve which the passing oil raises off its seat. As the oil level rises inside the main inner tubes, air trapped is compressed, thereby forming an air buffer acting as auxiliary to the main springs. This displacement of oil upon impact imposes a certain amount of damper effect, the extent of which increases with the violence of the shock, or in other words, the bigger the bump the greater the damping effect. Upon the recoil movement, the damper disc valve returns to its seat and the oil trapped between this valve and the plunger sleeve above has no other source of escape but past this sleeve and the adjacent small metered bleed hole. This intentionally restricted passage causes a considerable damper effect to the recoil action. It will thus be gathered that on the shock movement of the fork, slight damper action occurs, with a greatly increased damper action on the reverse movement, both actions automatically increasing in effect the more violent the movement. Before concluding this description, it should be mentioned that upon a very violent impact, as a result of which the main springs are almost fully compressed, the damping of the upward movement of the sliders is intentionally increased by the automatically greatly restricted passage for the displaced oil, brought about by the lower ends of the main tubes encircling the tapered enlarged ends of the damper tubes as the sliders near the limit of their upward movement. Thus bottoming is prevented, no matter how violent the impact. For ordinary purposes the recommended oil content is $6\frac{1}{2}$ ozs. (184·6 c.c.) each leg of one of the S.A.E. 20 oils specified. To deal with heavier loads than normal, the oil content may be increased to a permissible maximum of 10 fluid ozs. (284 c.c.) per leg. To increase damping oil of heavier grade may be used. It will be found, however, that for normal purposes the recommended grade and quantity of oil will give the most comfortable ride.

FRONT FORK " TOPPING UP "

No part of the **TELEDRAULIC** Front Fork requires individual lubrication, but it is advisable to check the oil content, once every five thousand miles. The normal content as already stated, is $6\frac{1}{2}$ fluid ounces (184·6 c.c.) each side.

Support motor cycle vertically with weight on both wheels. A steady under each footrest is the best method.

Lever off snap on dome caps and unscrew the hexagonal plugs at top of fork inner tubes. These are on level with handlebars and attached to them are the damper rods. Have a graduated measure of not less than 10 fluid ozs. capacity available in which to catch and measure the oil. Remove the drain plug from the bottom of a slider and catch the oil which drains out. Then reinsert drain plug and work the top plugs to which damper rods are attached up and down (pumping action), making upward strokes as violent as possible but using only fingers to do so. This pumping action is to eject any oil trapped in the damper tubes above the damper disc valve. Wait two minutes and again remove drain plug. Repeat the action until no further oil can be drained off when, if the fork had the correct oil content, about 6 fluid oz. (170·4 c.c.) will have been drained off. If less, add to make this quantity, or reduce if an excess quantity has been drained off. Next refit drain plug and carefully pour into the top of the tube being checked exactly 6 fluid ozs. (170·4 c.c.), after which the top plug may be replaced.

NOTE—Although the normal oil content of each side is specified as $6\frac{1}{2}$ fluid ozs., it is not possible to drain all the oil via the drain plug. This explains the lesser quantity of 6 fluid ozs. (170·4 c.c.) referred to above. However, if the fork is at any time completely dismantled and then reassembled in a dry state, it should be noted that in that event the correct quantity of oil to add to each leg is $6\frac{1}{2}$ fluid ozs. (184·6 c.c.).

TO REMOVE THE COMPLETE FRONT FORK ASSEMBLY

Support the machine with the front wheel clear of the ground. (A box, of suitable height, under each footrest is the best method.)

Remove the front wheel as described in Wheel Section.

Remove the front stand and front mudguard.

Slaken the screw on headlamp top, gently prise out the rim and reflector assembly, detach with a slight rotary and lifting movement the cap to which headlamp wires are attached and take away rim and reflector assembly.

Gently ease back the rubber sleeves covering the pilot lamp wire snap connectors and pull latter apart.

Remove the nuts on the tubular bolts through which the pilot lamp wires pass which enables the pilot lamps to be taken away, leaving the head lamp shell, etc., free to be gently suspended by the wiring loom.

Disconnect the driving cable from the speedometer head and draw same down through fork crown.

Remove the handlebar half clip and lay the handlebars, complete with controls, upon a pad on top of the petrol tank.

Detach the front brake cable from the forks. (First remove the slotted yoke end and then completely unscrew the cable adjuster.)

Remove the snap on dome caps and unscrew the hexagon plug on top of each inner tube, raise same and slacken the lock nuts securing the damper rods attached. Then, before removing the hexagon plugs, attach a piece of wire about 18 inches long underneath each damper rod lock nut, to enable the damper rods to be raised for reassembly.

Remove domed nut at top of steering column.

Remove lock nut on steering column.

Use a soft mallet to tap upward the handlebar lug until it disengages with the fork stem (steering column) and main tubes. The fork assembly can then be withdrawn. (Take care to avoid loss of any of the 56 steering head steel balls.)

To re-fit a complete front fork assembly

Secure, with grease, 28 balls in fork crown ball race.

Secure, with grease, 28 balls in main frame top ball race.

Proceed to fit fork assembly by reversing the instructions given above to dismantle, carefully retightening the damper rod locknuts before inserting the hexagonal headed plugs to which they are attached.

TO REMOVE A FORK SLIDER (either side) (Dealers' service only)

Support the motor cycle with the front wheel clear of the ground, and unscrew the tubular slider extension from the slider which it is intended to remove. Special articulated clamp tool required. (Available in workshop tools).

Next remove the front wheel, front stand and mudguard as detailed above. Then with a thin tubular box key, remove the bolt securing the damper tube. The hexagonal head of the bolt is sunk in the upper half of the wheel spindle clamp. Place a receptacle underneath to catch the oil which will drain out upon removing the bolt, and take care of the fibre washer located under the head. A sharp jerk downward should now enable the slider to be withdrawn, but should difficulty be experienced, apply a little heat to the enlarged top end of the slider. This will cause sufficient expansion to release the oil seal which is normally a snug push-in fit, in the top of the slider. The re-assembly is carried out in exactly the reverse order, again if necessary applying a little heat to enable the oil seal to be pushed down into the slider top before screwing in the slider extension. After completion, the oil which has escaped **MUST** be returned via the top. (See Front Fork " Topping up.")

TO REMOVE A FORK INNER TUBE ASSEMBLY (either side) (Dealers' service only)

Remove the snap on dome caps, then unscrew the hexagonal plug at the top of the inner tube it is intended to remove, and after slackening the lock nut by which the damper rod is secured to this plug, unscrew the plug, allowing the rod to fall. Next proceed to remove the slider as already detailed, except do not disturb the bolt securing the damper tube. This damper tube and protruding rod can be removed intact with the slider. Now loosen the fork crown clamping screw when it should be possible to draw the entire inner tube assembly down through the crown lug. Upon reassembly, the inner tube is first pushed home as far as possible by hand and then pulled right home by screwing down the top hexagonal plug. With this plug tightened down, then proceed to tighten the crown clamping screw, after which the hexagonal plug may be removed and a piece of wire passed down through the inner tube. Loop the bottom end of this wire underneath the damper rod lock nut. The slider is then carefully pushed upward while at the same time pulling on the wire until the top end of the damper rod projects sufficiently to permit the screwed plug to be attached and secured with the lock nut, after which the wire may be removed. It may be found necessary to apply a little heat to enable the oil seal to be pressed home with the fingers before screwing on the tubular extension.

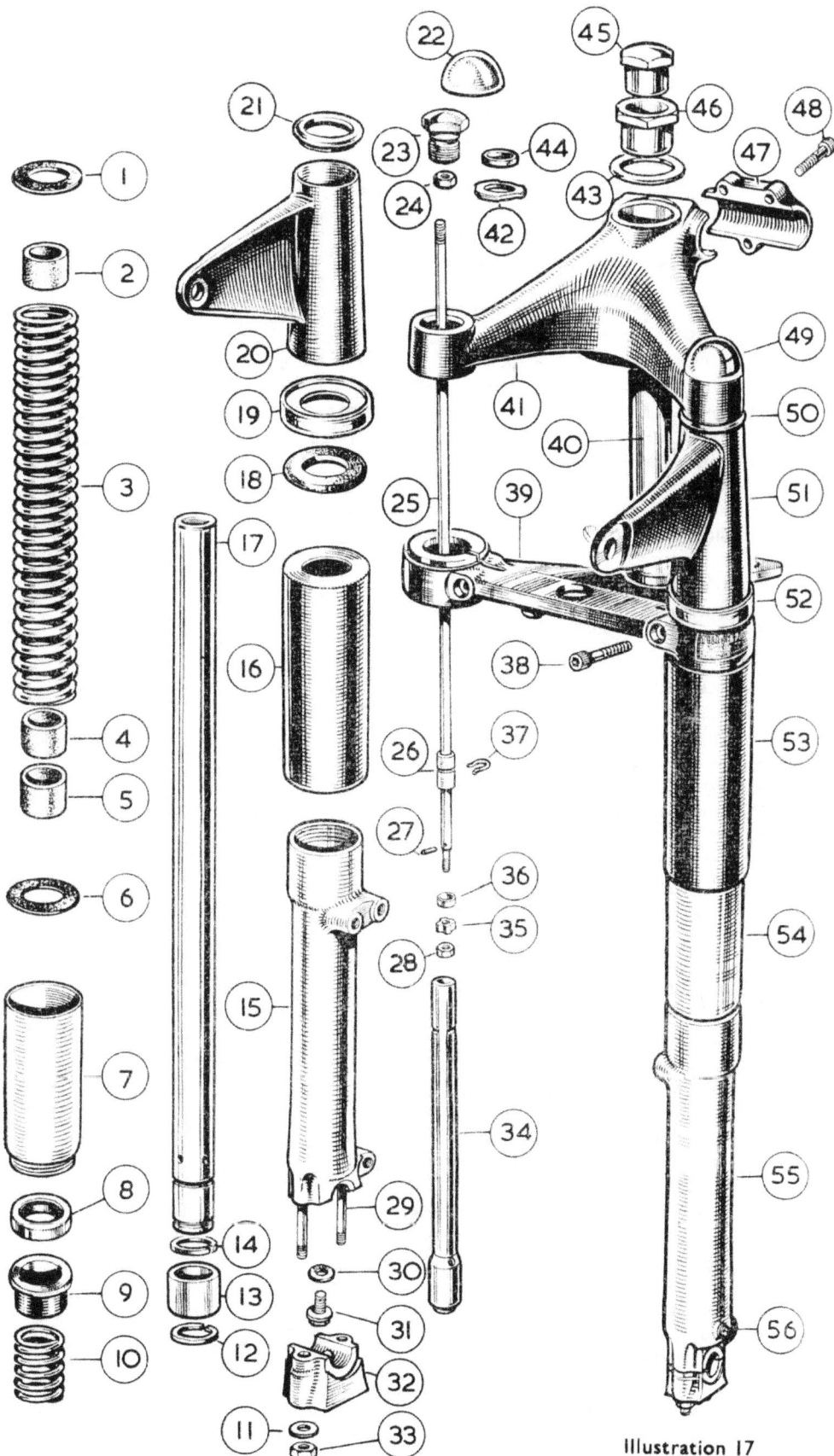

Illustration 17

REF. NO.	DESCRIPTION

1. WASHER, LEATHER, FOR FORK SPRING TOP SEATING.
2. BUFFER, RUBBER, FOR FORK INNER TUBE
3. SPRING, MAIN, FOR FRONT FORK.
4. BUFFER, RUBBER, FOR FORK INNER TUBE.
5. BUFFER, RUBBER, FOR FORK INNER TUBE.
6. WASHER, LEATHER, FOR FORK SPRING BOTTOM SEATING.
7. EXTENSION, FOR FORK SLIDER.
8. OIL SEAL, FOR FORK INNER TUBE.
9. BUSH, TOP, PLASTIC, FOR FORK INNER TUBE.
10. SPRING, BUFFER, FOR FRONT FORK.
11. WASHER, PLAIN, FOR FORK SLIDER CAP SECURING STUD.
12. CIRCLIP, LOCATING FORK INNER TUBE BOTTOM BUSH.
13. BUSH, BOTTOM, STEEL, FOR FORK INNER TUBE.
14. CIRCLIP, LOCATING, FORK INNER TUBE BOTTOM BUSH.
15. SLIDER FOR FORK WITH STUDS (RIGHT HAND).
16. TUBE, FORK, COVER, BOTTOM.
17. TUBE, FORK, INNER.
18. RUBBER RING FOR TOP COVER TUBE HOUSING RING.
19. HOUSING RING, TOP COVER TUBE.
20. TUBE, FORK COVER, TOP, RIGHT, WITH LAMP LUG.
21. SPIGOT RING TOP COVER TUBE.
22. SNAP ON DOME CAP.
23. BOLT, TOP, FOR FORK INNER TUBE.
24. NUT, LOCK, FOR TOP END OF DAMPER ROD.
25. ROD, FOR FORK DAMPER.
26. SLEEVE, PLUNGER, ON FORK DAMPER ROD.
27. PIN, STOP, FOR FORK DAMPER VALVE.
28. NUT, LOCK, FOR DAMPER VALVE SEAT.
29. STUD, SECURING CAP TO FORK SLIDER.
30. WASHER, FIBRE, FOR DAMPER TUBE BOLT.
31. BOLT, FIXING DAMPER TUBE TO SLIDER.
32. CAP, FOR FORK SLIDER.
33. NUT, FOR FORK SLIDER CAP SECURING STUD
34. TUBE, FOR FORK DAMPER.
35. SEAT, FOR FORK DAMPER VALVE.
36. VALVE, FOR FORK DAMPER.
37. CLIP, RETAINING DAMPER ROD SLEEVE.
38. SCREW, PINCH, FOR FORK CROWN.
39. FORK CROWN } NOT SOLD SEPARATELY
40. STEM, FOR FORK CROWN
41. LUG, FOR HANDLEBAR AND STEERING HEAD.
42. WASHER, SPECIAL FOR INNER TUBE TOP BOLT.
43. WASHER FOR FORK STEM ADJUSTING NUT.
44. RING, RUBBER, SEALING, FOR INNER TUBE TOP BOLT.
45. NUT, LOCK FOR FORK STEM.
46. NUT, ADJUSTING, FOR FORK STEM.
47. CLIP (HALF ONLY), FOR HANDLEBAR LUG.
48. SCREW, PINCH, FOR HANDLEBAR CLIP.
49. SNAP ON DOME CAP.
50. SPIGOT RING TOP COVER TUBE.
51. TUBE, FORK COVER, TOP, LEFT, WITH LAMP LUG.
52. HOUSING RING TOP COVER TUBE.
53. TUBE, FORK COVER, BOTTOM.
54. EXTENSION, FOR FORK SLIDER.
55. SLIDER FOR FORK WITH STUDS (LEFT SIDE)
56. SCREW, PLUG, WITH FIBRE WASHER, FOR FORK SLIDER OIL DRAIN HOLE.

REAR SUSPENSION

The rear wheel is mounted in a fork that is hinged just behind the gear box. The hinge has robust plain bearings lubricated from a reservoir of 1½ fluid ounces (42.6 c.c.) of heavy gear oil which is sufficient to last almost indefinitely. Provision is, however, made for replenishment should same be required. A small screw will be observed in the right-hand end cap of the hinge bearing, upon removal of this screw, oil can be injected into the reservoir, the screw orifice operating as a level control.

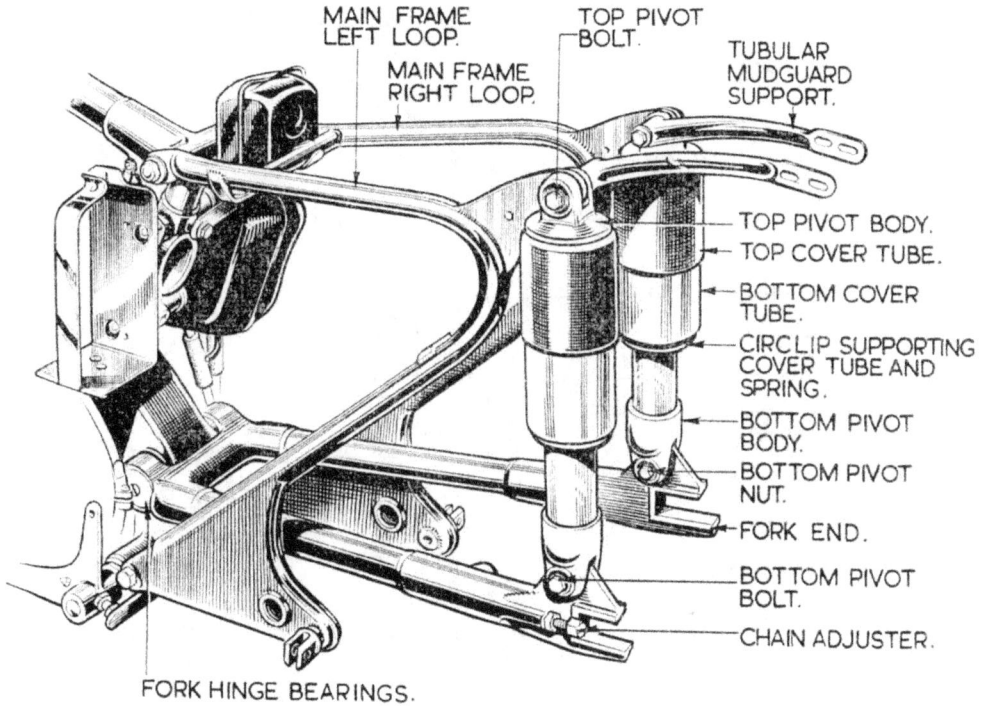

Illustration 18

Showing rear sprung frame and " TELEDRAULIC " legs

The rear wheel fork is suspended on springs located in the two " **TELEDRAULIC** " legs joining the rear of the fork to the main frame rear loops, and the spring action is damped by hydraulic dampers identical in design to those used in the "**TELEDRAULIC**" Front Fork Assembly.

The hydraulic fluid used is one of the grades of oil specified in the Lubrication Section for use in the " **TELEDRAULIC** " Front Forks.

The recommended quantity for each leg is 85 c.c. or a trifle under 3 fluid ozs. of S.A.E. 20 grade of one of the brands specified. For abnormal loads, or sustained high speed, the next heavier S.A.E. grade may be used, but unlike the front fork, recoil damping as well as maximum load capacity is increased by this alteration of grade alone, and under no circumstances should the oil content of each leg exceed 90 c.c. or roughly 3⅛ fluid ozs. Unless serious doubt exists as to the correct functioning of the rear legs, owners are advised to leave well alone. Should the need arise, however, the oil content of each leg should be separately checked as follows :

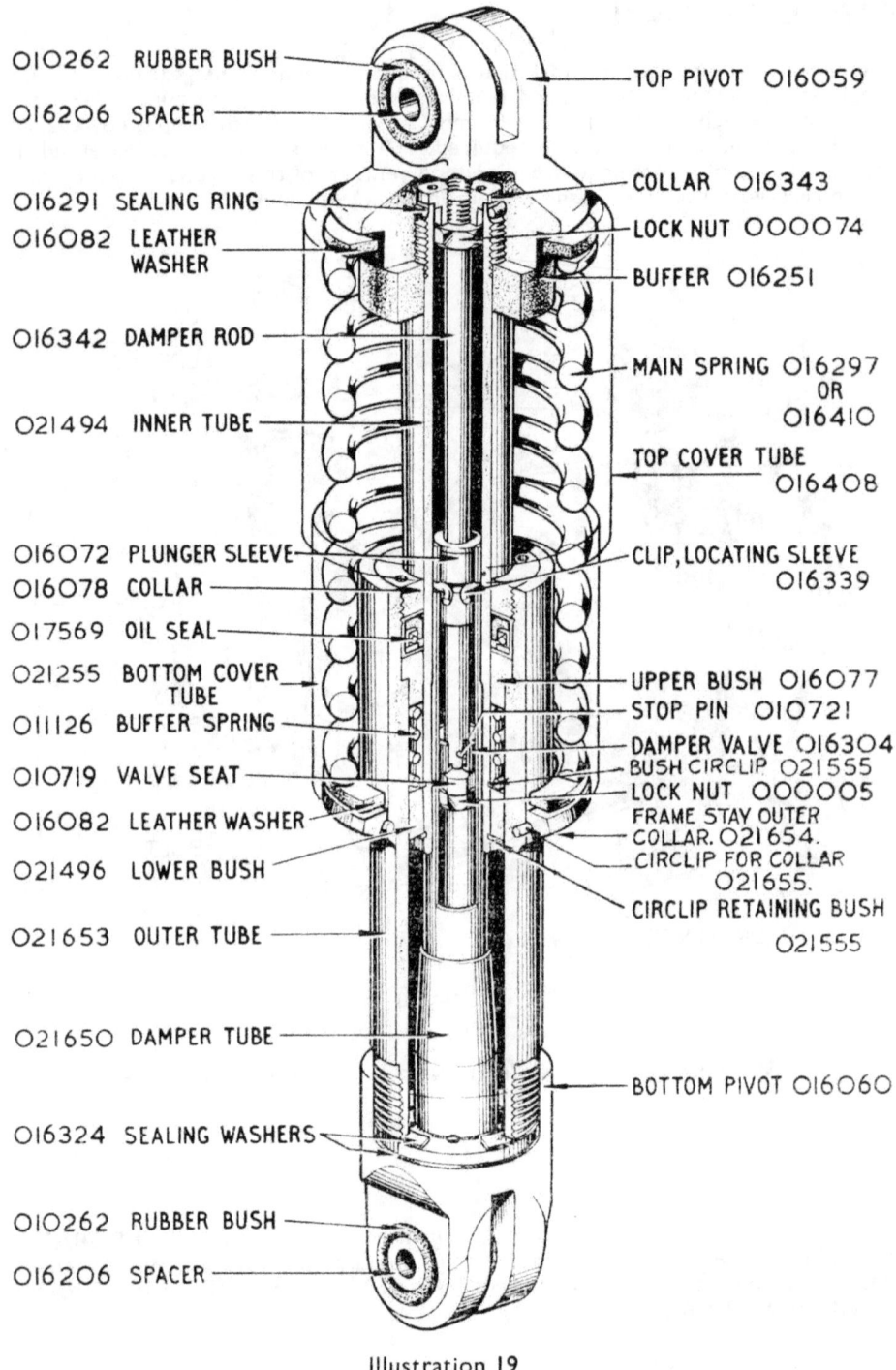

Illustration 19

Showing "Ghost" view of "TELEDRAULIC" leg

To check oil content of " TELEDRAULIC " leg and top-up :

Dealing with one leg at a time, remove top securing bolt, taking care to observe the location of the spacing washers on it. Remove bottom securing bolt and take away the leg.

Using a suitable clamp encircling the outer tube adjacent to the bottom pivot lug, grip in a vice and loosen the pivot lug.

Then holding leg vertically, bottom end uppermost, carefully remove the loosened pivot lug, and gripping the exposed end of the damper tube with the fingers, raise and lower several times (pumping action) after which pour the oil contents into a graduated measure.

It may be necessary to repeat the pumping action to eject oil from underneath the damper valve, and finally the open end of tube should be supported above the measure and left to drain for several minutes.

If the leg contained the correct amount of oil, 75 c.c. ($2\frac{5}{8}$ ozs.) should have been drained out into the graduated measure, leaving 10 c.c. ($\frac{1}{3}$ oz.) which cannot be withdrawn.

All that now remains is to pour carefully back into the leg exactly 75 c.c. ($2\frac{5}{8}$ ozs.) of oil, after which the pivot lug may again be screwed on and securely tightened down to prevent oil leakage when the leg is re-fitted, after which the other leg may be dealt with in a similar manner.

NOTE.—Shortage of oil is evidenced by very lively action.

PROP STAND

The prop stand hinges on a bolt which passes through a lug brazed to the frame and screws into the jaw of the stand leg. It is then locked by a nut and split pin. Care in tightening this bolt is necessary to avoid pinching, and it is essential to observe after securely tightening the lock nut that the stand is perfectly free. Smear the hinge bolt with engine oil before replacing it.

CENTRE STAND (Spring Frame Models)

The centre stand is mounted on a bolt set across the bottom rear of the main frame and is removed by taking off a nut of the centre bolt and pushing bolt through the frame. During removal and replacement the stand should be in a horizontal position in order to take off as much of the tension off the return spring as is possible.

FRONT STAND

The front stand is intended to operate **only as a support** and care is necessary, when using, to avoid passing the vertical position. No stops are provided and dragging the machine backward, with the stands down, is likely to fracture the lugs on the aluminium sliders of the forks to which the stand is attached.

Do not attempt to use the FRONT STAND unless the machine is already supported by the main stand.

REAR STAND (Rigid Frame Models)

A plain steel washer is fitted under the **HEAD** of each of the two bolts that retain the rear stand to the fork ends. The washers should **NOT** be fitted **UNDER** the nuts of those bolts.

TO REMOVE OIL TANK AND BATTERY CARRIER

Drain oil tank.

Disconnect wires from battery terminals.

Remove battery.

Disconnect oil feed pipe from bottom of oil tank.

Disconnect oil return pipe from bottom of oil tank.

Disconnect vent pipe from back of oil tank.

Remove bolt retaining oil tank stay to frame.

Remove screw in base of battery carrier, retaining carrier to stay from front chain case.

Remove the two nuts and washers retaining battery carrier to the two mounting studs and remove carrier.

Oil tank with supporting studs can then be withdrawn.

To refit reverse the above instructions.

TO REMOVE THE REAR CHAIN GUARD (Spring Frame Models)

Remove the rear wheel.   (See Wheel Section.)

Remove the bolt retaining the front end of the chain guard to the rear fork.

Remove the bolt retaining the rear end of the chain guard to the rear fork. (There is a spacer on this bolt, between the two sides of the guard.)

TO REMOVE THE REAR CHAIN GUARD (Rigid Frame Models)

Remove

The rear portion of rear mudguard.

The bolt retaining the front, top, end of the chain guard to the front chaincase.

The bolt retaining the front, bottom, end of the chain guard to the rear frame.

The bolt retaining the rear, top, end of the chain guard to the rear frame.

The chain guard is then free to be taken away.

BY USING GENUINE SPARES YOU ARE ASSURED THEY WILL FIT ACCURATELY AND GIVE SATISFACTORY SERVICE

WHEELS AND BRAKES

TO REMOVE FRONT WHEEL

Place machine on both stands.

Remove the split pin, and pin, retaining yoke end of front brake cable to the brake expander lever.

Remove bolt retaining brake anchor stay to brake cover plate.

Slacken the nut on the left-hand end of front wheel spindle.

Remove the four nuts retaining the caps to the fork sliders, which will permit the removal of the two caps and, putting pressure on the front wheel (in order to decrease the effective height of the wheel spindle) the wheel can be withdrawn towards the front.

NOTE—The two caps **MUST** be re-fitted in same order and position as originally. Therefore, lay them aside so that the order and position of assembly will be correctly made.

Do not attempt to use the FRONT STAND unless the machine is supported by the centre stand (on SPRING FRAME MODELS) or by the REAR STAND (on RIGID FRAME MODELS).

TO RE-FIT FRONT WHEEL

Holding the left side cap on the wheel spindle, offer wheel up so as to engage the cap with its securing studs. Then apply fixing nuts and washers but only loosely tighten.

NOTE—To pass the wheel spindle into position it may be necessary to apply pressure to flatten the tyre so as to enable the spindle to pass the forward fixing studs.

Next, fit the right side cap and again only loosely tighten the securing nuts. Now attach the brake anchor arm and refit the yoke end pin.

Next fully tighten the nuts securing the left side cap, taking care to keep the gap fore and aft approximately equal. Then tighten the left side spindle nut and lastly the nuts securing the right side cap.

Should any fork stiffness be apparent after re-fixing the front wheel, loosen the nuts securing the right side cap and after working the fork up and down violently, re-tighten.

This action will ensure that the wheel clamp occupies its natural position on the spindle end on which it is intentionally not positioned.

TO REMOVE DETACHABLE REAR WHEEL (Spring Frame Models)

Place the machine on the centre stand. Loosen the bolt in the rearmost position on each tubular member to which the detachable rear portion of the mudguard is secured. Also slacken off the two bolts securing the two portions of mudguard together. Disconnect the snap connectors of the rear lamp wire when the rear portion of mudguard is free to be taken away.

Disconnect speedometer drive by unscrewing the cable gland nut and withdrawing drive cable end from the speedometer gear box. Then remove the wheel spindle end nut and washer and withdraw spindle together with distance collar which will fall as spindle is withdrawn. The wheel is now free to be removed.

In refitting it will be found best to offer up the wheel, insert spindle without the distance collar and after engaging the driving pegs hold wheel *in situ*, withdraw the spindle and insert the distance collar.

Upon tightening the spindle end nut make certain the collar end of the spindle is in contact with the chain adjusting screw to ensure correct wheel alignment. Also see that the speedometer gear box is positioned correctly.

TO REMOVE REAR WHEEL (Rigid Frame Models)

Place machine on rear stand.
Disconnect rear lamp wire at connection near rear wheel spindle.
Disconnect speedometer driving cable. (Unscrew gland nut on cable.)
Disconnect rear chain connecting link. (Allow chain to hang clear of the rear wheel sprocket without becoming disengaged from the gear box small sprocket.) Engage a gear to prevent sprocket revolving.
Slacken the two bolts securing rear portion of rear mudguard to its front portion.
Loosen nut and washer from bolt securing mudguard side bridge and tool box stay to tubular stay.
Remove adjusting nut from rear brake rod.
Slacken the two nuts (unscrew about four turns) retaining the rear mudguard side stays to their studs.
Slacken the two nuts on the rear wheel spindle.
Remove the rear portion of the rear mudguard, with its stays, leaving tool box and stay in position.
Remove the rear wheel from the fork ends by twisting it sideways to release and clear the rear brake cover plate anchor bolt and then withdrawing it to the rear.
Re-fit in the reverse order but, before finally tightening the rear wheel spindle nuts, ensure the speedometer gear box is so positioned that the speedometer driving cable can be correctly replaced. Also make certain that the slotted end of the brake cover plate is correctly located on its anchoring bolt. See illustration 20.
When the wheel alignment is correct a piece of thin string stretched taut across both wheels, about four inches from, and parallel to, the ground, should just touch each tyre at both sides of the wheel centres.
Alternatively, a straight wooden batten, about five feet long, is handy to use for checking wheel alignment. This should be applied, as in the case of string, parallel to and about four inches from the ground.
NOTE—Above remarks on wheel alignment applies only to Models with similar width tyres back and front.
On Models with larger rear tyre than front observe equal gap each side of latter when checking.

TO RE-FIT REAR WHEEL (Spring Frame Model)

Reverse the removal procedure, see that the speedometer drive dogs are engaged, but leave the tightening of the nut that locates the speedometer gear box for the final operation, i.e., after the speedometer cable has been re-connected and the exterior axle nuts have been tightened. (This also applies to Rigid Frame Models.)

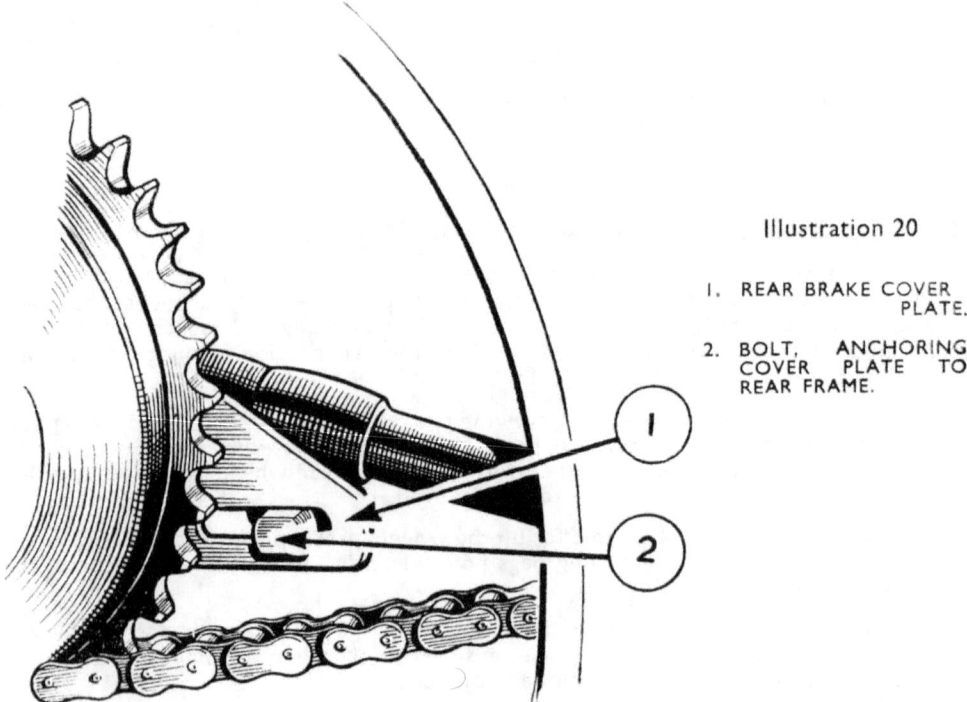

Illustration 20

1. REAR BRAKE COVER PLATE.
2. BOLT, ANCHORING COVER PLATE TO REAR FRAME.

On rigid frame models it will be found easier to re-fit the wheel to the fork ends with the brake cover plate hanging free and then, holding the wheel on its left-hand side, as far forward in the fork end as is possible, to swing the right-hand side backwards, lifting up the free cover plate so that the slot in it is positioned to engage with the square headed anchor bolt and then swinging the right-hand end of the axle forwards till engagement has been completed.

After re-fitting the rear wheel, check the rear chain adjustment, and, if necessary, re-set it. Then check the rear brake adjustment and, if necessary, re-set it. Also check that brake cover plate anchorage is correct (see illustration 20.)

WHEEL BEARINGS AND ADJUSTMENT

The wheel bearings are of taper roller type. See illustrations. The outer cups for the rollers are pressed into the hub shell. They have a fixed location one side and an adjustable location on the other. The fixed location is provided by a circlip in a groove cut in one end of the hub shell, while the adjustable location is regulated by a screwed ring that is threaded into the opposite end of the hub and the position of which can be locked by an encircling nut.

On all wheels the adjusting ring is located on the right-hand side.

It is rarely necessary to make adjustment to wheel bearings. It is most important they are not adjusted too tightly as this would quickly ruin them. There must always be a slight amount of end play. This should be about .002", which represents a just perceptible rim rock. (Not more than $\frac{1}{64}$" rock.)

A service method of ensuring correct adjustment is :

Slacken the lock nut.

Tighten the adjusting ring until all slackness has been taken up.

Slacken back the adjusting ring exactly one-half turn.

Tighten the lock nut, making sure that, when doing so, the adjusting ring does not creep round and that the cover disc is positioned to permit grease gun application to the nipple.

TO DISMANTLE FRONT WHEEL BEARINGS

Remove wheel from machine.

Remove nut securing brake cover plate, withdraw cover plate with brake shoes, etc.

Then remove brake cover positioning nut and washer.

Then turn to the right-hand side of wheel, remove adjusting ring lock nut and lift off cover disc.

Then completely unscrew the adjusting ring.

Now carefully apply pressure to the threaded end of the wheel spindle which will eject from the opposite end of the hub, the washer (7), oil seal (8) and oil seal cup (9) together with the bearing outer ring (6). The wheel spindle with its two sets of rollers in cages may now be lifted out leaving *in situ* only the fixed bearing ring together with the oil seal, washer and cup for that side bearing.

If it is desired to remove these pressure is first applied to the visible washer, by which the assembly is forced inward sufficiently to permit extraction of the retaining circlip, after which through the medium of a mandrel or a piece of tubing of external diameter, a trifle smaller than the hub bore, apply pressure to the inner edge of the fixed bearing ring so that it is forced out of the hub end. As it emerges it will push out the end washer (2), the oil seal (3) and the oil seal encircling collar (4) and the inner washer (5).

To refit reverse the above procedure remembering that after bearing ring (6), washer (5), spacer (4), oil seal (3) and washer (2) have been inserted, to refit the circlip (1) snugly in its groove and to then apply pressure to the inner edge of the bearing ring to force the assembly tightly back against the retaining circlip.

Finally, position the disc when tightening the adjusting ring lock nut so that access to the grease nipple is possible.

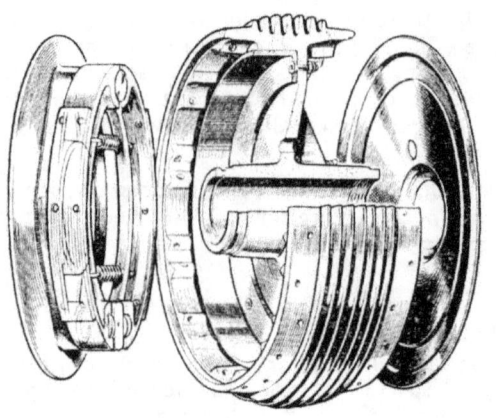
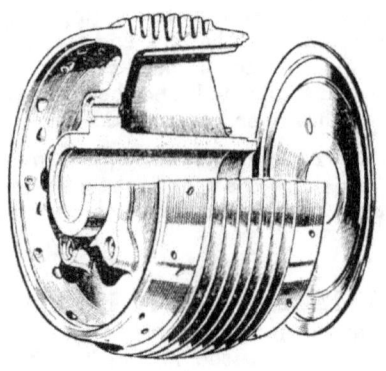

Illustration 21

Showing front hub and brake also rear hub

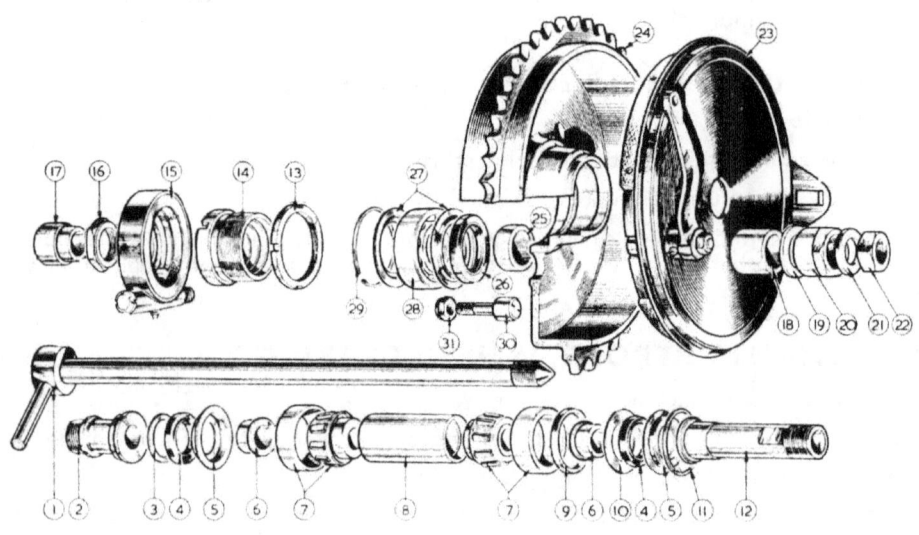

Illustration 22

**Showing rear wheel bearings and brake drum
(Spring Frame Models)**

1	WITHDRAWABLE WHEEL SPINDLE.	17	SPACER FOR WITHDRAWABLE SPINDLE.
2	SPEEDOMETER GEAR BOX SLEEVE.	18	OUTER SPACER FOR BRAKE COVER PLATE.
3	RING RETAINING OIL SEAL (Small).	19	WASHER FOR COVER PLATE FIXING NUT.
4	OIL SEAL.	20	BRAKE COVER PLATE FIXING NUT.
5	CUP FOR OIL SEAL.	21	SPINDLE END WASHER.
6	OIL SEAL DISTANCE PIECE.	22	SPINDLE END NUT.
7	TAPER ROLLER BEARING COMPLETE.	23	BRAKE COVER PLATE COMPLETE.
8	SPACER BETWEEN BEARINGS.	24	REAR BRAKE DRUM.
9	BEARING SPACING COLLAR (Brake Side).	25	INNER SPACER FOR BRAKE COVER PLATE.
10	RING RETAINING OIL SEAL (Large).	26	BRAKE DRUM BEARING OIL SEAL.
11	CIRCLIP.	27	BRAKE DRUM OIL SEAL WASHERS.
12	BRAKE DRUM DUMMY SPINDLE.	28	BRAKE DRUM BALL BEARING.
13	LOCK NUT FOR ADJUSTING RING.	29	CIRCLIP RETAINING BEARING.
14	ADJUSTING RING.	30	DRIVING PEG (5 Off).
15	SPEEDOMETER GEAR BOX COMPLETE.	31	NUT SECURING DRIVING PEG (5 Off).
16	SPEEDOMETER GEAR BOX FIXING NUT.		

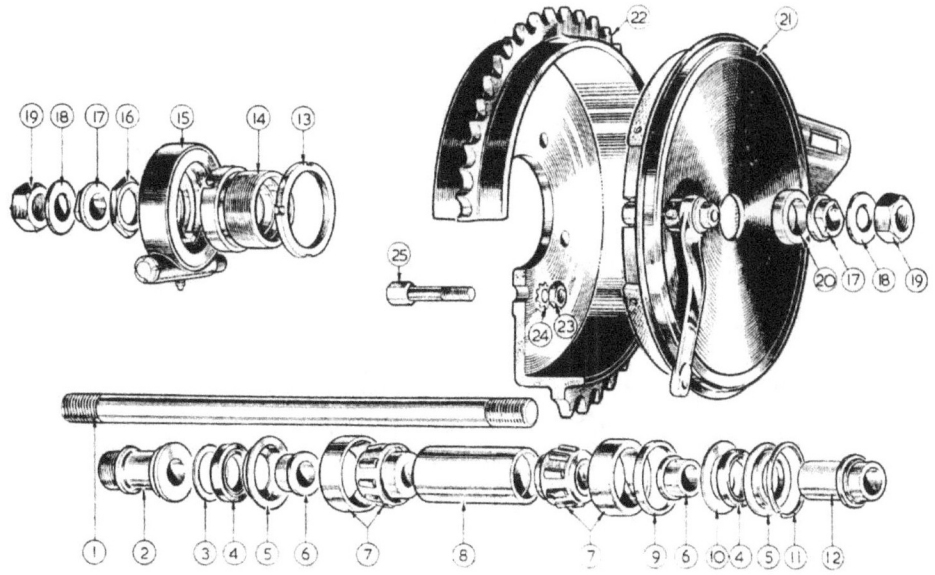

Illustration 23
**Showing rear wheel bearings and brake drum
(Rigid Frame Models)**

1. CENTRE SOLID WHEEL SPINDLE.
2. SPEEDOMETER GEAR BOX SLEEVE.
3. RING RETAINING OIL SEAL (Small).
4. OIL SEAL.
5. CUP FOR OIL SEAL.
6. OIL SEAL DISTANCE PIECE.
7. TAPER ROLLER BEARING COMPLETE.
8. SPACER BETWEEN BEARINGS.
9. BEARING SPACING COLLAR (Brake Side).
10. RING RETAINING OIL SEAL (Large).
11. CIRCLIP.
12. INNER SPACER FOR BRAKE COVER PLATE.
13. LOCK NUT FOR ADJUSTING RING.
14. ADJUSTING RING.
15. SPEEDOMETER GEAR BOX COMPLETE.
16. SPEEDOMETER GEAR BOX FIXING NUT.
17. SPACER FOR FORK END.
18. SPINDLE END WASHER.
19. SPINDLE END NUT.
20. OUTER SPACER FOR BRAKE COVER PLATE.
21. BRAKE COVER PLATE COMPLETE.
22. BRAKE DRUM.
23. BRAKE DRUM FIXING BOLT NUT.
24. BRAKE DRUM FIXING BOLT LOCK WASHER.
25. BRAKE DRUM FIXING BOLT.

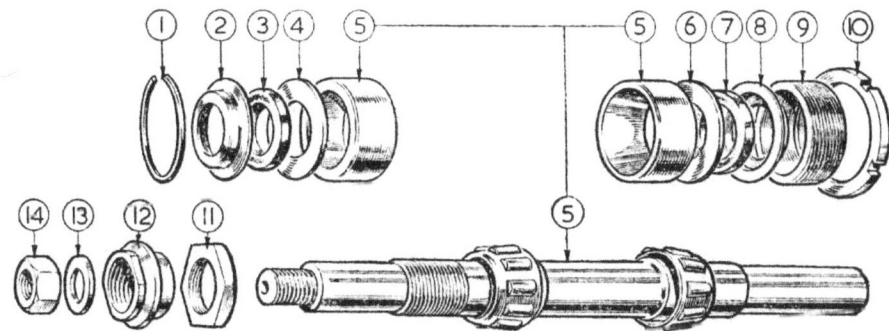

1. CIRCLIP
2. OIL SEAL CUP
3. OIL SEAL
4. WASHER RETAINING SEAL
5. WHEEL SPINDLE COMPLETE
6. WASHER RETAINING SEAL
7. OIL SEAL
8. OIL SEAL CUP
9. ADJUSTING RING
10. ADJUSTING RING LOCKNUT
11. NUT LOCATING BRAKE COVER PLATE
12. NUT SECURING BRAKE COVER PLATE
13. SPINDLE END WASHER
14. SPINDLE END NUT

Illustration 24
Front wheel bearings

TO DISMANTLE REAR WHEEL BEARINGS

With wheel still *in situ* first of all slacken the nut (16), securing the speedometer drive gear box. Then remove the wheel from cycle when the above nut should be removed and the speedometer gear box withdrawn. (If wheel is of non-detachable type remove the brake cover plate and withdraw the solid centre spindle together with all spacers attached).

Next, slacken the adjuster sleeve lock nut (13) and completely unscrew the adjuster sleeve (14) which will come away together with the sleeve upon which speedometer drive is mounted and also the cover disc. Then withdraw the washer (3), the oil seal (4) and the oil seal cup (5).

Now turn to the brake side of wheel and using a short bar of $\frac{7}{8}''$ external diameter apply pressure to the end of the projecting sleeve (6), which pressure will force out wheel bearing ring (7) together with the two taper roller bearings (7) and the spacing sleeve (8), leaving *in situ* only the bearing ring on the brake side together with oil seal, washers and retaining circlip.

If it is desired to remove this bearing ring pressure must be applied to the washer immediately under the circlip, until it is possible to extract the circlip. The outer seal cup (5), the oil seal (4) and the retaining washer (10) are then free to be withdrawn. The bearing ring may then be forced out of the end of the hub bore by applying pressure to its inner edge, through the medium of a bar or tube of suitable diameter, passed through the hub bore.

Reassembly is carried out in exactly reverse order, care being necessary after pressing in the brake side bearing ring sufficiently far to permit fitting the circlip, to then force the ring back until seal cup (5) is tightly in contact with the retaining circlip before proceeding with further assembly.

Final adjustment of the bearings should allow the slightest possible degree of end play, and when correctly adjusted just perceptible rim rock upon refitting the wheel should be observable.

NOTE—Upon tightening the adjusting ring nut (13) the cover disc must be positioned to permit application of the gun to the grease nipple, the hole in disc being provided for that purpose.

FRONT BRAKE COVER PLATE

It is most important the front brake cover plate is correctly positioned.

It is retained to the front wheel spindle by an inside nut (part number 021931) and an outside nut (part number 018071).

The inside nut must be positioned so that when the cover plate is applied, the outer face of the latter lies flush with the hub shell edge.

The outside nut is fitted so that its hexagonal side is against the brake cover plate

BRAKE DRUMS

The front wheel brake drum is a shrunk in fit in the hub shell (assembled under heat) and secured additionally by five screws.

The rear wheel brake drum is integral with the rear chain sprocket and on the rigid frame model is secured to the rear hub by five bolts and nuts. Under each nut is a lock washer of the tab type and it is essential these are always in position.

Harshness in transmission can be caused by the drum retaining bolts and nuts being loose.

On spring frame models the rear brake drum is mounted on a separate ball bearing and the drive to rear wheel is by means of five studs projecting from the hub face which engage with holes in the drum back face, thereby permitting removal of the wheel with the brake drum still *in situ*.

BRAKE SHOES

The front and rear brake shoes, springs and expanders are interchangeable. The two shoes in each brake are **NOT** identical, they are " handed."

One end of each shoe bears on a fulcrum fixed in the brake cover plate. The other end accommodates a detachable thrust pin. By inserting washers under a thrust pin its effective height can be increased, thereby compensating for wear on the brake linings.

BRAKE SHOE ADJUSTMENT

Brake adjustment, to compensate for lining wear, is normally made by means of a finger adjuster on the rear brake rod and a cable adjuster for the front brake cable.

After a very considerable mileage this continual adjustment causes the brake cam to occupy a position whereby the available leverage is considerably reduced and, as a result, the brake loses efficiency. See illustrations 26, 27 and 28.

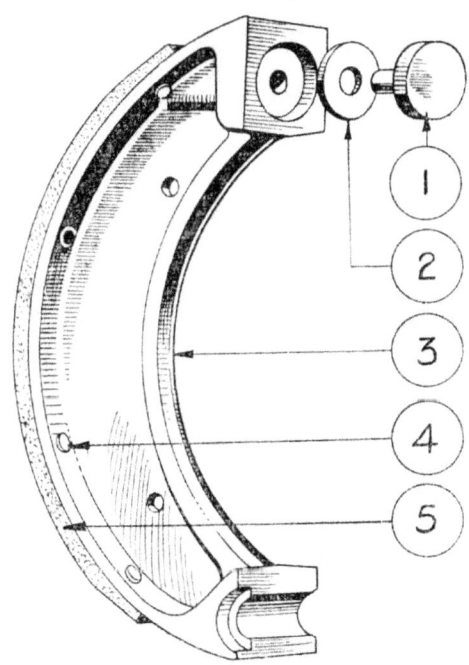

Illustration 25

To overcome this a hardened headed thrust pin is fitted to each shoe to enable a packing washer to be fitted under the head as, and when, required. Eight of these washers (000174) are provided in the tool kit. When wear of the brake linings is taken up in this manner it is then necessary to unscrew considerably the adjusting nut on the rear brake rod, or screw in the cable adjuster of the front brake cable, and afterwards adjust the brake, as described afterwards.

When a brake cover plate has been disturbed, it is advisable, upon re-assembly, to centralise the shoes in the brake drum to ensure equal pressure to each. In the case of the front wheel this is best done before re-fitting the wheel to the machine, but in the case of the rear wheel it is best done after re-fitting. If brake shoes tend to squeak, when the brake is applied it is generally an indication the brake shoes are not centralised in the drum.

(1) **Brake shoe thrust pin.**
(2) **Thrust pin packing washer.**
(3) **Brake shoe.**
(4) **Rivet, securing brake shoe lining.**
(5) **Brake shoe lining.**

Centralise brake shoes, Front or Rear, by :

Ensure the nut securing the cover plate and also the fulcrum stud nut (front only) are slightly slacked off.

Place on the brake expander lever a tubular spanner (to increase the leverage), and, while maintaining pressure on the tubular spanner (to expand fully the brake shoes), fully tighten the spindle nut binding the cover plate to the spindle and also the nut on fulcrum stud.

FRONT BRAKE ADJUSTMENT

Major adjustment of the frontbrake shoes is made on the brake thrust pins, by fitting packingwashers under the pins, as already described.

Minor adjustment of the front brake shoes is made by altering the position of the brake cable adjuster on the fork assembly. Unscrew the adjuster to "take up" the front brake. The adjuster is locked in position by a nut.

Adjust front brake by :

Place machine on both stands.

Slacken lock nut on cable adjuster.

Unscrew the cable adjuster till, by rotating the front wheel, it can be felt the brake shoes are just touching the brake drum.

Then screw back the adjuster two complete turns and tighten the lock nut.

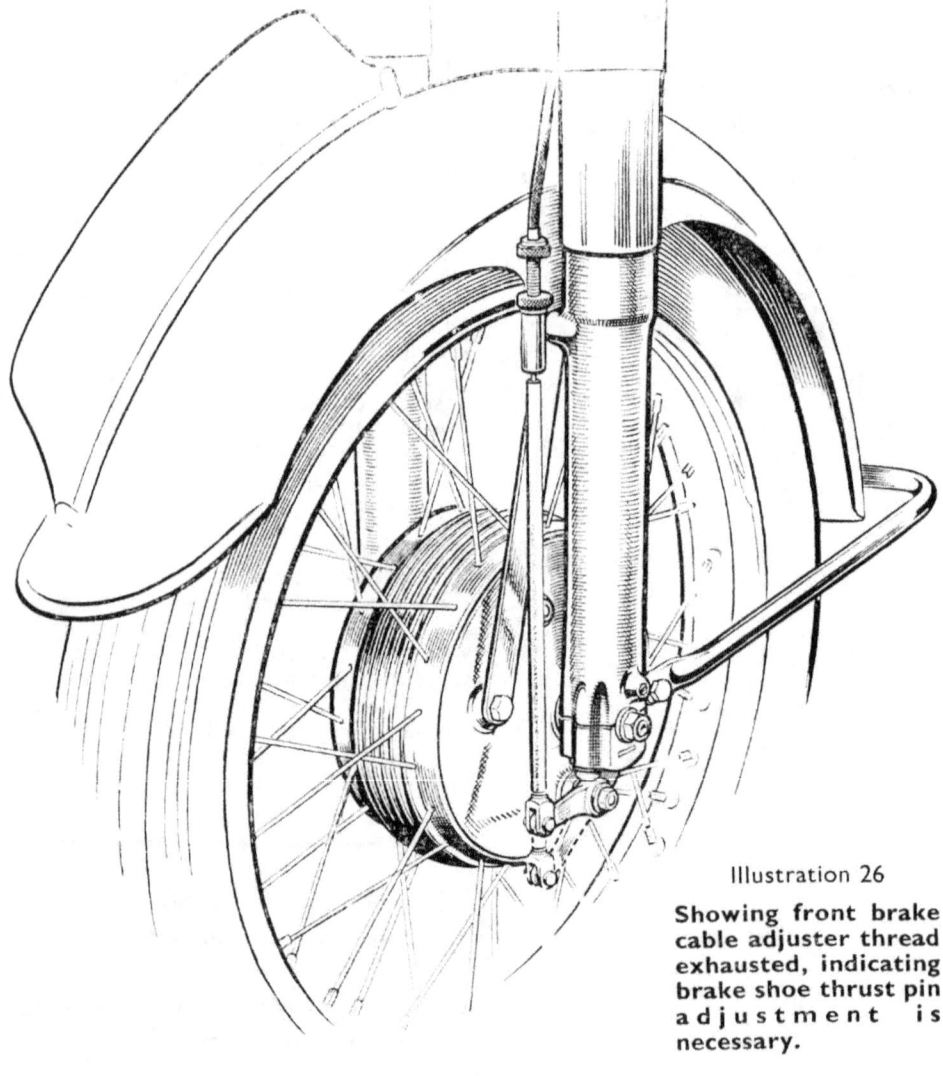

Illustration 26

Showing front brake cable adjuster thread exhausted, indicating brake shoe thrust pin adjustment is necessary.

REAR BRAKE ADJUSTMENT

Major adjustment of the rear brake shoes is made on the brake thrust pins, by fitting packing washers under the pins, as already described.

Minor adjustment of the rear brake shoes is made by altering the position, on the brake rod, of the knurled adjusting nut. Screw the nut further on the rod to " take up " the rear brake.

Adjust rear brake by :

Place machine on centre stand if spring frame, otherwise on rear stand.

Screw further on the brake rod the knurled adjusting nut till, by rotating the wheel, it can be felt the brake shoes are just touching the brake drum.

Then unscrew the adjusting nut two complete turns. (The adjusting nut is automatically locked in position in virtue of the two projecting noses on it engaging in accommodating slots cut in the clip which connects the brake rod and brake expander lever and being retained in that position by the spring which encircles the rear end of the brake rod.)

BRAKE PEDAL ADJUSTMENT

The position of the rear brake pedal can be adjusted within narrow limits. This is done by means of a bolt screwed into the heel of the pedal. The adjusting bolt is locked by a nut.

The best position, for normal use, is to position the pedal so that, when the brake is " off," it is just clear of the under-side of the footrest arm.

After altering the adjustment of the brake pedal, rear brake adjustment should be checked.

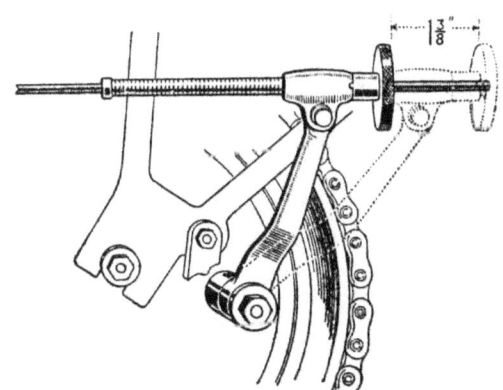

Illustration 27

Showing brake rod adjustment exhausted, indicating brake shoe thrust pin adjustment is essential.
RIGID FRAME MODELS)

RIMS AND SPOKES

The front and rear rims are each drilled for forty spokes, but owing to differing spoke angularity are not interchangeable.

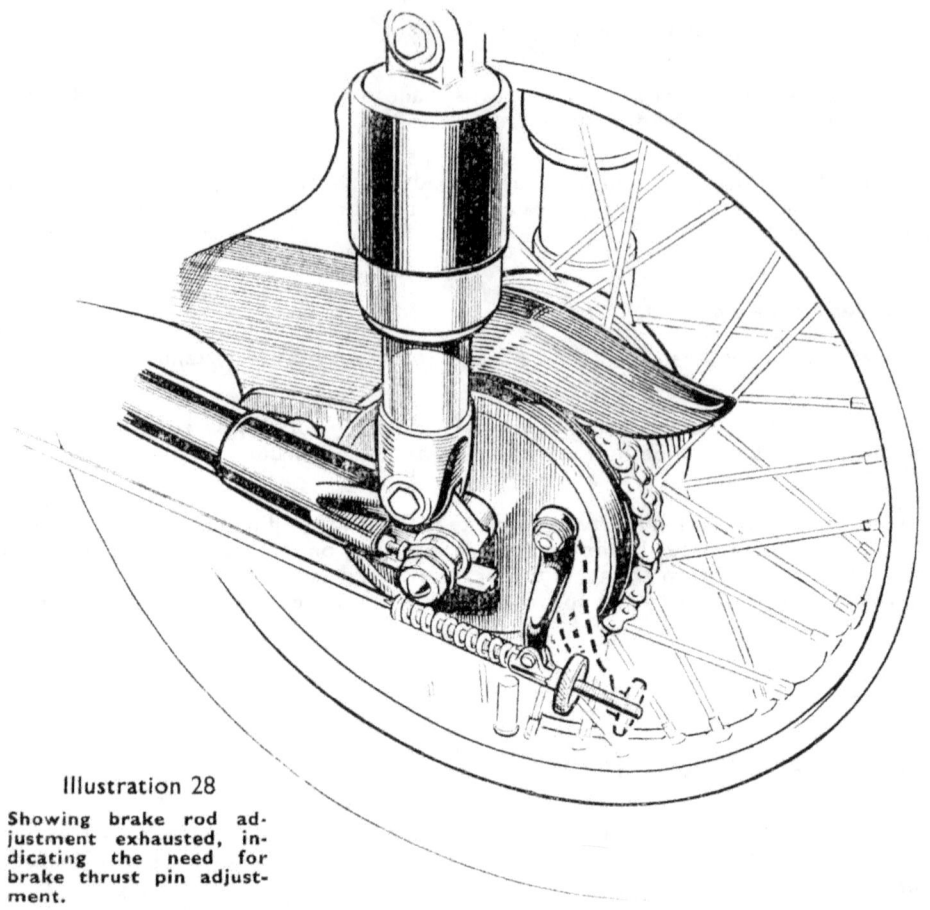

Illustration 28

Showing brake rod adjustment exhausted, indicating the need for brake thrust pin adjustment.

TYRES AND SERVICE (SPRING FRAME MODELS)

Obtaining satisfactory life and service from the tyres is largely a matter within the user's control because the first essential is correct inflation. Check tyre pressures with a low pressure gauge at least once a week. Inflate as may be necessary.

Avoid unnecessary, or "stunt," acceleration and fierce braking, which wear out tyres by causing wheel spin and skid.

Do not drive in tram lines. It is dangerous, especially when wet, and the uprising edges of worn rails will damage the tyres.

Remove flints, etc., that become embedded in the tread and, if any oil gets on the tyres or spokes, clean it off with petrol.

Make sure the front and rear wheels are in track. When the wheel alignment is correct, a piece of thin string stretched taut across both wheels, about four inches from, and parallel to, the ground, should just touch each tyre at both sides of the wheel centres. Alternatively, a straight wooden batten, about five feet long, is handy to use for checking wheel alignment. This should be applied, as in the case of string, parallel to and about four inches from the ground.

Always check the rear chain adjustment, and the rear brake adjustment, after making an alteration to the rear wheel position.

NOTE—Above remarks on wheel alignment applies only to Models with similar width tyres back and front.

On Models with larger rear tyre than front observe equal gap each side of latter when checking.

TYRE REMOVAL

It is not essential to remove a wheel from the machine to repair a puncture but it will usually be found desirable and more convenient to do so.

Take off outer cover and remove inner tube by :

Remove cap from tyre valve.

Remove nut from tyre valve.

Remove the " inside " from tyre valve. This allows inner tube to deflate. Most valve caps have a reduced and slotted top to engage with the valve " inside " in order to unscrew it.

Push edge of cover, that is diametrically opposite to the valve, **RIGHT INTO WELL OF RIM** and, using tyre lever 017007, pick up edge of cover **NEAR VALVE** so that it comes off over the edge of the rim.

Work off the remaining edge of the cover till it is clear of the rim. This is quite easy and there is no reason to use force.

Push upwards **valve stem** through its hole in the rim, and the inner tube is then free to be taken away.

Remove cover from rim by pushing it right into well of rim and, diametrically opposite, picking it up with the tyre lever and then working it off all the way round.

TYRE FITTING

Re-fit inner tube and outer cover by :

Place one edge of cover right into well of rim, with the three white dots on the cover side **adjacent to the valve hole**, and, commencing diametrically opposite, and using the hands only, work the cover over the edge of the rim.

Replace the valve "inside" and slightly inflate the inner tube. (Do not distend the tube.) Fit the valve into its hole in the rim and replace its nut, only screwing it on the valve stem about half an inch.

Tuck in the inner tube so that it lies snugly in the cover. Ensure it is not twisted. Smear some soapy water round the free edge of the cover. This is a great help in fitting and in ensuring the cover centralises itself on the rim and should always be employed if at all possible.

Introduce the free edge of the cover into the rim at the spot diametrically opposite to the valve. Get this edge right into the well of the rim and then, by working round the cover, equally on either side of the valve position, the cover will slip into place without excessive exertion, fitting the part nearest to the valve last of all.

Slightly inflate the inner tube and inspect for the inner tube being trapped between the outside edge of the cover and the rim at the spots where the valve is located.

Half inflate tyre, spin wheel and test for trueness because it is essential the pattern of the tread runs evenly and the cover must be manipulated till that occurs. This **centralisation of the cover is most important.**

Inflate to required pressure.

Screw fully home the nut on the valve.

Replace the valve cap.

TYRE PRESSURES

The following are correct minimum inflation pressures for specified loads per tyre :

Load per tyre,	200 lb.	Pressure	16 lb.	per square inch
do.	240 lb.	do.	18 lb.	do.
do.	280 lb.	do.	20 lb.	do.
do.	350 lb.	do.	24 lb.	do.
do.	400 lb.	do.	28 lb.	do.
do.	440 lb.	do.	32 lb.	do.

The best method of ascertaining the correct pressure is to actually weigh the loads on the front and rear tyres. This should be done on a weighbridge and is a service that can usually be provided by British Railways at a Goods Depot or by a Corporation at its Depot.

When the weights are known the table above can then be used.

As a rough guide it may be stated that, with a rider of average weight and with normal equipment, solo, the pressure should be 18 lb. for the front tyre and 22 lb. for the rear.

USEFUL INFORMATION

In the following five paragraphs are particulars of failures and troubles that can occur, together with the probable reasons. These troubles are arranged in the order of their probability.

TRACING TROUBLES

Engine fails to start, or is difficult to start, may be due to:

Water on high-tension pick-up.
Moisture on sparking plug.
Oiled up, or fouled, sparking plug.
Throttle opening too large.
Pilot jet choked.
Air lever in open position, or bad air leak at carburetter flange.
Lack of fuel because of insufficient flooding (cold only).
Lack of fuel because of pipe, or tap, obstruction.
Excessive flooding of carburetter (with hot engine only).
Stuck up engine valve.
Weak, or broken, valve spring.
Valve not seating properly.
Contact points dirty.
Incorrect contact point gap.

Engine misses fire may be due to:

Defective, or oiled, sparking plug.
Incorrect contact point gap.
Contact breaker points loose.
Rocker adjustment incorrect.
Oil on contact breaker points.
Defective sparking plug wire.
Partially obstructed petrol supply.

Loss of power may be due to:

Faulty sparking plug.
Lack of oil in tank.
Weak, or broken, valve spring.
Sticky valve stem.
Valve not seating properly.
Brakes adjusted too closely.
Badly fitting, or broken, piston rings.
Punctured carburetter float.
Engine carbonised.
Choked silencer.

Engine overheats may be due to :

Lack of proper lubrication.   (Quality or quantity of oil.)
Faulty sparking plug.
Air control to carburetter out of order.
Punctured carburetter float.
Engine carbonised.
Weak valve springs.
Pitted valve seats.
Worn piston rings.
Ignition setting incorrect.
Choked silencer.

Engine stops suddenly may be due to :

No petrol in tank, or choked petrol supply.
High-tension wire detached from sparking plug.
Choked main jet.
Oiled up, or fouled, sparking plug.
Water on high-tension pick-up, or sparking plug.
Water in float chamber.
Vent hole in petrol tank filler cap choked.
Stuck up valve.

EXCESSIVE OIL CONSUMPTION

Excessive oil consumption may be due to :
Clogged, or partly clogged, oil filter.
Stoppage, or partial stoppage, in the pipe returning oil from the engine to the oil tank.
Badly worn, or stuck up, piston rings.   (Causing high pressure in the crankcase.)
Air leak in dry sump oiling system.
Worn inlet valve stem or guide.
Improper non-return valve action.

EXCESSIVE PETROL CONSUMPTION

Excessive petrol consumption may be due to :
Leaks in the petrol feed system.   (Damaged fibre washers, loose union nuts on piping, defective float needle action.)
Incorrect Ignition setting.   (Ignition not advanced sufficiently.)
Defective engine valve action.
Incorrect use of air control lever.
Moving parts of carburetter badly worn.   (Only possible after very considerable mileage.)
Bad air leak at carburetter junction.

STEERING UNSATISFACTORY

Incorrect steering head adjustment. (too tight or excessively slack.)
Pitted steering head ball races resulting from loose adjustment.
Wheels out of alignment.
Front and/or rear tyre tread not correctly manipulated to run true with wheel (causes handlebar oscillation at low road speed.)
Damaged front fork main tubes resulting from impact.

ABNORMAL TYRE WEAR

Abnormal tyre wear may be due to :

Incorrect tyre pressure.

Wheels not in alignment.

Harsh driving methods. (Misuse of acceleration and braking.)

CLEANING THE MACHINE

Do not attempt to rub, or brush, mud off the enamelled surfaces because this will soon destroy the sheen of the enamel. Mud, and other road dirt, should be soaked off with water.

The best method is to use a small hose, taking care not to direct water on to the engine, carburetter, magneto and other such parts. As a poorer substitute, a pail of water and a sponge may be used.

After washing down with water, the surplus moisture should be removed with a chamois leather, and, when the enamelled surfaces are thoroughly dry, they may be polished with a good wax polish and soft dusters.

Such parts as the engine crankcase and the gear box can be cleaned by applying paraffin with a stiff brush, and, with a final application of petrol, will come up like new.

CHROMIUM PLATING

Under some climatic conditions, a rusty looking deposit may be observed on ferrous parts that are chromium plated. This is not ordinary rust (ferric oxide) but is a salt deposit that, in most cases and in its early stages, can be quickly and easily removed with a damp chamois leather. In stubborn cases it may be necessary to use a special chromium cleaning compound.

Lack of attention will lead to more serious damage.

The safest precaution during Winter is to wipe over all chromium plated parts with a soft rag soaked in " **TEKALL**," which is a lanoline base rust preventative marketed in small tins and available at most garages. This material, so applied, leaves an almost invisible film that is impervious to moisture and its use cannot be too highly recommended to owners who value the appearance of their mounts.

In Summer, when those conditions do not prevail, chromium parts should be frequently cleaned with a damp chamois leather and afterwards polished with a soft duster, or, better still, with a polishing cloth of the " **Selvyt** " type.

If a polish is used it must be one of the special compounds for chromium plating only. Ordinary metal polishing liquids, in particular, must not, on any account, be used because these, almost without exception, contain acids, which attack chromium.

NOTE—" Tekall " is a product of **20th Century Finishes Ltd., 175-177, Kirkgate, Wakefield**, and is retailed in ½ pint and 1 pint tins. It can be obtained from our Spare Parts Department, as follows :

½ pint tin " Tekall," Part number 011957, price 2/-, plus 6d. postage.

1 pint tin " Tekall," Part number 011958, price 3/-, plus 6d. postage.

ELECTRICAL SERVICE

IGNITION

A Lucas magneto type SR-1 with automatic advance and retard is fitted to all Touring models.

A Lucas racing magneto type NR-1 is fitted to all Competition 350 c.c. and 500 c.c. models.

On the SR-1 magneto fitted to all Touring models, the contact breaker is exposed by removing the moulded end cover secured with 3 captive screws.

To remove the contact breaker lever, slacken the nut securing the end of the contact breaker spring which is slotted to permit easy withdrawal of the moving contact lever.

If dirty, oily or burnt, contact points must be cleaned with a fine carborundum stone or very fine emery cloth and afterwards wiped with a cloth moistened with petrol.

Adjustment of contact breaker (Magneto type SR-1)

If and when adjustment is necessary slacken the two screws securing the fixed contact plate and adjust the position of the plate until the gap, when the contacts are fully opened, is set to the thickness of the gauge. The correct gap should be .010 to .012.

Special Notes (all models)

Check the contact breaker gap after the first 500 miles. Owing to the initial settling down there is a tendency for the gap to alter in the first few hundred miles of use.

Subsequent adjustment will only be required at long intervals, but it is nevertheless advisable to check every two thousand miles.

Lubrication

All magnetos are provided with ball bearings on the driving shaft. These bearings are packed with grease upon assembly and require no attention for a considerable time.

About every two years or when the engine is undergoing a general overhaul the magneto should be dismantled at a Lucas Service Depot and the bearings re-packed with high melting point grease.

SPARKING PLUG

The K.L.G. Type FE80 "Corundite" Plug is fitted to all models.

It has a thread of 14 mm. and the reach is ⅜". The point gap is ·020 to ·022". Check the point gaps every time the engine is decarbonised and, if necessary, re-set the points.

See that the plug is fitted with its external seating washer.

Coat the thread with "Oil Dag" or Graphite paste. (See page 36.)

Firmly tighten the plug by using the standard box spanner and tommy bar (Part No. 017252.) All that is required is a GAS-TIGHT joint. Therefore do not over tighten, which will **not** make a gas-tight joint more gas-tight, but can, and possibly will, **distort and damage the body of the plug.**

Set the gaps to ·020 to ·022". Never try to move the central electrode. To widen or narrow the gap between the electrodes only move the earth (side electrodes). Check the gaps first with a gap gauge. If they are too wide tap the earth (side electrodes) towards the central electrode using preferably a small copper drift and light hammer. Check the gaps between each tap and stop when the gauge is a nice sliding fit between the central electrode and the three earth side electrodes.

If the gaps are too small to start with gently lever the earth electrodes away from the centre electrode using a small screwdriver and then tap them back as described above. Avoid damaging the centre electrode and do not attempt to move the electrodes apart by forcing anything between them.

For maximum efficiency, plugs should be cleaned at every 3,000 miles. To take the plug to pieces for cleaning, unscrew the gland nut by holding the smaller hexagon on the gland nut upside down in a vice and then using the box spanner to unscrew the larger hexagon on the body.

Then lift away the central electrode assembly which should be washed in petrol or paraffin. Then, using fairly coarse glass paper, remove the carbon deposit and wash again.

The central firing point should be cleaned with fine emery cloth. The inside of the body should be scraped clean with a knife and finally rinsed in petrol.

There is an internal washer, between the insulator and its seating in the body. On re-assembly lightly smear this with thin oil and then screw up the gland nut sufficiently tight to give a gas-tight joint.

Finally adjust the gap to ·020 to ·022".

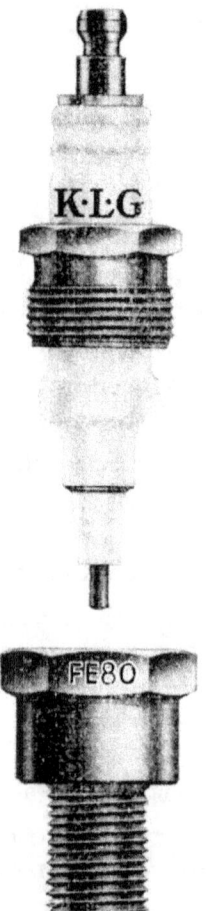

Illustration 29

CHARGING

A LUCAS type E3-N dynamo is fitted. It is anti-clockwise in rotation. The cutting in speed is 1250-1500 r.p.m. at 7 volts and at 1,850 to 2,200 revolutions per minute it gives an output of 5 amps at 7 volts. The replacement part number is 20028A. The negative brush is insulated and the positive brush is earthed. The two exterior terminals are marked " D " and " F," indicating the respective terminals for the Positive and Field wires that lead to similarly marked terminals on the Regulator Unit.

Inspect commutator and brush gear every 5,000 to 6,000 miles. *(Maker's Recommendation.)*

Remove the cover band to inspect commutator and brush gear.

The brushes are held in contact with the commutator by means of springs. Move each brush, see they are free to slide in their holders, if dirty, or if sticking, remove and clean with a cloth moistened with petrol. Take care to replace brushes in their original positions, otherwise they will not " bed " properly on the commutator.

If, after long service, the brushes have become worn to such an extent that the brush flexible wire is exposed on the running face, or if the brushes do not make good contact with the commutator, they must be replaced by genuine LUCAS brushes.

The commutator must be free from any trace of oil or dirt and should have a highly polished appearance. Clean a dirty, or blackened, commutator by pressing a fine dry cloth against it while the engine is slowly turned over by means of the kick-starter. (It is an advantage to remove the sparking plug before doing this). If the commutator is very dirty, moisten the cloth with petrol.

At every 10,000 miles, the complete dynamo should be handed to a **Lucas Service Station** for dismantling, replacement of worn parts, cleaning and lubrication.

Electrical breakdown of the dynamo is most unusual and therefore before assuming this unit is defective, it should be tested as follows :

Check that the dynamo, regulator and battery are correctly connected.

To remove the dynamo (see page 78)

Test Dynamo in position by :

(a) Remove the two wires from the dynamo terminals and connect the two terminals with a short length of wire.

(b) Start the engine and set to run at normal idling speed.

(c) Connect the negative lead of a moving coil voltmeter (calibrated not less than 0 to 10 volts) to either of the two dynamo terminals and connect the positive lead to a good earth point on the dynamo or engine.

(d) Gradually increase the engine speed, when the voltmeter reading should rapidly rise and without fluctuation.

Do not allow the voltmeter reading to rise above 10 volts.

Do not race the engine in an attempt to increase the voltage. It is sufficient to run up the engine to a speed of 1,000 r.p.m.

If the above reading is obtained the dynamo is in order.

If there is no reading, check the brush gear.

If there is a low reading of approximately $\frac{1}{2}$ volt, the field winding may be at fault.

If there is a low reading of approximately $1\frac{1}{2}$ to 2 volts, the armature winding may be at fault.

If the tests, mentioned above, clearly indicate the dynamo is not charging, it is then desirable to remove the dynamo from the machine in order to make further tests and repairs or replacements.

TO REMOVE THE DYNAMO

Remove the left side foot rest arm.

Place a tray under primary chaincase to catch the oil.

Remove chaincase band binding screw and remove metal band and also endless rubber band.

Remove nut and washer in centre of chaincase when outer half can be taken away.

Remove spring circlip, locking plate and nut securing dynamo sprocket and withdraw sprocket with a suitable tool. (Use spanner 017254 to hold sprocket while nut is being slackened, this relieves the dynamo shaft of all bending strain).

Detach dynamo cables and loosen dynamo clamping bolt to fullest extent.

Twist dynamo by hand until the locating strip on its body is in line with the keyway cutaway in the rear engine plate housing the dynamo, in which position same can be withdrawn tilting upwards to clear gear box while doing so (see illustration 30.)

To re-fit the dynamo, reverse the foregoing taking care to accurately locate the dynamo sprocket key when applying the sprocket. See separate instructions for correct dynamo chain adjustment and re-fitting outer half of chaincase. Ensure that dynamo sprocket securing nut is well tightened before refitting locking plate and retaining circlip.

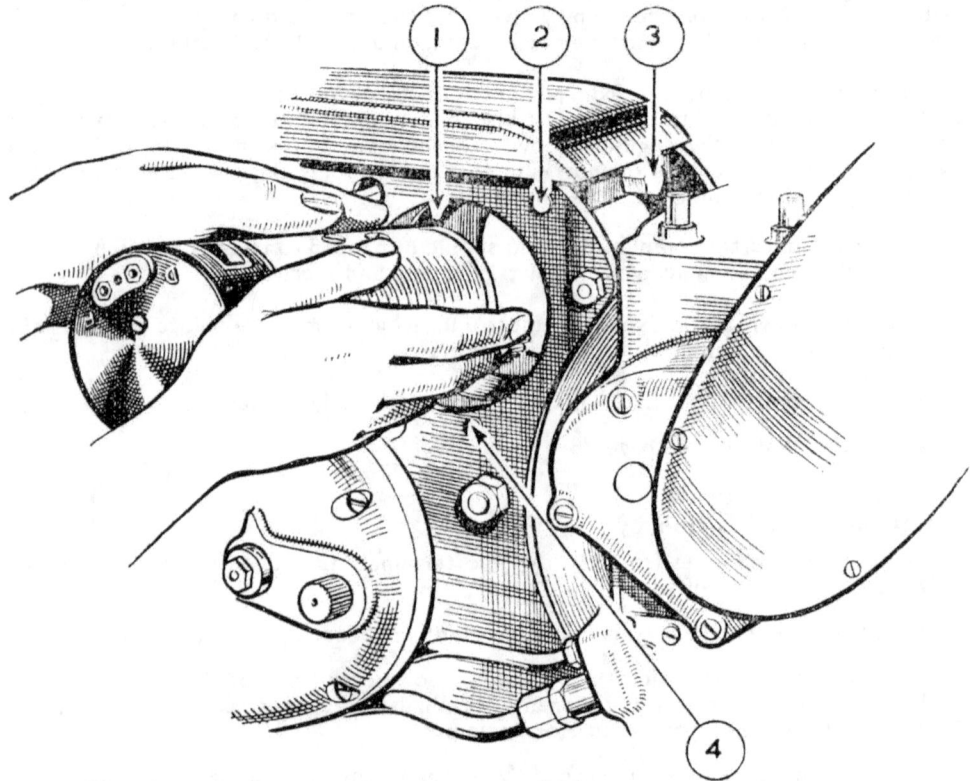

Illustration 30

1. STRAP (metal) CLAMPING DYNAMO IN POSITION.
2. SQUARE CROSSBAR, TO ACCOMMODATE THE BOLT WHICH TIGHTENS DYNAMO CLAMPING STRAP.
3. BOLT, FOR TIGHTENING DYNAMO CLAMPING STRAP.
4. HINGE PIN FOR ANCHORING LOWER END OF DYNAMO CLAMPING STRAP

The cut-out and regulator unit (A.V.C.), is type **MCR-2,** and the replacement part number is 37144-A.

Although the voltage regulator and the cut-out are combined structurally, they are electrically separate.

The regulator is set to maintain a pre-determined generator voltage at all speeds and regulates the output of the dynamo to the battery according to the state of charge of the battery. The charge rate is at its maximum when the battery is discharged, automatically tapering off to a minimum as the battery becomes charged and its voltage rises.

Normally, during day-time running, when the battery is in good condition, the dynamo gives only a trickle charge, so that the ammeter reading will seldom exceed 1 to 2 amperes, i.e. half to one division on scale. The cut-out is an automatic switch which is connected between the dynamo and the battery. When the engine is running fast enough to cause the voltage of the dynamo to exceed that of the battery the cut-out allows the battery to be charged by the dynamo. On the other hand, when the engine speed is low, or the engine is stationary, the cut-out disconnects the battery from the dynamo, thereby preventing current flowing back from the battery to the dynamo, a proceeding that would soon cause the battery to become completely discharged.

The regulator and cut-out are accurately set during manufacture. If, under normal running conditions, it is found that the battery is continually in a low state of charge, or is being constantly over-charged, then the regulator setting should be checked by a qualified electrician and, if necessary, re-set. Whenever possible, this should be carried out by a Lucas Service Depot or Agent.

The A.V.C. Unit is retained by two bolts with self-locking nuts. The self locking nature of the nuts prevents subsequent slacking off. The four terminals of the A.V.C. Unit are plainly marked by the letters F.A.D.E. Wires from F and D go to similarly marked terminals on the dynamo. The A terminal is connected to one of the ammeter terminals and the E terminal is " earthed."

We specially warn against unskilled meddling with the settings of the regulator and the cut-out contacts.

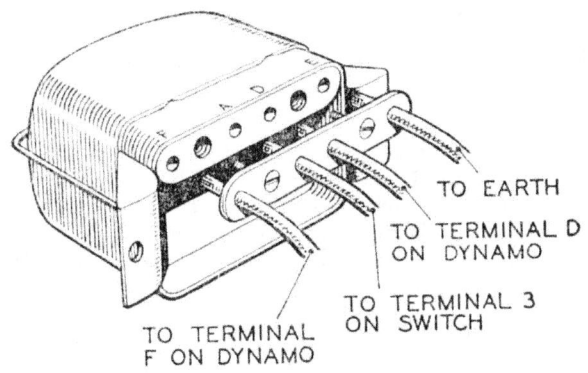

Illustration 31

Showing connections to regulator and cut-out unit Type MCR-2

Later machines may be fitted with a new A.V.C. Unit type **RB-107**, but the foregoing notes will still apply with the exception of terminal grouping which will be F.A.E.D.

Battery

The battery fitted is LUCAS type **PU7E/9** This is a lead-acid battery in which the electrolyte is in free liquid form. The voltage is 6 and the capacity is 12 ampere hours.

Maintenance once every 14 days

Remove battery cover, brush dirt from top of battery and remove vent plugs. (There are three vent plugs.)

NOTE—**NEVER** bring a naked light near a battery when the vent plugs have been removed, or when the battery is being charged, as the gas given off by the electrolyte is highly explosive.

The specific gravity of the electrolyte indicates the state of charge of the battery. With a fully charged battery the specific gravity of the electrolyte should be 1·280 to 1·300. Check the gravity by means of a hydrometer, and if it is below 1·150 the battery should be charged as soon as possible by the normal running of the motor cycle. If this cannot be arranged, the battery should be charged from an external source.

If the level of the electrolyte is so low that a hydrometer reading cannot be taken, no attempt should be made to take a reading after adding distilled water until the battery has been on charge for at least 30 minutes.

NEVER transfer the electrolyte from one cell to another.

NEVER leave a battery in a discharged condition. It must be put on charge as soon as possible.

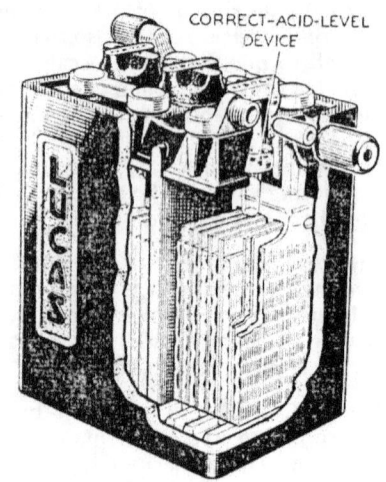

Illustration 32

Lucas PU7E/9 Battery

Check if the electrolyte in each cell is level with the top of the separators. Top-up, if necessary, with distilled water. Do not allow the distilled water to come into contact with metals—always only use a glass or earthenware container and funnel. See filling instructions on underside of battery lid. Beware excessive filling.

If a battery is found to need an excessive amount of topping-up, steps should be taken to find out the reason. For example, the battery may be receiving an excessive charge, in which case the regulator setting may need adjustment. If one cell in particular needs topping-up more than another, it is likely the case, or container, is cracked, in which event the battery must be replaced and arrangements made to clean up the battery carrier.

Metal parts should be well cleaned and, if possible, washed, with a solution of ammonia, or bicarbonate of soda, in water.

Vent plugs should be kept clean and air passages in them kept free. Re-fix vent plugs tightly.

Keep the battery, and surrounding parts, particularly the tops of the cells, clean and dry. Brush away any sand, dust or road slush.

Battery electrolyte, which contains sulphuric acid in a diluted form, is destructive to practically everything except rubber, lead, glass or earthenware. Therefore, rags used to clean battery tops, etc., should be thrown away afterwards. If put back in the tool box they will cause the tools to rust.

Assuming the temperature of the electrolyte is about 60° F. a test with a hydrometer quickly shows the state of charge, as under :

>Reading 1.280 to 1.300 indicates fully charged.
>Reading about 1.210 indicates half discharged.
>Reading below 1.150 indicates fully discharged.

If the electrolyte exeeds this, ·002 must be added to the hydrometer reading for each 5° F. rise to give the specific gravity at 60° F. Similarly, ·002 must be subtracted from the hydrometer reading for every 5° F. below 60° F.

LIGHTING AND ACCESSORIES

Headlamp

A LUCAS headlamp is fitted and snugly mounted on each side is a neat torpedo shaped pilot lamp. These pilot lamps and also the headlamp are secured to the front fork arms by means of tubular bolts through which a wire passes to each pilot lamp. The headlamp bulb has two filaments one of which provides the main driving beam and the other a dipped beam brought into operation as required by the dipping switch on the left handlebar. The headlamp reflector and glass are made up as one assembly and are in consequence not sold separately as spares. The main bulb is of the pre-focus type and the design of its holder is such that the bulb is correctly positioned in the reflector.

No focussing is therefore necessary when a replacement bulb is fitted. See Controls page 7 for switch functions.

To remove headlamp rim and light unit

Slacken the screw on the top of the lamp body at the front, pull the rim outward from the top and, as the front comes away, lower slightly to disengage the bottom tag from the lamp shell. Twist the back cap in an anti-clockwise direction and pull it off, the bulb can then be removed. The light unit is secured to the rim by means of spring clips.

These can be disengaged from the turned up inner edge of the rim by pressing with a screwdriver blade and, at the same time, working away from the edge.

To replace the headlamp rim and light unit

Lay the light unit in the rim so that the location block on the unit back engages with the forked bracket on the rim.

Replace, by springing in, the spring clips so that they are evenly spaced around the rim.

To replace the back cap engage the projections on the inside of the back cap with the slots in the holder, press on and secure by twisting it to the right.

Engage bottom tag on lamp rim with the small slit in the shell and gently force the top of the rim back into the shell, after which re-tighten the locking screw on the top of the lamp body.

Access to the pilot lamps interior for bulb removal is obtained by removing the screw at the rear end and gently pulling forward on the glass rim.

Rear lamp

A LUCAS rear lamp is fitted. The body, with bulb holder, is secured to the rear number plate.

Details of lamp bulbs are given in "**DATA.**"

Horn

The horn push switch, situated on the right handlebar.

Fuses

There are no detachable fuses in LUCAS motor cycle electrical equipment.

Snap wire connector

The LUCAS snap connector, as shown in Illustration 33, is made up of four components. Two are tubular sleeves, having pointed extremities, and which are soldered to the ends of the two wires to be connected. The third part is the centre split ferrule, into which the two sleeves snap and the fourth component is a rubber sleeve which covers the whole connector. That rubber sleeve serves the dual purpose of insulating the various metal parts and also preventing same from separation as the result of vibration.

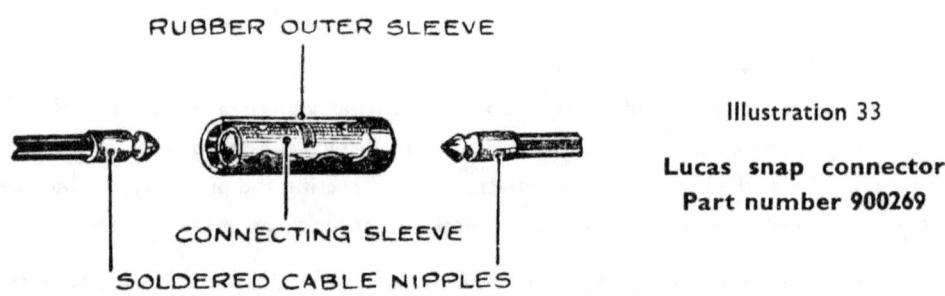

Illustration 33

**Lucas snap connector
Part number 900269**

One snap connector is used in the rear lamp wire and another is used in the wire connecting the regulator unit to the output side of the ammeter in the head lamp.

Two more are used in the headlamp interior (pilot lamp wires).

Terminals

All models have the POSITIVE battery terminal connected to "EARTH".

The earth wires (two—one from regulator, the other from terminal of battery) and the high-tension wire (on sparking plug end of wire from magneto to sparking plug) have terminals of the solid sleeve type having an eye at the extreme end. To make such a connection, it is necessary to bare the end of the wire for $\frac{3}{8}''$, pass the terminal over the wire so that the bared end fully enters the reduced core of the terminal and then flatten that part by either pinching in a vice or by hammering.

The two earth wires, mentioned above, are connected to the "earth" by securing them to the seat lug (which is situated just under the saddle) by means of a nut, washer and a screw. It is essential that the connections are kept clean and the screw must be kept fully tight.

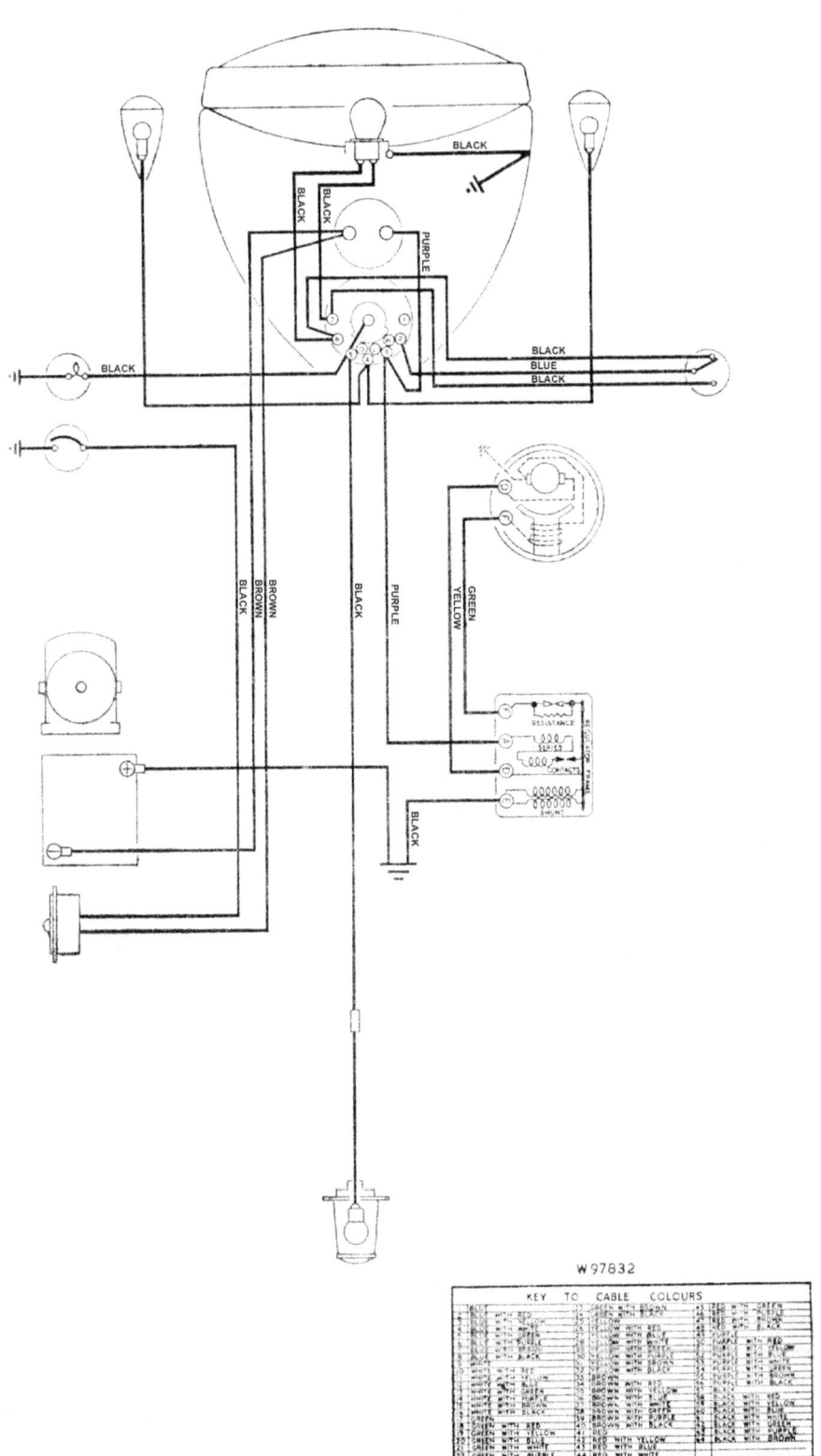

Illustration 34

Wiring diagram

REPAIRS AND SERVICE

REPAIRS

The instructions regarding repairs should be clear and definite, otherwise the cost may be greater than that expected. We shall be pleased to give estimates for repairs if parts are sent to us for that purpose. If the estimate is accepted, no charge is made for the preliminary examination, but, should it be decided not to have the work carried out, it **MAY** be necessary to make a charge to cover the cost of whatever dismantling and re-assembly may have been done to prepare the estimate.

Customers desiring that old parts which are replaced with new during the course of overhaul or repair be retained must make the fact known prior to the work being put in hand because, normally, such parts, having no further useful life, are scrapped upon removal.

Parts sent to us as patterns, or for repair, should have attached to them a label bearing the sender's full name and address. The instructions regarding such parts should be sent under separate cover.

If it is necessary to bring a machine, or parts, to the Works for an urgent repair, **IT IS ESSENTIAL** you **MAKE AN APPOINTMENT** beforehand to **AVOID DISAPPOINTMENT.** This can be done by letter or telephone.

CORRESPONDENCE AND ORDERS

Our routine is organised into different departments, therefore delay cannot be avoided if matters relating to more than one department are contained in one letter.

Consequently, it is desirable, when communicating with more than one department, to do so on **SEPARATE SHEETS,** each of which should bear your name and address. When writing on a technical matter, or when ordering spares, it is essential to quote the **COMPLETE ENGINE NUMBER.** Some numbers have one, or more, letters incorporated in them and these letters **MUST BE QUOTED,** otherwise model identification is not possible.

Orders should always be sent in list form and not as part of a letter.

Owners are strongly advised to purchase a Spare Parts List so that correct part numbers can be quoted. Most parts are clearly illustrated in this list which makes it very easy to recognize the part or parts required.

PROPRIETARY FITTINGS

No expense is spared to secure and fit the most suitable, and highest quality, instruments and accessories for the standard equipment of our machines.

Nevertheless, our Guarantee does not cover such parts and, in the event of trouble being experienced, the parts in question should be returned to, and claims made, direct on the actual manufacturers who will deal with them on the terms of their respective guarantees.

Those manufacturers are :

Carburetters	Messrs. Amalgamated Carburetters Ltd., Holford Road, Witton Birmingham, 6
Chains	The Renold and Coventry Chain Co. Ltd., Didsbury, Manchester
Electrical Equipment	Messrs. Joseph Lucas Ltd., Great King Street, Birmingham, 19
Gear Boxes	Messrs. Burman & Sons Ltd., Wychall Lane, King's Norton, Birmingham, 30
Sparking Plugs	K.L.G. Sparking Plugs Ltd., Putney Vale, London, S.W.15
Speedometers	Messrs. S. Smith & Sons (M.A.) Ltd., Cricklewood, London
Tyres	Messrs. Dunlop Rubber Co. Ltd., Fort Dunlop, Birmingham
Air Filter	Messrs. Vokes Ltd., Henley Park, Nr. Guildford, Surrey

All the above manufacturers except S. Smith & Sons (M.A.) Ltd., issue instructive literature regarding their products which is obtainable by writing to them.

SERVICE

The **Service and Repair Department** is situated in **Burrage Grove, Plumstead, London, S.E.18,** and is open on Mondays to Fridays from 8.30 a.m. to 12.55 p.m.—2.0 p.m. to 5.30 p.m. It is closed on Saturdays, Sundays and National Holidays.

It exists for the purposes of :

    (a) Giving technical assistance verbally or through the post.

    (b) Supplying spare parts over the counter or through the post.

    (c) Repairing and re-conditioning machines, or parts of machines, of our make.

Burrage Grove is the first turning on the left from Burrage Road when entering Burrage Road from the Plumstead Road. (See final paragraph below.)

The nearest Railway Station is WOOLWICH ARSENAL, SOUTHERN REGION RAILWAY. This Station is five minutes walk from our Service Depot in Burrage Grove. There is an excellent service of electric trains from Charing Cross, Waterloo, Cannon Street and London Bridge Stations, Southern Region Railway.

Bus routes 53, 53a, 54, 99 and 122. Trolleybus routes, 696 and 698 pass the end of Burrage Road (one minute from the Service Depot).

Bus routes 21a, 75 and 161 serve **Beresford Square** which is three minutes walk from the **Service and Repair Department.**

Visitors from the North can pass into Woolwich via the Free Ferry between North Woolwich and Woolwich. North Woolwich is a British Railways terminus and is also served by Bus and Trolleybus routes 101, 569, 669 and 685. There is also a tunnel under the River Thames at this point for foot passengers. The Free Ferry accommodates all types of motor vehicles and there is a very frequent service. The Southern landing stage is less than a mile from the Service Depot.

Visitors arriving by road, if they are strangers to the locality, should enquire for **Beresford Square, Woolwich.** Upon arrival there, the road skirting the Royal Arsenal should be followed in an Easterly direction for about four hundred yards, and Burrage Road is the second turning on the right after leaving the Square. Burrage Grove is then the first turning on the left.

THE DRIVER AND THE LAW

The driver of a motor cycle **MUST** be **INSURED** against Third Party Claims and **MUST** be able to produce an **INSURANCE CERTIFICATE** showing that such an insurance is in force.

If your Insurance Certificate specifies you can only drive one particular machine you **MUST NOT DRIVE** any other machine unless its owner has a current Certificate covering **" ANY DRIVER "** and it is advisable to remember that, in the absence of such a provision the penalties for doing so are very heavy.

The driver of a motor cycle **MUST** hold a current **DRIVING LICENCE.** If you are a learner and hold a Provisional Driving Licence, your machine must show, front and back, the standard " L " plates in red and white and you must not take a **PILLION PASSENGER** unless that passenger is the holder of a current **UNRESTRICTED** driving licence.

As soon as you receive your driving licence, sign it in the appropriate place and do so each time it is renewed. It is an offence not to.

Make sure you are well acquainted with the recommendations set down in the " Highway Code," a copy of which can be obtained from any main Post Office.

THE MACHINE AND THE LAW

Every motor cycle used on the public roads must be registered and carry the registration numbers and licence disc allotted to it. The dealer, from whom the machine is bought, will, generally, attend to all matters legally essential before it is used on the public roads.

To register a new machine

Send to the Local Registration Authority the following :

(a) Form " RFI/2," duly completed.
(b) The certificate of insurance.
(c) The invoice you received from your dealer when you purchased the machine.
(d) The appropriate registration fee.

In due course you will receive :

(1) A Registration Book. (Commonly called the " log " book).
(2) A Licence Disc.
(3) Your Insurance Certificate.
(4) Your Invoice.

The Registration Book and the Licence Disc will bear the registration numbers that have been allotted to your machine and will also show the date the Road Licence expires.

Your number plates must then be painted, in white upon a black background, with the registration numbers in characters of even thickness as follows :

The numbers on the front plate must be $1\frac{3}{4}''$ high, $1\frac{1}{4}''$ wide and $\frac{5}{16}''$ thick with spaces of $\frac{1}{2}''$ between each two characters.

The numbers on the rear plate must be $2\frac{1}{2}''$ high, $1\frac{3}{4}''$ wide and $\frac{3}{8}''$ thick with spaces $\frac{1}{2}''$ between each two characters.

The Licence Disc must be enclosed in a water-tight container, having a transparent front, and this must be fixed to the machine in a conspicuous position, near the front and on the left-hand side.

It is not legally necessary to carry your Driving Licence, Insurance Certificate and Registration Book while driving your machine.

Ignition Suppressors

As required by law all 1956 models for the Home Market are issued with an approved type of radio interference suppressor already installed.

Speedometer

A speedometer MUST be fitted and it MUST BE so ILLUMINATED that it is possible to read the dial after lighting up time.

Lamps

During the official " **LIGHTING UP** " hours the machine must exhibit a white light facing forwards and a red light facing rearwards. The rear number plate must be adequately illuminated by a white light.

Each front electric light bulb **MUST** be marked with its " Wattage." (Beware of cheap, imported, bulbs that do not have this marking).

All motor cycles made by us have electric equipment that complies with the law regarding position, size of bulbs, marking on bulbs and the correct illumination of the rear number plate.

GUARANTEE

We give the following guarantee with our motorcycles, motorcycle combinations and sidecars, which is given in place of any implied conditions, warranties or liabilities whatsoever, statutory or otherwise, all such implied conditions, warranties and liabilities being in all cases excluded. Any statement, description, condition or representation contained in any catalogue, advertisement, leaflet or other publication shall not be construed as enlarging, varying or overriding this guarantee. In the case of machines (a) which have been used for " hiring-out " purposes or (b) any motorcycle and/or sidecar used for any dirt track, cinder track or grass track racing or competitions (or any competition of any kind within an enclosure for which a charge is made for admission to take part in or view the competition) or (c) machines from which the trade mark, name or manufacturing number has been removed, no guarantee, condition or warranty of any kind is given or is to be implied.

We guarantee, subject to the conditions mentioned below, that all precautions which are usual and reasonable have been taken by us to secure excellence of materials and workmanship, but this guarantee is to extend and be in force for six months only from date of purchase, and damages for which we make ourselves responsible under this guarantee are limited to the free supply of a new part in exchange for the part of the motorcycle, motorcycle combination or sidecar which may have proved defective. We do not undertake to replace or refix, or bear the cost of replacing or refixing, such new part in the motorcycle, motorcycle combination or sidecar. We undertake, subject to the conditions mentioned below, to make good at any time within six months any defects in these respects. As motorcycles, motorcycle combinations and sidecars are easily liable to derangement by neglect, or misuse, this guarantee does not apply to defects caused by wear and tear, misuse or neglect.

The term " misuse " shall include amongst others the following acts :—

1. The attaching of a sidecar to a motorcycle in such a manner as to cause damage or calculated to render the latter unsafe when ridden.

2. The use of a motorcycle or of a motorcycle and sidecar combined, when carrying more persons or a greater weight than that for which the machine was designed by the manufacturers.

3. The attaching of a sidecar to a motorcycle by any form of attachment not provided, supplied or approved by us or to a motorcycle which is not designed for such use.

Any motorcycle, motorcycle combination or sidecar sent to us to be plated, enamelled or repaired will be repaired upon the following conditions, i.e., we guarantee that all precautions which are usual and reasonable have been taken by us to secure excellence of materials and workmanship, such guarantee to extend and be in force for three months only from the time such work shall have been executed or until the expiration of the six months above referred to, and this guarantee is in lieu and in exclusion of any common law or statute warranty or condition, and the damages recoverable are limited to the cost of any further work which may be necessary to amend and make good the work found to be defective.

CONDITIONS OF GUARANTEE

If a defective part should be found in our motorcycles, motorcycle combinations or sidecars, or in any part supplied by way of exchange before referred to, it must be sent to us CARRIAGE PAID, and accompanied by an intimation from the owner that he desires to have it repaired or exchanged free of charge under our guarantee, and he must also furnish us at the same time with the number of the machine, the date of the purchase or the date when the alleged defective part was exchanged as the case may be.

Failing compliance with the above, such articles will lie here AT THE RISK OF THE OWNER, and this guarantee and any implied guarantee, warranty or condition shall not be enforceable.

We do not guarantee specialities such as tyres, saddles, chains, electrical equipment, lamps, etc., or any component parts supplied to the order of the Purchaser differing from standard specifications supplied with our motorcycles, motorcycle combinations, sidecars or otherwise.

NOTICE

We do not appoint agents for the sale on our behalf of our motor cycles or other goods, but we assign to motor cycle dealers areas in which we supply to such dealers exclusively for re-sale in such areas. No such Dealer is authorised to transact any business, give any warranty, make any representation or incur any liability on our behalf.

TOOLS AND SPECIAL EQUIPMENT

TOOLS

The standard tool kit, issued with each new machine, contains :

1	017253	Tool bag.
1	017114	Tyre inflator.
2	017007	Tyre lever.
1	017248	Pliers.
1	011188	Gudgeon pin circlip pliers.
1	017256	Screwdriver.
1	017246	Grease gun.
1	017249	Adjustable wrench.
1	017252	Sparking plug box spanner and tommy bar.
1	017254	Dynamo spanner and clutch spring nut key.
1	018178	Double end spanner, 1·010 in. by 1·200 in.
2	017052	Double end spanner. Small.
1	017053	Double end spanner. Large.
1	021889	Contact point screwdriver and gauge (Touring).
1	015023	Contact point spanner and gauge. (Competition)
1	017257	Double end spanner.
1	018055	Handlebar clip screw key.
1	018153	Single spanner for petrol tap.
1	018657	Key for fork crown clamp screw.

OPTIONAL EQUIPMENT

The following items of optional equipment are available. They are described and priced in the Spares List.

Stop rear light.

Air cleaner.

Mudguard type pillion seat (Rigid Frame Models).

Pillion footrests, bolted on, to fold up when not in use and specially designed for these machines. (Not on competition).

Detachable luggage carrier. (Not on competition).

Timing disc 022011. A circular timing disc, graduated in degrees and made of ivorine. A very useful device.

Valve holder, for valve grinding. Part number 017482.

Valve spring compressor. Part number 018276. (See page 28).

Pannier frames and bags for spring frame and rigid models.

SPARES LIST

An illustrated and priced spares list is available at a cost of 2/6 post free. (See page 28).

GASKET SETS

For convenience in ordering, standard sets of engine washers and gaskets as well as the washers used in the petrol and oil feed systems are stocked. Full details of contents and prices are included in the Spares List.

BADGES

Neat monogram badges are now available at a cost of 1/6, plus 6d. postage. They can be supplied as a tie pin, as a brooch or for fitting in a button hole. When ordering state type required.

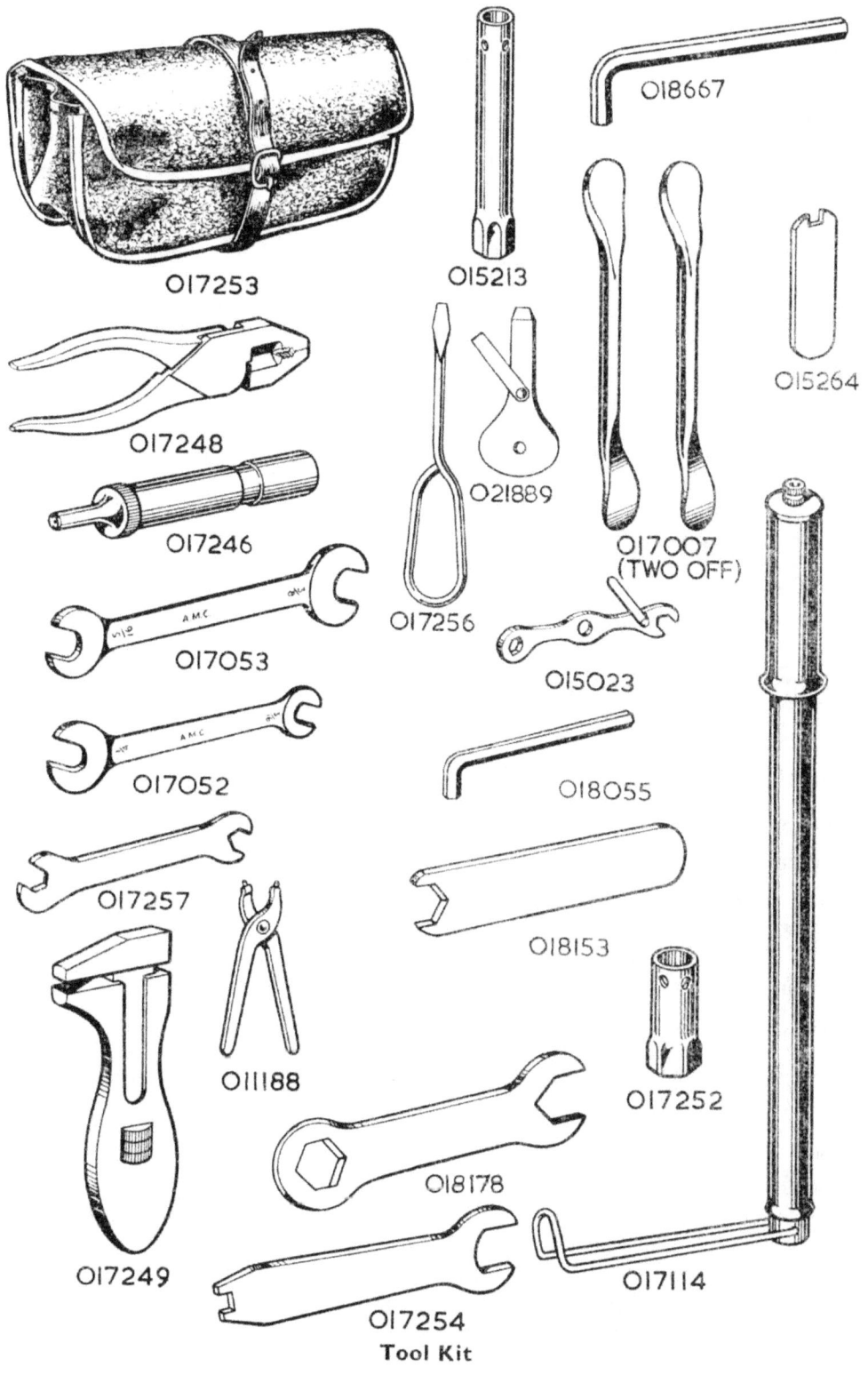

Tool Kit

Illustration 35

ILLUSTRATIONS

	Illustrations	Page
Battery	32	80
Brake adjustment, front	26	68
Brake adjustment, rear (rigid frame)	27	69
Brake adjustment, rear (spring frame)	28	70
Brake anchorage, rear	20	62
Brake shoe adjustment	25	67
Carburetter	13	37
Clutch	15	46
Controls	1	8
Cut-out unit	31	79
Dynamo Removal	30	78
Engine lubrication	4	16
Flywheels	9	29
Fork component details	17	55
Fork damper details	16	52
Gear box	14	40
Gear lever positions	2	10
Hub bearing details	22	64
Hub, rear and front	21	64
Leg, teledraulic, rear	19	58
Lubrication chart	6	21
Oil tank	3	13
Oil pump	12	35
Rear spring frame	18	57
Sparking plug	29	76
Tank fixing details	7	25
Tappet adjustment	11	33
Timing valve	10	32
Tools	35	89
Valve lubrication	5	18
Valve spring compressor	8	28
Wire connector, snap type	33	82
Wiring diagram	34	83

SPARES LIST

FOR

1955 A·J·S

350 MODEL 16M RIGID FRAME (TOURING)
350 MODEL 16MS SPRING FRAME (TOURING)
350 MODEL 16MC RIGID FRAME (COMPETITION)
350 MODEL 16MCS SPRING FRAME (COMPETITION)

---

500 MODEL 18 RIGID FRAME (TOURING)
500 MODEL 18S SPRING FRAME (TOURING)
500 MODEL 18C RIGID FRAME (COMPETITION)
500 MODEL 18CS SPRING FRAME (COMPETITION)

---

350 —	Bore 69 mm.	Stroke 93 mm.	Capacity 347 c.c.
500 —	Bore 82·5 mm.	Stroke 93 mm.	Capacity 498 c.c.

Compiled and Issued by the Manufacturers

A·J·S MOTOR CYCLES

(Proprietors : ASSOCIATED MOTOR CYCLES LIMITED)

Registered Offices :
**PLUMSTEAD ROAD, PLUMSTEAD
LONDON, S.E.18 . ENGLAND**

Nearest Station :
WOOLWICH ARSENAL
Southern Region Railway)

Factories :
BURRAGE GROVE and MAXEY ROAD
PLUMSTEAD, S.E.18

Telegrams and Cables : "ICANHOPIT, WOL-LONDON"
Telephone : WOOLWICH 1223 (7 Lines)
Codes : A.B.C. 5th and 6th Edition ; Bentley's ; and Private Codes

---

All correspondence to :—
A ' J ' S MOTOR CYCLES, PLUMSTEAD ROAD, LONDON, S.E.18

Price : TWO SHILLINGS and SIXPENCE

INDEX

BADGES	Page
Button hole	59
Coat	59
Tie	59

BRAKES
Cables	45
Front	53
Levers	44
Rear	54
Rods	55

CABLES
Clips	60
Control	45 to 46
Electric	58
Speedometer	60

CARBURETTERS
Air cleaners	16
Complete	15 to 16
Jets	16
Mixing bodies	15
Valves	15

CARRIAGE Charges ... 2

CARRIERS
Battery	39
Luggage	34
Pannier Bags	59
Pannier Frames	59

CHAINS
Complete	19
Links	19

CORRESPONDENCE
Instructions	3

DAMPERS
Rear Leg	28
Steering	32

ELECTRICAL
Battery	56
Battery carrier	39
Bulbs	58
Cable clips	60
Dynamos	56
Dynamo Fixing Parts	56
Horns	58
Lamps, Head	56
Lamps, Rear	57
Magneto	55
Magneto Fixing Parts	55
Sparking plugs	58
Sundries	58
Switches	58
Voltage Regulator	56

ENGINE	Page
Axles	7
Bearings	8
Big-end	7
Bolts	8
Bush (gudgeon)	7
Connecting Rod	7
Cover Tubes	10
Crankcases	7 to 8
Crankpin	7
Cylinder	5
Cylinder Heads	5
Flywheels	7
Gaskets	61
Heads (cylinder)	5
Oil Pump	10
Push Rods	10
Re-boring	7
Release Valve	10
Rings (piston)	6
Rocker Box	11
Rocker Box Stay	11 to 12
Rockers	11
Small End Bush	7
Tappets	10
Timing Gear	10
Valve Lifter	11
Valves	5

FORKS
Front	29 to 30
Front Assemblies	29
Rear	25

FOOTRESTS
Pillion	40
Riders	40

FRAME
Bolts	27
Engine Plates	27
Front Fork	29 to 30
Front Frame	25
Rear Fork	27
Rear Frame	25
Rear Leg	28

GASKETS Sets of ... 61

INDEX

	Page
GEARBOX	
Bearings	21
Clutch	23
Clutch Operating Parts	24
Complete Boxes	17
Fixing Parts	19
Gear Operating Parts	23
Gears	21
Kick-starter	24
Shafts	21
Shells	19
Small Sprockets	21
GUARANTEE Terms of	3
GUARDS	
Chaincase, Front	37
Chainguard, Rear	39
Mudguard, Front	33
Mudguard, Rear, Competition	35
Mudguard, Rear, Touring	34
HANDLEBAR	
Bar only	31
Control Levers	42 to 45
Grips	42
IDENTIFICATION	
Machine Numbers	2
INSTRUCTION BOOK	
Details of	3
LEG Rear	28
LEVERS (Control)	
Air	44 to 45
Brake	44
Clutch	44
Exhaust	45
Ignition	44 to 45
Twist Grip	42
MUDGUARDS See Guards	
PACKING Cost of	2
PATTERNS Identification	3
PIPES	
Exhaust	13
Oil	49
Petrol	49
Vent	49
PLATES	
Engine	27
Number, Front	35
Number, Rear	37

	Page
REPAIRS	
Conditions	3
Proprietary Parts	3
RUST PREVENTATIVE	
Tekall	59
SEATS	
Pillion	41
Riders	40 to 41
SERVICE	
Details	2
Location	61
SILENCERS	
Boxes and Extensions	13
SPARES How to Order	2
SPEEDOMETERS	
Complete	60
Components	60
SPROCKETS	
Clutch	23
Dynamo	17
Engine	17
Gear Box	21
Magneto	17
Rear Wheel	54
STANDS	
Centre	32
Front	32
Prop	33
Rear	33
TANKS	
Oil	49
Petrol	48
TERMS OF BUSINESS	
Details	2
TOOLS	
Boxes	41
Complete Kits	59
Separate Tools	59
Special Tools	59
TRANSFERS	
Complete Sets	42
Separate Items	42
WHEELS	
Bearings, Front	51
Bearings, Rear	53
Wheels, Front	50
Wheels, Rear	51

(1) TERMS OF BUSINESS.

Our terms are :—   CASH WITH ORDER,
CASH AGAINST PRO-FORMA INVOICE, OR
APPROVED LEDGER ACCOUNT.

Customers who wish to avoid delay can open deposit accounts and the usual deposit is £5.

Orders from abroad should be accompanied by a remittance to cover the costs of goods and postal charges.

We do not send goods by "CASH ON DELIVERY" (C.O.D.).

(2) PRICES AND SPECIFICATIONS.

All prices, specifications and conditions are subject to alteration without notice. The prices of spares do not include the costs of packing and carriage.

(3) CARRIAGE AND PACKING.

All invoices for spare parts will be SURCHARGED by 5 PER CENT. to cover the cost of packing and postage, or carriage, and the minimum surcharge is sixpence. (Home orders only.)

A special packing case, or crate, is required for some spares to ensure freedom from damage in transit. In such circumstances a special charge for the value of the case, or crate, will be made in addition to the 5 per cent. surcharge but the special charge will be credited in full if the container is promptly returned to our factory carriage paid and in good condition.

(4) HOW TO ORDER SPARES.

STATE :— (a) The Model of the machine.
(b) The complete engine number. (See paragraph 5.)
(c) The frame number. (See paragraph 5.)
(d) The part numbers of the spares required.
(e) A description of each spare.
(f) The quantity required of each item.
(g) How the spares are to be sent. (Post, Parcels Post, Passenger train or Goods train.)
(h) Your full name and address. These particulars are best written in BLOCK LETTERS.
(i) Mention if, or not, you have an account with us.

ALSO :—   Unless you have a deposit or ordinary account, enclose a remittance to cover the cost of the spares plus the 5 per cent. surcharge. (See paragraph 3.)

When cash is sent any excess will be refunded without prior application.

NOTE :— When sending orders by telegram or cable do not omit your name and address from the message.

(5) IDENTITY.

To ensure the supply of correct spares it is essential we can identify the machine for which they are required. The ONLY WAY to do that is for us to know the COMPLETE ENGINE and frame numbers.

The engine number is stamped on the left crankcase, under the cylinder, and may have one or more letters incorporated in it. THE COMPLETE NUMBER MUST BE QUOTED.

The frame number is stamped on the right-hand side of the frame lug that is below the saddle.

(6) SERVICE.

The **SERVICE AND REPAIR DEPARTMENT** is situated in **BURRAGE GROVE, PLUMSTEAD, LONDON, S.E.18**, and is open on Mondays to Fridays from 8.30 a.m. to 12.55 p.m.—2 p.m. to 5.30 p.m. It is closed on Saturdays, Sundays and National Holidays.

It exists for the purpose of :—
(a) Giving technical assistance verbally or through the Post.
(b) Supplying spare parts over the counter or through the Post.
(c) Repairing and re-conditioning machines, or parts of machines, of our make.

If it is considered necessary to bring a machine, or parts, to the factory for an urgent repair IT IS ESSENTIAL you make an appointment beforehand to avoid disappointment. This can be done by letter or telephone.

(7) REPAIRS.

The instructions regarding repairs should be clear and definite, otherwise the cost may be greater than that expected. We shall be pleased to give estimates for repairs if parts are sent to us for that purpose. If the estimate is accepted, no charge is made for the preliminary examination, but, should it be decided not to have the work carried out, it may be necessary to make a charge to cover the cost of whatever dismantling and re-assembly may have been done to prepare the estimate.

(8) REPAIRS TO PROPRIETARY FITTINGS.

We do not repair carburetters, chains, electrical equipment, saddles, sparking plugs, speedometers and tyres. On page 84 of the "MAINTENANCE MANUAL AND INSTRUCTION BOOK" will be found the names and addresses of the manufacturers of the proprietary equipment we fit, all of whom service and repair equipment they make.

(9) PATTERNS.

Parts sent to us as patterns, or for repair, should have attached to them a label bearing the sender's full name and address. The instructions regarding such parts should be sent under separate cover.

(10) GUARANTEE.

All parts made by us, and sold as spares, are subject to the same Limited Guarantee as that issued with each new motor cycle and that guarantee is printed in full on Page 87 of the "MAINTENANCE MANUAL AND INSTRUCTION BOOK."

(11) INSTRUCTION BOOK.

A "MAINTENANCE MANUAL AND INSTRUCTION BOOK" has been compiled and published by us.

One copy is supplied free, upon application, with each new motor cycle. Replacement copies are two shillings and sixpence each.

(12) CORRESPONDENCE.

Our routine is organised into different departments. Therefore delay cannot be avoided if matters relating to more than one department are contained in one letter.

Consequently when communicating with more than one department it is desirable to do so on SEPARATE SHEETS. Each sheet should bear the sender's name and address. **IN PARTICULAR, requests** for TECHNICAL ADVICE should not be on the same sheets as ORDERS FOR SPARE PARTS.

A·J·S MOTOR CYCLES,
PLUMSTEAD, LONDON, S.E.18.

NOTE

The numbers, in brackets, that appear in the "Description" columns relate to the numbered foot notes regarding items so specially indicated.

The quantities per machine of each item are entered in the "Qty." columns. "R" indicates as may be required.

The illustrations are not to scale and are not necessarily accurate in detail.

Some items are not illustrated.

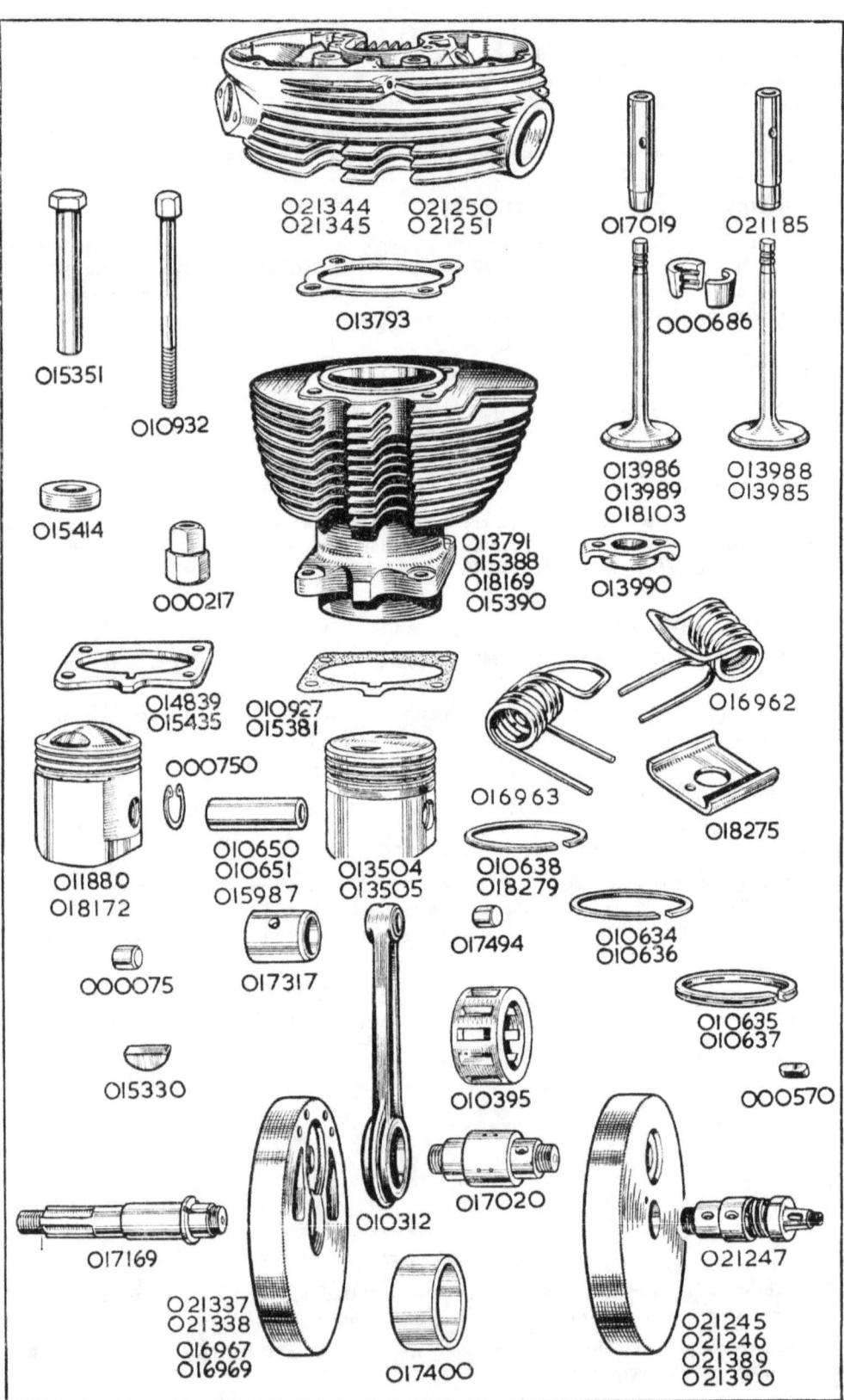

ENGINE SECTION.

PART NUMBER.	DESCRIPTION.	QTY.	USED ON.	PRICE EACH £ s. d.

CYLINDER.
013791	Barrel, cylinder	1	16M, 16MS	
015388	Barrel, cylinder	1	16MC, 16MCS	
018169	Barrel, cylinder	1	18, 18S	
015390	Barrel, cylinder	1	18C, 18CS	
014839	Plate, compression, $\frac{1}{16}$ in. thick, not Std. fitting (15)	1	16MC, 16MCS	
015435	Plate, compression, $\frac{1}{8}$ in. thick, not Std. fitting (15)	1	18C, 18CS	
010927	Washer, paper, cylinder base	1	16M, 16MS, 18, 18S	
015381	Washer, paper, cylinder base	1	16MC, 16MCS, 18C, 18CS	
015381	Washer, paper, compression plate	1	16MC, 16MCS, 18C, 18CS	
000217	Nut, retaining cylinder to crankcase	4	16M, 16MS, 18, 18S	
015351	Nut, sleeve, retaining cylinder head and barrel to crankcase	4	16MC, 16MCS, 18C, 18CS	
015414	Spacer, $\frac{1}{4}$ in. long, for cylinder head sleeve nut	4	18C, 18CS	
000008	Washer, plain, for cylinder head sleeve nut	4	16MC, 16MCS	
Note 15	Compression plate used to obtain medium compression ratio when high compression piston is fitted.			

CYLINDER HEADS.
021355	Head, cylinder, with valve guides	1	16M, 16MS	
021356	Head, cylinder, with valve guides	1	16MC, 16MCS	
021357	Head, cylinder, with valve guides	1	18, 18S	
021358	Head, cylinder, with valve guides	1	18C, 18CS	
021344	Head, cylinder, less valve guides	1	16M, 16MS	
021345	Head, cylinder, less valve guides	1	16MC, 16MCS	
021250	Head, cylinder, less valve guides	1	18, 18S	
021251	Head, cylinder, less valve guides	1	18C, 18CS	
010643	Screw, needle adjusting, inlet valve oil feed. (Screws into cylinder head)	1	All	
011373	Nut, lock, needle adjusting screw	1	All	
010932	Bolt, securing head to barrel, $3\frac{27}{32}$ ins. by $\frac{3}{8}$ in. by 20	4	16M, 16MS, 18, 18S	
000010	Washer, plain, for head securing bolt	4	16M, 16MS, 18, 18S	
013793	Gasket, for cylinder head	1	16M, 16MS, 18, 18S	
000291	Stud, fixing carburetter, 2 ins. by $\frac{5}{16}$ in. by 22 and 26	2	All	
000004	Nut, for carburetter stud	2	All	

ENGINE VALVES.
013985	Valve, inlet	1	All 350	
013988	Valve, inlet	1	All 500	
013986	Valve, exhaust	1	16M, 16MS	
018103	Valve, exhaust	1	16MC, 16MCS	
013989	Valve, exhaust	1	All 500	
016963	Spring, for valve, wide prong	2	All	
016962	Spring, for valve, narrow prong	2	All	
013990	Collar, for valve spring	2	All	
018275	Seat, for valve spring	2	All	
000686	Collet, for valve (each in two pieces)	2	All	
017019	Guide, for inlet valve	1	All	
021185	Guide, for exhaust valve	1	All	

PISTONS.
018301	Piston, complete C.R.6.5 No compression plate	1	16M, 16MC 16MS	
018925	Piston, complete C.R.7.5 No compression plate	1	16MC/S	
018304	Piston, complete C.R.9.4 No compression plate	1	All 350	
016858	Piston, complete C.R.6.3 No compression plate	1	18, 18S	
016858	Piston, complete C.R.6.3 — 015435 Compression plate	1	} 18C	
016858	Piston, complete C.R.7.3 No compression plate	1		

PART NUMBER.	DESCRIPTION.	QTY.	USED ON.	PRICE EACH £ s. d.

PISTONS—continued.

Part Number	Description	Qty	Used On
018927	Piston, complete C.R.7·3 — 015435 Compression plate	1	} 18CS
018927	Piston, complete C.R.8·3 No compression plate	1	
018171	Piston, complete C.R.8·3 No compression plate	1	18, 18S
018171	Piston, complete C.R.8·3 — 015435 Compression plate	1	18C, 18CS
018171	Piston, complete C.R.9·8 No compression plate	1	18C, 18CS
013504	Piston, bare C.R.6·5 No compression plate	1	16M, 16MC, 16MS
018924	Piston, bare C.R.7·5 No compression plate	1	16MCS
011880	Piston, bare C.R.9·4 No compression plate	1	All 350
013505	Piston, bare C.R.6·3 No compression plate	1	18, 18S
013505	Piston, bare C.R.6·3 — 015435 Compression plate	1	} 18C
013505	Piston, bare C.R.7·3 No compression plate	1	
018926	Piston, bare C.R.7·3 — 015435 Compression plate	1	} 18CS
018926	Piston, bare C.R.8·3 No compression plate	1	
018172	Piston, bare C.R.8·3 No compression plate	1	18, 18S
018172	Piston, bare C.R.8·3 — 015435 Compression plate	1	18C, 18CS
018172	Piston, bare C.R.9·8 No compression plate	1	18C, 16CS
018279	Ring, compression, $2\frac{23}{32}$ ins. by $\frac{1}{16}$ in. (chrome plated)	1	All 350
010634	Ring, compression, $2\frac{23}{32}$ ins. by $\frac{1}{16}$ in.	1	All 350
010636	Ring, compression, $3\frac{1}{4}$ ins. by $\frac{1}{16}$ in.	1	All 500
010638	Ring, compression, $3\frac{1}{4}$ ins. by $\frac{1}{16}$ in. (chrome plated)	1	All 500
010635	Ring, scraper, $2\frac{23}{32}$ ins. by $\frac{1}{8}$ in.	1	All 350
010637	Ring, scraper, $3\frac{1}{4}$ ins. by $\frac{1}{8}$ in.	1	All 500
010650	Pin, gudgeon	1	All 350
015987	Pin, gudgeon (special for H.C. piston)	1	All 350
010651	Pin, gudgeon	1	All 500
000750	Circlip, for gudgeon pin	2	All

New machines have the lowest C.R. specified above.

The following oversize parts can be supplied:

Part Number	Description	Used On	Price
018302	Piston, complete ·020 O/S For 018301		Price as normal size
018303	Piston, complete ·040 O/S For 018301		,, ,,
018948	Piston, complete ·020 O/S For 018925		,, ,,
018949	Piston, complete ·040 O/S For 018925		,, ,,
018305	Piston, complete ·020 O/S For 018304		,, ,,
016938	Piston, complete ·020 O/S For 016858		,, ,,
016857	Piston, complete ·040 O/S For 016858		,, ,,
018950	Piston, complete ·020 O/S For 018927		,, ,,
021392	Piston, complete ·040 O/S For 018927		,, ,,
018856	Piston, complete ·020 O/S For 018171		,, ,,
013621	Piston, bare ·020 O/S For 013504		,, ,,
014723	Piston, bare ·040 O/S For 013504		,, ,,
018929	Piston, bare ·020 O/S For 018924		,, ,,
018930	Piston, bare ·040 O/S For 018924		,, ,,
013711	Piston, bare ·020 O/S For 011880		,, ,,
013622	Piston, bare ·020 O/S For 013505		,, ,,
015267	Piston, bare ·040 O/S For 013505		,, ,,
018932	Piston, bare ·020 O/S For 018926		,, ,,
021391	Piston, bare ·040 O/S For 018926		,, ,,
018857	Piston, bare ·020 O/S For 018172		,, ,,
018280	Ring, compression, $2\frac{23}{32}$ ins. plus ·020 in. by $\frac{1}{16}$ in. (chrome plated)	1	All 350
016443	Ring, compression, $2\frac{23}{32}$ ins. plus ·020 in. by $\frac{1}{16}$ in.	1	All 350
018281	Ring, compression, $2\frac{23}{32}$ ins. plus ·040 in. by $\frac{1}{16}$ in. (chrome plated)	1	All 350
016444	Ring, compression, $2\frac{23}{32}$ ins. plus ·040 in. by $\frac{1}{16}$ in.	1	All 350
013661	Ring, compression, $3\frac{1}{4}$ ins. plus ·020 in. by $\frac{1}{16}$ in.	1	All 500
016447	Ring, compression, $3\frac{1}{4}$ ins. plus ·040 in. by $\frac{1}{16}$ in.	1	All 500
016449	Ring, compression, $3\frac{1}{4}$ ins. plus ·020 in. by $\frac{1}{16}$ in. (chrome plated)	1	All 500
016450	Ring, compression, $3\frac{1}{4}$ ins. plus ·040 in. by $\frac{1}{16}$ in. (chrome plated)	1	All 500
016445	Ring, scraper, $2\frac{23}{32}$ ins. plus ·020 in. by $\frac{1}{8}$ in.	1	All 350
016446	Ring, scraper, $2\frac{23}{32}$ ins. plus ·040 in. by $\frac{1}{8}$ in.	1	All 350
013662	Ring, scraper, $3\frac{1}{4}$ ins. plus ·020 in. by $\frac{1}{8}$ in.	1	All 500
016448	Ring, scraper, $3\frac{1}{4}$ ins. plus ·040 in. by $\frac{1}{8}$ in.	1	All 500

"Piston, complete" includes—Piston, one ordinary compression ring, one chrome plated compression ring, one scraper ring, gudgeon pin and two circlips.

PART NUMBER.	DESCRIPTION.	QTY.	USED ON.	PRICE EACH £ s. d.

RE-BORING.

Cylinders may be re-bored to ·020 in. or to ·040 in. oversize and normal compression pistons (with rings) (one chrome plated) supplied to suit.
350 Model £2 11s. 8d. (New gudgeon pins and circlips 7s. 1d. extra).
500 Model £3 1s. 2d. (New gudgeon pins and circlips 7s. 6d. extra).

Cylinders sent for re-boring should be packed in stout cases which will be used by us for their return. Carriage is additional. If a complete machine, or engine, is sent to us for cylinder re-boring, there will be an additional charge, according to the time taken, for dismantling and assembly.

FLYWHEELS.

Part	Description	Qty	Used On
021337	Flywheel, bare, driving side	1	All 350, Except 16MC
021245	Flywheel, bare, timing side	1	All 350, Except 16MC
021338	Flywheel, bare, driving side	1	All 500, Except 18C
021246	Flywheel, bare, timing side	1	All 500, Except 18C
021247	Axle, timing side flywheel	1	All
017169	Axle, driving side flywheel	1	All
015330	Key, driving side flywheel axle	2	All
021249	Nut, timing side flywheel axle	1	All
000234	Nut, driving side flywheel axle	1	All
021389	Flywheel, bare, timing side	1	16MC
016967	Flywheel, bare, driving side	1	16MC
021390	Flyweeel, bare, timing side	1	18C
016969	Flywheel, bare, driving side	1	18C

CONNECTING ROD.

Part	Description	Qty	Used On
010312	Rod, connecting with liner and bush	1	All
017400	Liner, for big-end bearing	1	All
017317	Bush, for gudgeon pin	1	All
000075	Roller, crankpin, $\frac{1}{4}$ in. by $\frac{1}{4}$ in.	30	All
010395	Cage, for crankpin rollers	1	All
017020	Crankpin	1	All
000233	Nut, for crankpin	2	All

The following oversize part can be supplied, but we recommend only skilled mechanics should fit same, because it is almost general that the big-end journals and sleeves require " lapping " to ensure a correct fit.

Part	Description	Qty	Used On
017494	Roller, crankpin, $\frac{1}{4}$ in. plus ·001 in. diameter by $\frac{1}{4}$ in. long	30	All

CRANKCASE.

Part	Description	Qty	Used On
021956	Crankcase, complete (2)	1	16M, 16MS, 18, 18S
021957	Crankcase, complete (3)	1	16MC, 16MCS, 18C, 18CS
021958	Crankcase, driving side only (4) (6)	1	16M, 16MS, 18, 18S
021959	Crankcase, driving side only (4) (6)	1	16MC, 16MCS, 18C, 18CS
021960	Crankcase, timing side only (5) (6)	1	16M, 16MS, 18, 18S
021961	Crankcase, timing side only (5) (6)	1	16MC, 16MCS, 18C, 18CS
000575	Plug, drain, for timing side crankcase	1	All
000485	Screw, plug, for crankcase oil holes $\frac{1}{4}$ in. by $\frac{1}{4}$ in. by 26	3	All
000203	Washer, fibre, for oil hole screws	3	All
000576	Plug, for cylinder oil feed valve	1	All
010934	Body, for cylinder oil feed valve	1	All
000021	Ball ($\frac{1}{4}$ in. steel), for cylinder oil feed valve	1	All
000701	Spring, for cylinder oil feed valve	1	All
000300	Stud, for cylinder base, $1\frac{5}{32}$ in. by $\frac{3}{8}$ in. by 26 and 20	4	16M, 16MS, 18, 18S

PART NUMBER.	DESCRIPTION.	QTY.	USED ON.	PRICE EACH £ s. d.

CRANKCASE—continued.

Part	Description	Qty	Used On	Price
015350	Stud, for cylinder base, $7\frac{7}{16}$ in. by $\frac{3}{8}$ in. with top end threaded $\frac{3}{8}$ in. by 26 and bottom end threaded $\frac{7}{16}$ in. by 18.	4	16MC, 16MCS, 18C, 18CS	
000577	Peg, dowel, locating timing gear cover	2	All	
017182	Washer, paper, for timing gear cover	1	All	
010770	Cover, timing gear, with bushes	1	All	
000482	Screw, fixing timing gear cover, $1\frac{1}{16}$ in. by $\frac{1}{4}$ in. by 26	5	All	
000765	Cap, in timing gear cover, for cam bush	1	All	
021342	Cover, magneto chaincase	1	18, 18S, 16M, 16MS	
010816	Cover, magneto chaincase	1	16MC, 16MCS, 18C, 18CS	
000455	Screw, fixing magneto chaincase cover, $1\frac{1}{4}$ in. by 2.BA	4 or 6	All	
021383	Screw, fixing magneto chaincase cover, 2 ins. by 2.BA	2	18, 18S, 16M, 16MS	
Note 2	Comprises items 021958 and 021960.			
Note 3	Comprises items 021959 and 021961.			
Note 4	Comprises crankcase half and two cylinder base studs.			
Note 5	Comprises crankcase half, bush for timing side flywheel axle with peg, two camshaft bushes, cylinder oil feed valve assembled, two cylinder base studs and two dowel pins for the timing cover.			
Note 6	Halves of crankcases must be "matched" in the Factory. Therefore it is necessary to send the sound half of a crankcase when ordering a new half.			

CRANKCASE BEARINGS.

Part	Description	Qty	Used On	Price
021962	Bush, timing side flywheel axle	1	All	
012233	Peg, securing timing side bush	1	All	
021872	Ball bearing, for driving side axle, 1 in. by $2\frac{1}{2}$ in by $\frac{3}{4}$ in.	1	All	
017191	Ball bearing, for driving side axle, 1 in. by $2\frac{1}{4}$ ins. by $\frac{5}{8}$ in.	1	All	
021859	Washer, spacing, between ball bearings	1	All	
000651	Bush, for exhaust cam, in crankcase	1	All	
000652	Bush, for exhaust cam, in timing cover	1	All	
000651	Bush, for inlet cam, in crankcase	1	All	
000651	Bush, for inlet cam in timing cover	1	All	

CRANKCASE BOLTS.

Part	Description	Qty	Used On	Price
010824	Stud, front, top position, $6\frac{9}{32}$ ins. by $\frac{5}{16}$ in. by 26 and 26	1	All	
000278	Stud, front, centre position, $4\frac{9}{16}$ ins. by $\frac{5}{16}$ in. by 26 and 26	1	All	
000277	Stud, front, bottom position, $4\frac{3}{8}$ ins. by $\frac{5}{16}$ in. by 26 and 26	1	All	
000278	Stud, bottom, rear position, $4\frac{9}{16}$ ins. by $\frac{5}{16}$ in. by 26 and 26. For the "Stud, bottom, front position" (which also unites the front and rear frames) see FRAME.	1	All	
000278	Stud, rear, top position, $4\frac{9}{16}$ ins. by $\frac{5}{16}$ in. by 26 and 26. For the "Stud, rear, centre position," see "000316 stud, fixing centre of chaincase," in FRONT CHAINCASE.	1	All	
014147	Bolt, rear, bottom position, $4\frac{5}{32}$ ins. by $\frac{5}{16}$ in. by 26	1	All	
000011	Washer, plain, for $\frac{5}{16}$ in. studs and bolt	8	All	
000004	Nut, $\frac{5}{16}$ in. by 26, for all $\frac{5}{16}$ in. studs and bolt	11	All	

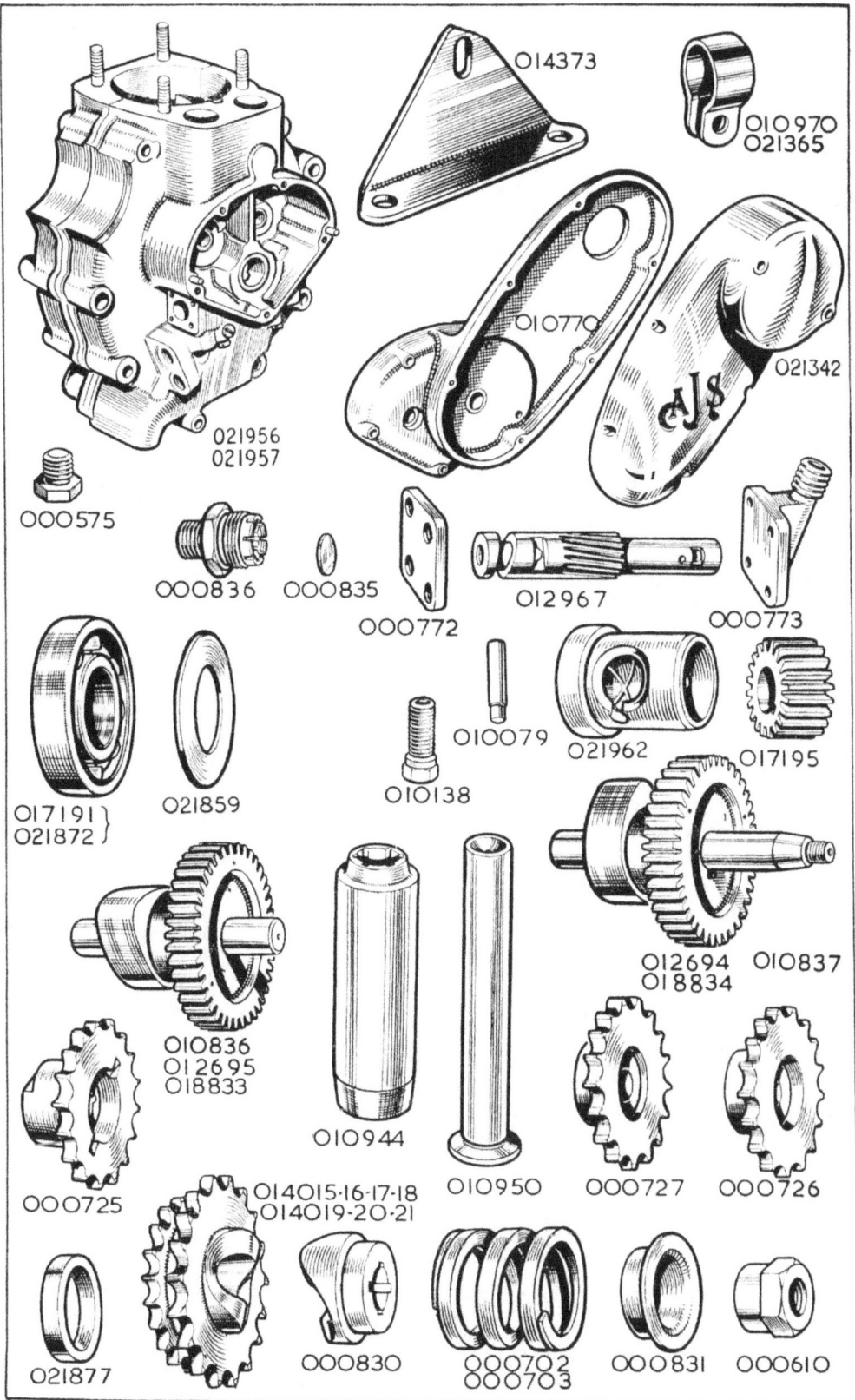

PART NUMBER.	DESCRIPTION.	QTY.	USED ON.	PRICE EACH £ s. d.

OIL PUMP.

012967	Plunger, oil pump	1	All	... ...
010138	Screw, guide, oil pump plunger	1	All	... ...
010079	Pin, guide screw, oil pump plunger	1	All	... ...
000773	Cap, front end, oil pump	1	All	... ...
000772	Cap, rear end, oil pump	1	All	... ...
000582	Washer, paper, pump end cap	2	All	... ...
000015	Screw, fixing front end cap, oil pump, $\frac{3}{8}$ in. by 3.BA	4	All	... ...
000591	Bolt, fixing rear end cap, oil pump, $\frac{5}{16}$ in. by 3.BA	4	All	... ...

RELEASE VALVE.

000836	Body, release valve	1	All	... ...
000835	Diaphragm, for release valve	1	All	... ...

TIMING GEAR.

012694	Camshaft, exhaust	1	16M, 16MS 18, 18S	...
010837	Camshaft, exhaust	1	16MC, 18C	...
018834	Camshaft exhaust	1	16MCS, 18CS	...
016847	Washer, shim, ·005 in. thick, for exhaust Camshaft	R.	All	... ...
016848	Washer, shim, ·010 in. thick, for exhaust Camshaft	R.	All	... ...
012695	Camshaft, inlet	1	16M, 16MS, 18, 18S	...
010836	Camshaft, inlet	1	16MC, 18C	...
018833	Camshaft inlet	1	16MCS, 18CS	...
017195	Pinion, timing, on flywheel axle	1	All	... ...
000570	Key, for timing pinion	1	All	... ...
000221	Nut, retaining timing pinion to axle (left hand thread)	1	All	... ...

TAPPETS.

010950	Tappet, bare	2	All	... ...
010944	Guide, for tappet	2	All	... ...

PUSH RODS.

018314	Rod, long, push, complete (8)	2	All Touring and 350 Comp.	...
018315	Rod, long, push, complete (8)	2	Comp. 500	...
018168	Rod, long, push, bare	2	All Touring and 350 Comp.	...
015511	Rod, long, push, bare	2	Comp. 500	...
000721	End, ball, bottom of long push rod	2	All	... ...
018266	Push rod top sleeve, tapped	2	All	... ...
000592	Screw, adjusting, top of long push rod	2	All	... ...
000216	Nut, lock, push rod adjusting screw	2	All	... ...
Note 8	"ROD, LONG, PUSH, COMPLETE" comprises—one long push rod with top sleeve end, one bottom, ball end and one adjusting screw with lock nut.			

PUSH ROD COVER TUBES.

010952	Tube, cover, for long push rod	2	All	... ...
010672	Gasket, rubber, top of cover tube	2	All	... ...
016944	Washer, metal, $\frac{3}{64}$ in. thick, located below 010672 rubber gasket	2	All	... ...
011087	Washer, metal, $\frac{3}{64}$ in. thick, located over 010672 rubber gasket when no compression plate fitted	2	All	... ...
011087	Washer, metal, $\frac{3}{64}$ in. thick, located over 010672 rubber gasket when compression plate fitted, (two in each location)	4	All 350	...
014603	Washer, metal, $\frac{1}{8}$ in. thick, located over 010672 rubber gasket when compression plate fitted	2	All 500	...
000691	Gland, rubber, bottom of cover tube	2	All	... ...

PART NUMBER.	DESCRIPTION.	QTY.	USED ON.	PRICE EACH £ s. d.

ROCKER BOX.

022142	Rocker box, assembled (10)	1	16M, 16MS, 18, 18S	
022143	Rocker box, assembled (10)	1	16MC, 16MCS, 18C, 18CS	
014364	Rocker box, with bushes (11)	1	16M, 16MS, 18, 18S	
015458	Rocker box, with bushes (11)	1	16MC, 16MCS, 18C, 18CS	
013958	Rocker box, bare	1	16M, 16MS, 18, 18S	
015422	Rocker box, bare	1	16MC, 16MCS, 18C, 18CS	
013984	Gasket, for rocker box	1	All	
017103	Bush, for rocker box	4	All	
013980	Cover, side, for rocker box	1	16M, 16MS, 18, 18S	
015678	Cover, side, for rocker box	1	16MC, 16MCS, 18C, 18CS	
014229	Fillet, rubber, rocker box side cover	1	All	
000251	Stud, fixing rocker box side cover $1\frac{1}{16}$ in. by 2.BA	3	All	
000623	Nut, for rocker box side cover stud	3	All	
000205	Washer, fibre, for rocker box side cover stud	3	All	
000508	Union, oil, in rocker box	1	All	
015353	Bolt, fixing rocker box, short, $1\frac{15}{16}$ ins. by $\frac{5}{16}$ in. by 22	4	All	
015354	Bolt, fixing rocker box, long, $2\frac{15}{16}$ ins. by $\frac{5}{16}$ in. by 22	2	All	
015355	Bolt, fixing rocker box, long, $2\frac{3}{4}$ ins. by $\frac{5}{16}$ in. by 22 with extension $\frac{5}{16}$ in. by 26	2	All except 16MC	
021444	Bolt, fixing rocker box, with extension	2	16MC	
015356	Bolt, fixing rocker box, centre position $3\frac{5}{16}$ ins. by $\frac{5}{16}$ in. by 22	1	All	
000011	Washer, plain, rocker box fixing bolts	9	All	

Note 10   Includes all parts listed in this paragraph (except gasket, fixing bolts and washers), and all those listed under "OVERHEAD ROCKERS" and "EXHAUST VALVE LIFTER."

Note 11   This is a "bare" rocker box to which is fitted four 017103 bushes, two 012722 felt rings and oil metering plug 018890.

OVERHEAD ROCKERS.

017192	Axle, rocker	2	All	
017292	Sleeve, for rocker axle	2	All	
022136	Arm, rocker, valve end, inlet	1	All	
022137	Arm, rocker, valve end, exhaust	1	All	
013948	Arm, rocker, tappet end, inlet and exhaust	2	All	
000010	Washer, plain, for rocker axle	4	All	
000003	Nut, for rocker axle	4	All	
012722	Ring, felt, for rocker axle sleeve	2	All	

EXHAUST VALVE LIFTER.

013969	Lever, exhaust lifter	1	All	
014523	Ring, sealing, for valve lifter lever	1	All	
013970	Spring, for valve lifter lever	1	All	
000451	Screw, anchor, valve lifter spring, $\frac{1}{2}$ in. by 2.BA	1	All	
000039	Washer, plain, valve lifter spring screw	1	All	

ROCKER BOX STAY.

014373	Stay, for rocker box	1	All	
000004	Nut, fixing stay to rocker box bolt extension	2	All	
000011	Washer, plain, rocker box bolt extension	2	All	
010970	Clip, for rocker box stay	1	All, except 16MC, 18C	
021365	Clip, for rocker box stay	1	16MC, 18C	

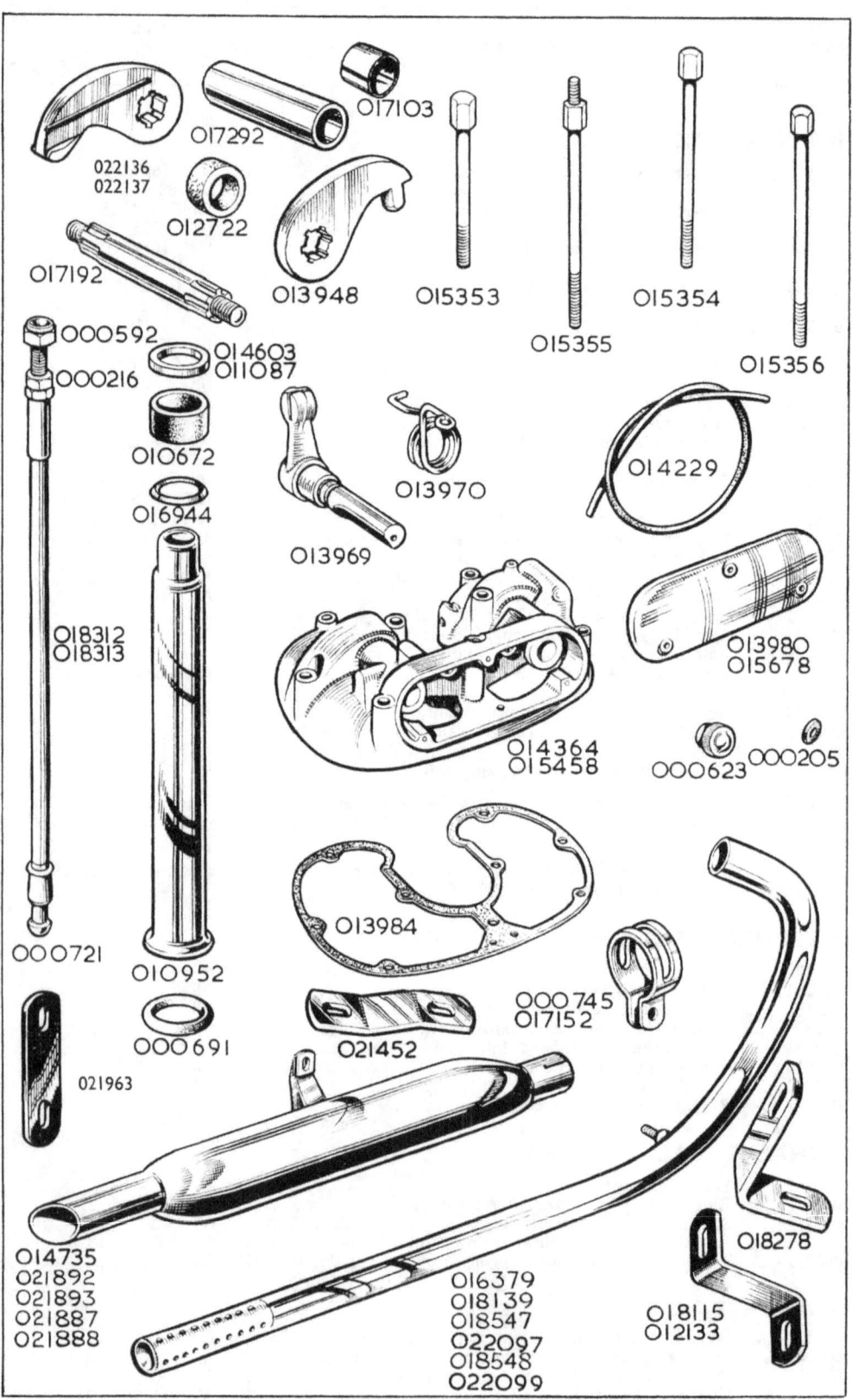

PART NUMBER.	DESCRIPTION.	QTY.	USED ON.	PRICE EACH £ s. d.

ROCKER BOX STAY—*continued.*

000364	Bolt, for rocker box stay clip, $\frac{15}{16}$ in. by $\frac{5}{16}$ in. by 26	1	All	
000011	Washer, plain, rocker box stay clip bolt	1	All	
000004	Nut, rocker box stay clip bolt	1	All	
000011	Washer, rocker box stay	R	All	

GASKETS.

Engine gaskets are supplied as separate spares and in complete sets.
Single gaskets are listed in the groups to which they belong.
Gaskets in sets are listed on page 61.

EXHAUST PIPE AND SILENCER SECTION.

PART NUMBER.	DESCRIPTION.	QTY.	USED ON.	PRICE EACH £ s. d.

EXHAUST PIPES.

016379	Pipe, exhaust, bare	1	16M, 16MS	
018547	Pipe, exhaust, bare	1	16MC	
022097	Pipe, exhaust, bare	1	16MCS	
018139	Pipe, exhaust, bare	1	18, 18S	
018548	Pipe, exhaust, bare	1	18C	
022099	Pipe, exhaust, bare	1	18CS	
016467	Pipe, extension, for exhaust pipe (12)	1	16MC, 16MCS, 18C, 18CS	
012133	Stay, for exhaust pipe	1	16M, 16MS	
018115	Stay, for exhaust pipe	1	18, 18S	
014748	Stay, for exhaust pipe	1	16MC, 18C	
018278	Stay, for exhaust pipe	1	16MCS, 18CS	
000004	Nut, fixing exhaust pipe to stay	1	All	
000174	Washer, plain, exhaust pipe fixing nut	1	All	
000192	Washer, spring, exhaust pipe fixing nut	1	All	
Note 12	This is an optional extra, and fits in place of the standard silencer.			

SILENCERS.

021892	Silencer, bare	1	16M	
021887	Silencer, bare	1	16MS	
014735	Silencer, bare	1	16MC, 18C, 16MCS, 18CS	
021893	Silencer, bare	1	18	
021888	Silencer, bare	1	18S	
017152	Clip, clamping silencer to exhaust pipe	1	16M, 16MS, 16MC, 16MCS, 18C, 18CS	
000745	Clip, clamping silencer to exhaust pipe	1	18, 18S	
000363	Bolt, for silencer clip $\frac{3}{4}$ in. by $\frac{5}{16}$ in. by 26	1	All	
000174	Washer, plain, for silencer clip bolt	1	All	
000004	Nut, for silencer clip bolt	1	All	
021963	Stay, for silencer	1	16MCS, 18CS	
000004	Nut fixing silencer to stay	1	All, except 16MS, 18S	
000174	Washer, plain, for silencer fixing nut	1	All, ditto	
000192	Washer, spring, for silencer fixing nut	1	All, ditto	
000363	Bolt, fixing silencer stay to frame	1	16MS, 16MCS, 18S, 18CS	
000011	Washer, plain, for silencer stay fixing bolt	1	ditto	
000192	Washer, spring, for silencer stay fixing bolt	1	ditto	

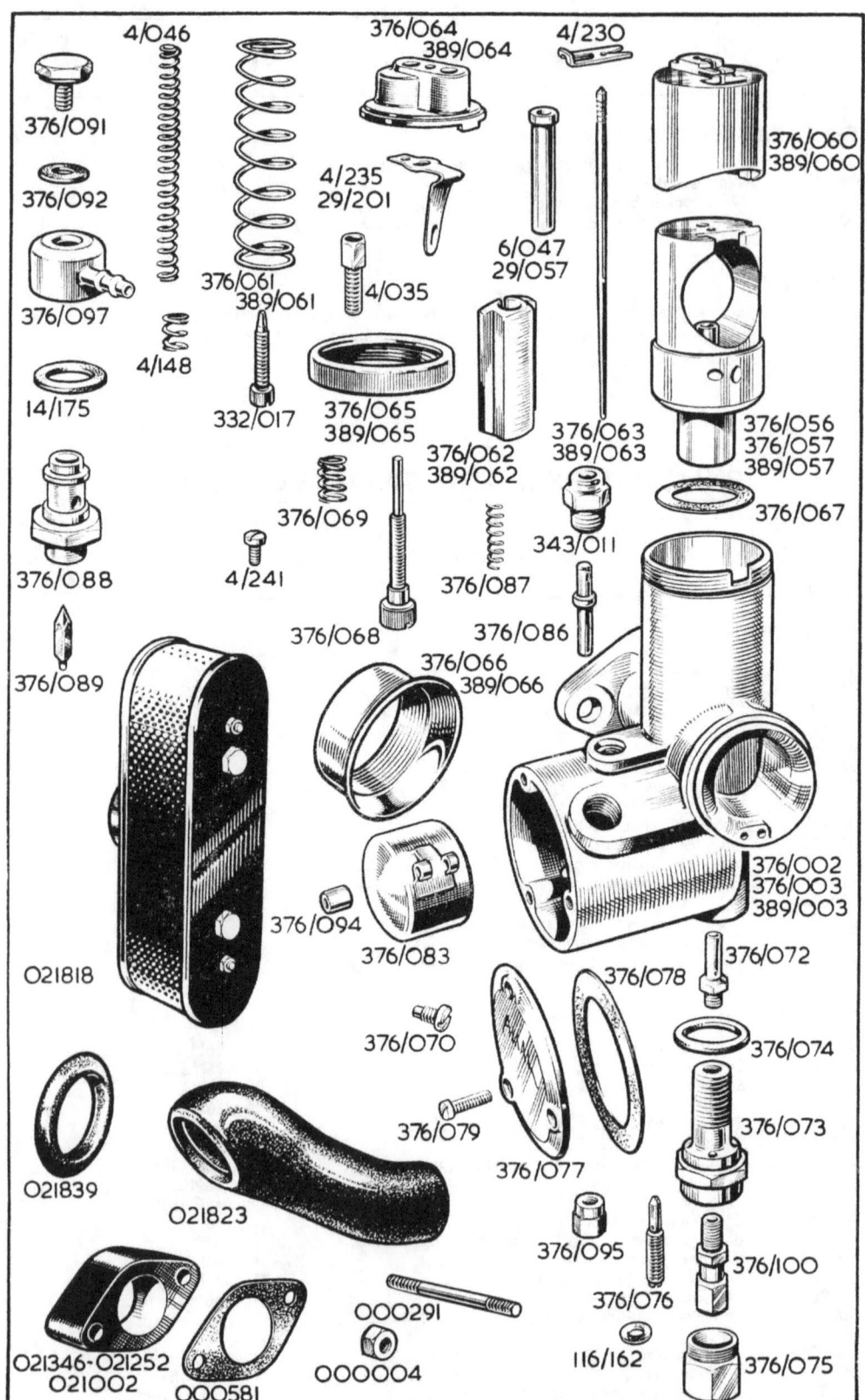

CARBURETTER SECTION.

PART NUMBER.	DESCRIPTION.	QTY.	USED ON.	PRICE EACH £ s. d.

CARBURETTER PARTS.

021873 ...	Carburetter, complete (less controls), type 376/1	1	16M, 18MS, 16MC ...	...
021874 ...	Carburetter, complete (less controls), type 389/1	1	18, 18S, 18C ...	★
018074 ...	Carburetter, complete (less controls), type 10/TT	1	16MCS ...	★
018881 ...	Carburetter, complete (less controls), type 10/TT10	1	18CS ...	★
021346 ...	Spacer, for carburetter, $\frac{3}{4}$ in. wide, $1\frac{1}{16}$ in. bore..........	1	16M, 16MS, 16MC ...	...
021252 ...	Spacer, for carburetter, $\frac{3}{4}$ in. wide, $1\frac{5}{32}$ in. bore..........	1	18, 18S	...
021002 ...	Spacer, for carburetter, $\frac{3}{4}$ in. wide, $1\frac{3}{16}$ in. bore	1	18C, 18CS	...
022103 ...	Spacer for carburetter, $\frac{3}{4}$ in. wide, $1\frac{1}{16}$ in. bore............	1	16MCS	...
000581 ...	Gasket, for carburetter	1	All ...	...
000581 ...	Gasket, for carburetter spacer	1	All ...	...
376-003 ...	Carburetter body	1	16M, 16MS, 16MC	
389-003 ...	Carburetter body	1	18, 18S, 18C ...	
376-077 ...	Side cover...	1	16M, 16MS 16MC, 18, 18S, 18C ...	
376-078 ...	Side cover jointing washer	1	ditto	
376-079 ...	Side cover screw..	3	ditto	
376-083 ...	Float	1	ditto	
376-094 ...	Float spindle bush	1	ditto	
376-089 ...	Float needle...	1	ditto	
376-088 ...	Float needle seating	1	ditto	
376-065 ...	Mixing chamber cap securing ring	1	16M, 16MS, 16MC ...	...
389-065 ...	Mixing chamber cap securing ring	1	18, 18S, 18C ...	
4-235 ...	Mixing chamber cap securing ring spring	1	16M, 16MS, 16MC ...	...
29-201 ...	Mixing chamber cap securing ring spring	1	18, 18S, 18C ...	
4-241 ...	Screw fixing cap securing ring spring...................	1	16M, 16MS, 16MC, 18, 18S, 18C	
376-064 ...	Mixing chamber cap	1	16M, 16MS, 16MC ...	...
389-064 ...	Mixing chamber cap	1	18, 18S, 18C ...	
4-035 ...	Control cable adjuster	2	16M, 16MS, 16MC, 18, 18S, 18C	
376-062 ...	Air valve	1	16M, 16MS, 16MC ...	...
389-062 ...	Air valve	1	18, 18S, 18C ...	
6-047 ...	Air valve guide	1	16M, 16MS, 16MC ...	...
29-057 ...	Air valve guide	1	18, 18S, 18C ...	
376-060 ...	Throttle valve	1	16M, 16MS, 16MC ...	...
389-060 ...	Throttle valve	1	18, 18S, 18C ...	
4-046 ...	Air valve spring	1	16M, 16MS, 16MC, 18, 18S, 18C ...	
376-061 ...	Throttle valve spring	1	16M, 16MS, 16MC ...	...
389-061 ...	Throttle valve spring	1	18, 18S, 18C ...	
376-068 ...	Throttle stop screw	1	16M, 16MS, 16MC, 18, 18S, 18C ...	
376-069 ...	Throttle stop screw spring	1	ditto	
332-017 ...	Pilot air adjusting screw	1	ditto	
4-148 ...	Pilot air adjusting screw spring	1	ditto	

★ *Price on application*

PART NUMBER.	DESCRIPTION.	QTY.	USED ON.	PRICE EACH £ s. d.

CARBURETTER PARTS—continued.

376-063	Taper jet needle	1	16M, 16MS, 16MC	...
389-063	Taper jet needle	1	18, 18S, 18C	...
4-230	Taper needle clip	1	16M, 16MS, 16MC, 18, 18S, 18C	...
376-072	Needle jet	1	ditto	
376-100	Main jet (specify size when ordering)	1	ditto	
376-073	Main jet holder	1	ditto	
376-074	Jet holder washer	1	ditto	
376-075	Main jet cover	1	ditto	
376-076	Pilot jet	1	ditto	
376-095	Pilot jet cover nut	1	ditto	
116-162	Pilot jet cover nut washer	1	ditto	
376-057	Jet block complete	1	16M, 16MS, 16MC	...
389-057	Jet block complete	1	18, 18S, 18C	
376-067	Jet block washer	1	16M, 16MS, 16MC, 18, 18S, 18C	...
376-070	Locating peg for jet block	1	ditto	
376-097	Petrol pipe banjo	1	ditto	
376-091	Petrol pipe banjo bolt	1	ditto	
376-092	Petrol pipe banjo bolt washer	1	ditto	
14-175	Banjo seating washing	1	ditto	
343-011	Tickler body	1	ditto	
376-086	Tickler plunger	1	ditto	
376-087	Tickler spring	1	ditto	
376-066	Air intake venturi	1	16M, 16MS, 16MC	...
389-066	Air intake venturi	1	18, 18S, 18C	...

The prices of parts of 10TT and 10TT/10 carburetters as fitted to C/S machines can be had upon application

AIR CLEANER. (This is optional extra equipment).

021818	Cleaner, air	1	All except competition	...
022128	Cleaner, air	1	16MC, 18C	... ★
022129	Adaptor, for air cleaner	1	16MC	... ★
022130	Adaptor, for air cleaner	1	18C	... ★
021823	Sleeve for air cleaner	1	All except competition	...
021839	Sealing ring rubber	1	ditto	
022075	Stud to frame	2	ditto	
016983	Set of air cleaner elements comprising filter element and two fabric end gaskets	1	All except competition	...

When an AIR CLEANER is fitted it is essential to :—

Fit a smaller jet, viz :—

for 350 use jet 376/100 (size 200) ... 1 ... ...
for 500 use jet 376/100 (size 250) ... 1 ... ...

★ Price on application.

BY USING GENUINE SPARES YOU ARE ASSURED THEY WILL FIT ACCURATELY AND GIVE SATISFACTORY SERVICE

TRANSMISSION SECTION.

PART NUMBER.	DESCRIPTION.	QTY.	USED ON.	PRICE EACH £ s. d.

ENGINE SPROCKET.

014016	Sprocket, engine, bare, 16 teeth	1	16MC, 16MCS	
014018	Sprocket, engine, bare, 18 teeth	1	16M, 16MS, 18C, 18CS	
014021	Sprocket, engine, bare, 21 teeth	1	18, 18S	
021877	Spacer, collar, for engine sprocket	1	All	
000702	Spring, engine shock absorber	1	All 350	
000703	Spring, engine shock absorber	1	All 500	
000830	Cam, engine shock absorber	1	All	
000831	Cap, engine shock absorber spring	1	All	
000610	Nut, lock, engine shock absorber	1	All	
012444	Washer, felt, between engine sprocket and crankcase	1	16MC, 16MCS, 18C, 18CS	
021117	Cage, for felt washer	1	ditto	

The following alternative engine sprockets can be supplied.

014015	Sprocket, engine, bare, 15 teeth	1	All	
014017	Sprocket, engine, bare, 17 teeth	1	All	
014019	Sprocket, engine, bare, 19 teeth	1	All	
014020	Sprocket, engine, bare, 20 teeth	1	All	

MAGNETO DRIVING SPROCKET.

000727	Sprocket, magneto, on engine camshaft	1	All	
000011	Washer, plain, for camshaft sprocket	1	All	
000004	Nut, retaining, for camshaft sprocket	1	All	
000726	Sprocket, magneto, on armature shaft	1	16MC, 16MCS, 18C, 18CS	
140074	Washer, plain, for armature sprocket	1	ditto	
171284	Nut, retaining, for armature shaft sprocket	1	ditto	
021354	Sprocket and automatic advance unit w/fixing bolt and washers (Lucas)	1	18, 18S	★
021680	Sprocket and Automatic advance unit w/fixing bolt and washers (Lucas)	1	16M, 16MS	★

DYNAMO SPROCKET.

000725	Sprocket, on dynamo shaft	1	All	
000572	Key, for dynamo sprocket	1	All	
000010	Washer, plain, for dynamo sprocket nut	1	All	
000164	Washer, lock, for dynamo sprocket nut	1	All	
000708	Ring, lock, for dynamo sprocket nut	1	All	
000611	Nut, retaining, for dynamo sprocket	1	All	

GEARBOX.

016708	Gearbox, complete with four plate clutch, foot gear lever and kick-starter lever	1	16M, 16MS	★
016709	Gearbox, complete with five plate clutch, foot gear lever and kick-starter lever	1	18, 18S	★
018981	Gearbox, complete with five plate clutch, foot gear lever and kick-starter lever	1	16MC, 18C	★
016711	Gearbox, complete with five plate clutch, foot gear lever and kick-starter lever	1	16MCS, 18CS	★

★ Price on application.

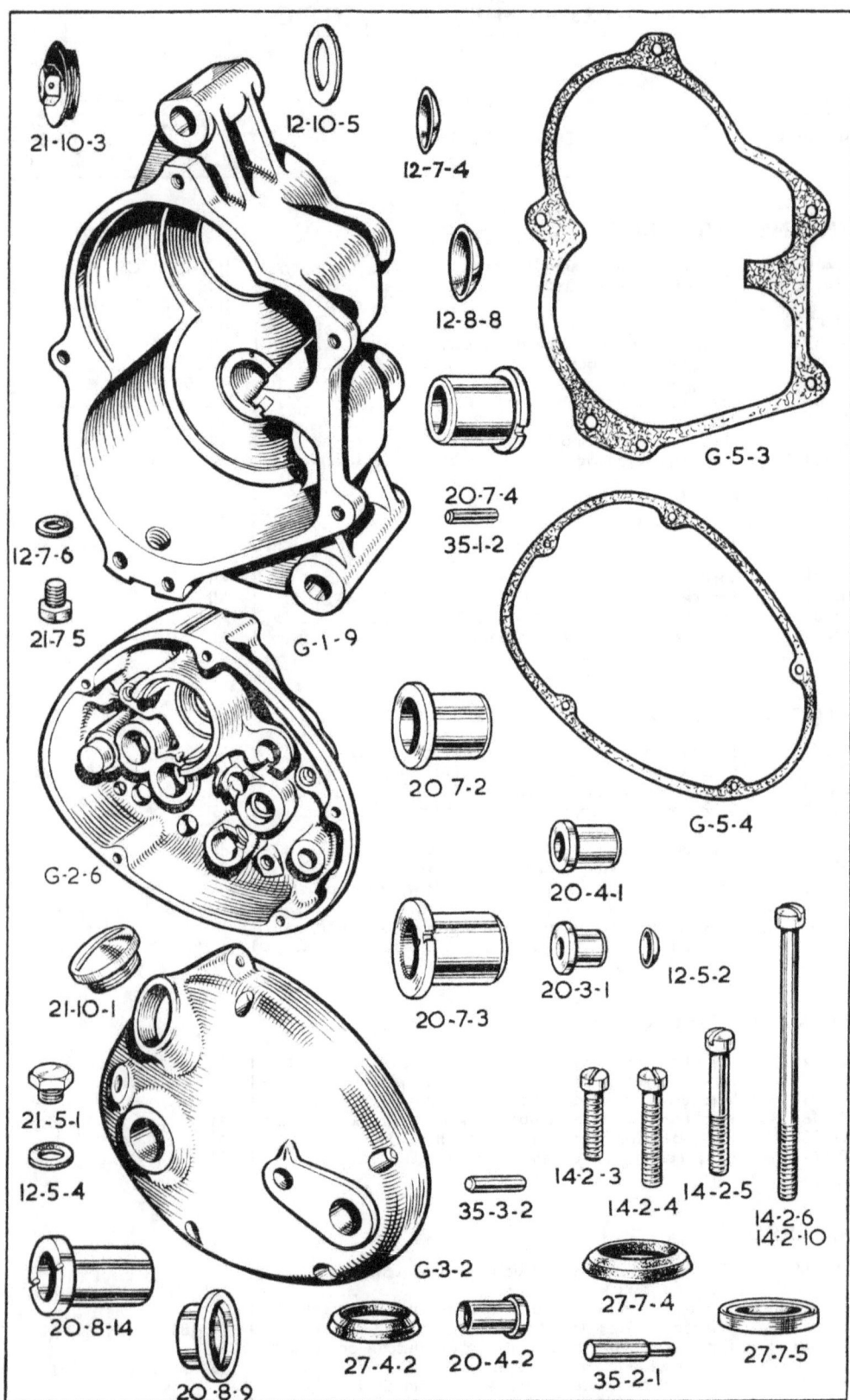

PART NUMBER.	DESCRIPTION.	QTY.	USED ON.	PRICE EACH £ s. d.

CHAINS.

017381	Chain, front, 65 links, $\frac{1}{2}$ in. by ·305 in. (13)	1	16MC, 16MCS	
017298	Chain, front, 66 links, $\frac{1}{2}$ in. by ·305 in. (13)	1	16M, 16MS, 18C, 18CS	
017299	Chain, front, 67 links, $\frac{1}{2}$ in. by ·305 in. (13)	1	18, 18S	
017380	Chain, rear, 90 links, $\frac{5}{8}$ in. by ·380 in. (13)	1	16MC, 18C	
017301	Chain, rear, 94 links, $\frac{5}{8}$ in. by ·380 in. (13)	1	16M, 18	
017376	Chain, rear, 98 links, $\frac{5}{8}$ in. by ·380 in. (13)	1	16MS, 16MCS, 18S, 18CS	
017296	Chain, dynamo, 49 links, $\frac{3}{8}$ in. by ·225 in. (14)	1	All	
017294	Chain, magneto, 46 links, $\frac{3}{8}$ in. by ·225 in. (14)	1	All	
110046-26	Link, connecting, for $\frac{1}{2}$ in. chains	R	All	
110056-26	Link, connecting, for $\frac{5}{8}$ in. chains	R	All	
110046-30	Link, cranked, for $\frac{1}{2}$ in. chains	R	All	
110056-30	Link, cranked, for $\frac{5}{8}$ in. chains	R	All	
110046-27	Clip, spring, for $\frac{1}{2}$ in. connecting links	R	All	
110056-27	Clip, spring, for $\frac{5}{8}$ in. connecting links	R	All	

Note 13 ... The prices of front and rear chains include spring connecting links, and these are also included in the number of links per chain. We do not sell odd lengths of chain.

Note 14 ... Magneto and Dynamo chains are endless. We do not sell connecting and cranked links for same.

GEAR BOX FIXING PARTS.

010957	Bolt, gearbox top fixing, $5\frac{3}{16}$ ins. by $\frac{7}{16}$ in. by 26	1	All	
000318	Stud, gearbox bottom fixing, $4\frac{9}{16}$ ins. by $\frac{7}{16}$ in. by 26	1	All	
012999	Spacer, $\frac{5}{16}$ in. wide, on top bolt, outside right	1	All	
000002	Nut, for gearbox top fixing bolt	1	All	
000002	Nut, for gearbox bottom fixing stud	2	All	
000009	Washer, plain, for top fixing bolt, left side	1	All	
013987	Eye-bolt, for front chain adjustment	1	All	
000215	Nut, for front chain adjustment eye-bolt	2	All	
000785	Crosshead, for front chain adjustment eye-bolt	1	All	
000361	Bolt, fixing crosshead to engine plate, $\frac{9}{16}$ in. by $\frac{5}{16}$ in. by 26	1	16M, 16MC, 18, 18C	
000011	Washer, plain, for crosshead fixing bolt	1	16M, 16MC, 18, 18C	

GEAR BOX SHELL.

G-1-9	Shell, gearbox,	1	All	
21-10-3	Inspection plug	1	All	
12-10-5	Inspection plug washer	1	All	
21-7-5	Plug, drain, for gearbox shell	1	All	
12-7-6	Washer, fibre, for gearbox shell drain plug	1	All	
12-7-4	Cap, in shell, covering bore for selector spindles	2	All	
35-3-2	Pin, dowel, locating, kick-starter case on gearbox shell	1	All	
G-2-6	Case, kick-starter	1	All	
G-5-3	Washer, paper, between shell and kick-starter case	1	All	
G-3-2	Cover, for kick-starter case	1	All	
G-5-4	Washer, paper, between kick-starter case and cover	1	All	
28-12-45	Piece, locating, between kick-starter case and cover	1	All	
35-1-1	Pin, dowel, locating fixed cam-plate in kick-starter case	2	All	
21-10-1	Cap, filler, for kick-starter case cover	1	All	
21-5-1	Plug, oil level, in kick-starter case cover	1	All	
12-5-4	Washer, fibre, for oil level plug	1	All	
35-2-1	Pin, anchor, in cover, for kick-starter spring	1	All	
14-2-3	Screw, $\frac{7}{8}$ in. under head	1	All	
14-2-4	Screw, $1\frac{1}{4}$ in. under head	3	All	
14-2-5	Screw, $1\frac{3}{8}$ in. under head	2	All	
14-2-6	Screw, $2\frac{7}{8}$ ins. under head	1	All	
14-2-10	Screw, $3\frac{1}{8}$ ins. under head	1	All	
12-2-5	Fibre washer (fits under screwhead)	8	All	

Above screws have cheese heads and are threaded $\frac{1}{4}$ in. whit.

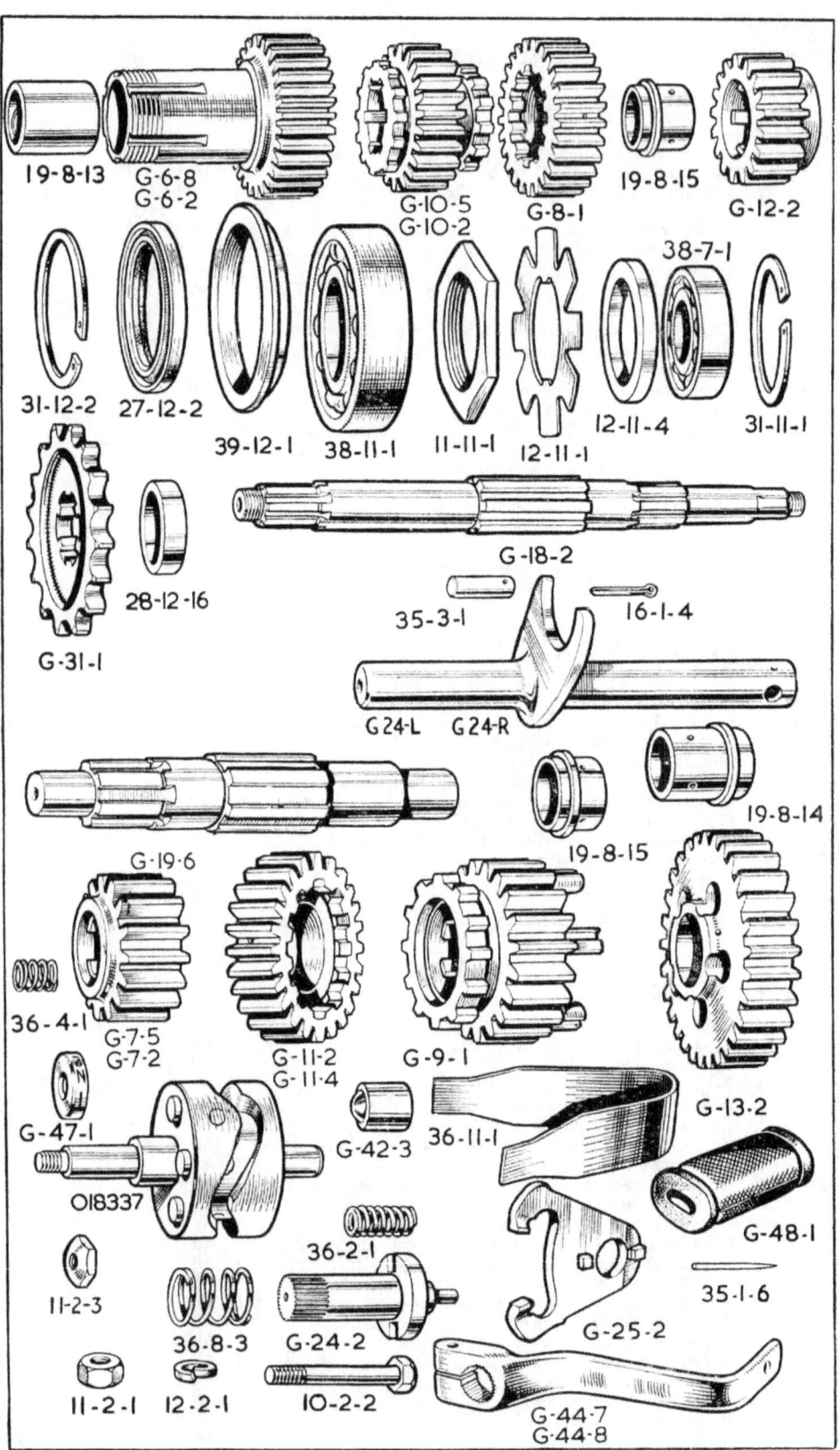

PART NUMBER.	DESCRIPTION.	QTY.	USED ON.	PRICE EACH £ s. d.

SHAFTS AND GEARS.

Part Number	Description	QTY.	Used On	Price
G-18-2	Mainshaft, for gearbox	1	All	
G-19-6	Layshaft, for gearbox (overall length 5½ ins.)	1	All	
G-6-2	Gear, driving, mainshaft, with bushes, 28 teeth	1	16M, 16MS, 16MCS, 18, 18S, 18CS	
G-6-8	Gear, driving, mainshaft with bushes, 30 teeth	1	16MC, 18C	
G-12-2	Gear, first, mainshaft, 17 teeth	1	All	
G-10-2	Gear, second, mainshaft, 22 teeth	1	16M, 16MS, 16MCS, 18, 18S, 18CS	
G-10-5	Gear, second, mainshaft, 20 teeth	1	16MC, 18C	
G-8-1	Gear, third, mainshaft, 25 teeth	1	All	
G-7-2	Pinion, on layshaft, 18 teeth	1	16M, 16MS, 16MCS, 18, 18S, 18CS	
G-7-5	Pinion on, layshaft, 16 teeth	1	16MC, 18C	
G-13-2	Gear, first, layshaft, with bush, 29 teeth	1	All	
G-11-2	Gear, second, layshaft, with bush, 24 teeth	1	16, 16MS, 16MCS, 18, 18S, 18CS	
G-11-4	Gear, second, layshaft, 26 teeth	1	16MC, 18C,	
G-9-1	Gear, third, layshaft, 21 teeth	1	All	
19-8-13	Bush, for mainshaft driving gear	2	All	
19-8-15	Bush, for mainshaft third gear	1	All	
19-8-15	Bush, for layshaft second gear	1	All	
19-8-14	Bush, for layshaft first gear	1	All	

GEARBOX BEARINGS, CAPS AND OIL-SEALS

Part Number	Description	QTY.	Used On	Price
38-11-1	Bearing, ball, 1 $\frac{9}{32}$ in. by 62 mm. by 16 mm. for driving gear on mainshaft	1	All	
27-12-2	Oil-seal, for driving gear bearing	1	All	
39-12-1	Housing, for driving gear bearing oil-seal	1	All	
31-12-2	Ring, split, retaining driving gear bearing	1	All	
38-7-1	Bearing, ball, 17 mm. by 40 mm. by 12 mm. for mainshaft (kick-starter end)	1	All	
31-11-1	Ring, split, retaining mainshaft ball bearing	1	All	
20-7-4	Bush, for layshaft (clutch end) (·968 in. long)	1	All	
35-1-2	Pin, dowel, locating layshaft bush	1	All	
12-8-8	Cap, in shell, covering bore, for layshaft	1	All	
20-7-3	Bush, for layshaft (kick-starter end) (·779 in. long)	1	All	
35-1-2	Pin, dowel, locating layshaft bush	1	All	
20-7-2	Bush, in kick-starter case, for kick-starter spindle	1	All	
20-8-14	Bush, in cover, for kick-starter spindle	1	All	
27-7-5	Oil-seal, in cover bush, for kick-starter spindle	1	All	
20-4-1	Bush, in kick-starter case, for cam spindle	1	All	
20-4-2	Bush, kick-starter case cover	1	All	
27-4-2	Oil-seal, in cover bush, for cam spindle	1	All	
20-3-1	Bush, in kick-starter case, for control quadrant spindle	1	All	
12-5-2	Cap, in kick-starter case, covering bore for control quadrant spindle	1	All	
20-8-9	Bush, in cover, for control quadrant spindle	1	All	
27-7-4	Oil-seal, in cover bush, for control quadrant spindle	1	All	

GEARBOX SMALL SPROCKET

Part Number	Description	QTY.	Used On	Price
G-31-1	Sprocket, gearbox, 16 teeth by $\frac{5}{8}$ in. by ·380 in.	1	All	
28-12-16	Collar, spacing, gearbox sprocket, ·435 in. wide	1	All	
12-11-3	Spacer, $\frac{1}{16}$ in. thick	2	All	
12-11-1	Washer, lock, for gearbox sprocket nut	1	All	
11-11-1	Nut, fixing gearbox sprocket to driving gear	1	All	
018494	Deflector, water, fits under nut 11-11-1	1	16MC, 18C, 16MCS, 18CS	

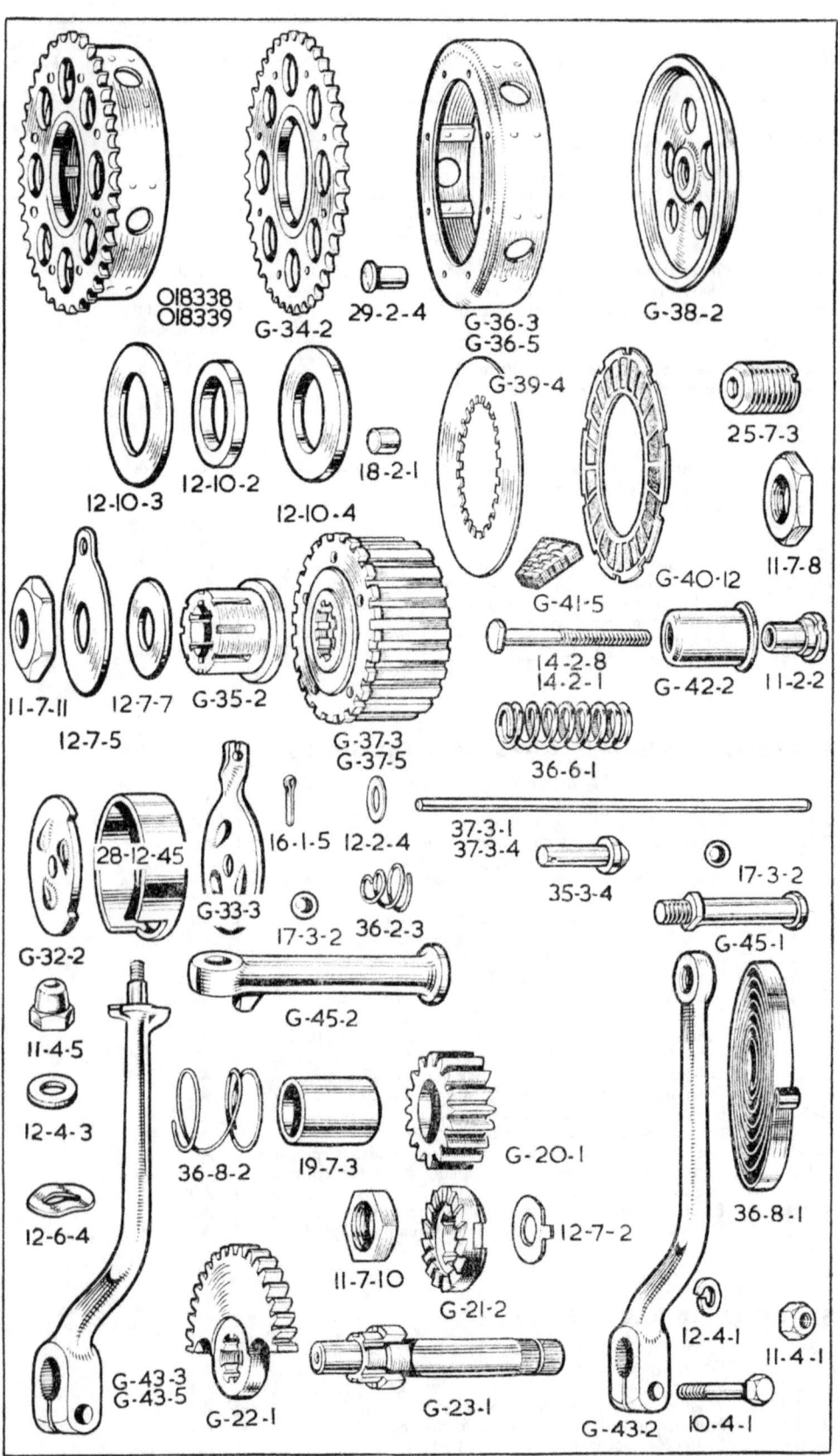

PART NUMBER.	DESCRIPTION.	QTY.	USED ON.	PRICE EACH £ s. d.

GEAR OPERATING PARTS

G-29-4	Spindle and fork, gear selection, left	1	All	
G-29-6	Spindle and fork, gear selection, right	1	All	
35-3-1	Peg, for selector spindles	2	All	
16-1-4	Pin, cotter, for selector spindle pegs	2	All	
018337	Cam assembly	1	All	

The cam assembly comprises:

1—G-27-2 Spindle.

1—G-28-1 Cam.

3—35-2-4 Pegs.

1—35-2-2 Locating pegs.

2—35-1-4 Cam stop pegs.

(Above parts not sold as separate spares)

G-42-3	Plunger, locating cam assembly	1	All	
36-2-1	Spring, for cam assembly locating plunger	1	All	
G-25-2	Quadrant, for control spindle	1	All	
35-2-6	Peg, quadrant drive	1	All	
G-24-2	Spindle, for gear control quadrant	1	All	
36-11-1	Spring, primary, for control quadrant	1	All	
36-8-3	Spring, secondary, for control quadrant	1	All	
G-47-1	Indicator	1	All	
36-4-1	Spring under indicator	1	All	
11-2-3	Nut, retaining indicator	1	All	
G-44-7	Lever, foot, for gear control	1	All	Except CS
G-48-1	Pad, rubber, for gear foot lever	1	All	
35-1-6	Pin, fixing gear foot lever rubber pad	1	All	
10-2-2	Bolt, clamping gear foot lever	1	All	
12-2-1	Washer, spring, for gear foot lever bolt	1	All	
11-2-1	Nut, for gear foot lever bolt	1	All	
G-44-8	Lever, foot, gear control	1	16MCS, 18CS	

CLUTCH

G-36-3	Case, for five plate clutch	1	All	
29-2-4	Rivet, for clutch case and chainwheel	8	All	
G-34-2	Chainwheel, 40 teeth by ½ in. by ·305 in.	1	All	
018339	Case and chainwheel, assembled	1	All	
G-35-2	Sleeve, for mainshaft	1	All	
12-10-2	Race, roller, for clutch bearing chainwheel	1	All	
18-2-1	Rollers, for chainwheel bearing............price per set of	24	All	
12-10-3	Washer, thin, chainwheel bearing	1	All	
12-10-4	Washer, thick, chainwheel bearing	1	All	
G-37-5	Centre, for four plate clutch	1	16M, 16MS	
G-37-3	Centre, for five plate clutch	1	All except 16M, 16MS	
12-7-7	Washer, plain, for centre retaining nut	1	All	
12-7-5	Washer, lock, for centre retaining nut	1	All	
11-7-11	Nut, retaining clutch centre	1	All	
G-39-4	Plate, clutch, plain, steel	5 or 6	All	
G-40-12	Plate, clutch, friction, with inserts	4	16M, 16MS	
G-40-12	Plate, clutch, friction, with inserts	5	16MC, 18, 18S, 18C, 18CS, 16MCS	

PART NUMBER.	DESCRIPTION.	QTY.	USED ON.	PRICE EACH £ s. d.

CLUTCH—continued.

G-41-5	... Inserts, fabric, for friction plate.........price per dozen	96	16M, 16MS	...
G-41-5	... Inserts, fabric, for friction plate.........price per dozen	120	16MC, 18, 18S, 18C, 18CS, 16MCS	...
G-38-2	... Plate, clutch, spring pressure..................................	1	All	... ...
25-7-3	... Cup thrust, for spring pressure plate......................	1	All	... ...
11-7-8	... Nut, lock, for pressure plate thrust cup.................	1	All	... ...
14-2-1	... Stud, for clutch spring, 1¾ in. long (four plate clutch)...	5	16M, 16MS	...
14-2-8	... Stud, for clutch spring, 2 ins. long (five plate clutch).....	5	16MC, 18, 18S, 18C, 18CS, 16MCS	...
36-6-1	... Spring, for clutch	5	All	... ...
G-42-2	... Cup, for clutch spring..	5	All	... ...
11-2-2	... Nut, adjusting, for clutch spring.................................	5	All	... ...

CLUTCH OPERATING PARTS

37-3-4	... Rod, thrust, 9⅞ ins. long (four plate clutch)...............	1	16M, 16MS,	...
37-3-1	... Rod, thrust, 10 3/16 ins. long (five plate clutch)...............	1	16MC, 18, 18S, 18C, 18CS, 16MCS	...
17-3-2	... Ball, 5/16 in., steel, for clutch thrust rod......................	1	All	... ...
G-32-2	... Cam-plate, fixed, actuating clutch.............................	1	All	... ...
G-33-3	... Cam-plate, moving, actuating clutch.........................	1	All	... ...
35-3-4	... Dowel, thrust (passes through both cam-plates).........	1	All	... ...
12-2-4	... Washer, plain, for cam-plate dowel............................	1	All	... ...
36-2-3	... Spring, for cam-plate dowel......................................	1	All	... ...
16-1-5	... Pin, split, for cam-plate dowel...................................	1	All	... ...
17-3-2	... Ball, 5/16 in., steel, for cam-plates...............................	3	All	... ...

KICK-STARTER

G-21-2	... Ratchet, driving, kick-starter....................................	1	All	... ...
G-20-1	... Pinion, ratchet, kick-starter......................................	1	All	... ...
19-7-3	... Bush, kick-starter ratchet pinion...............................	1	All	... ...
36-8-2	... Spring, kick-starter ratchet pinion.............................	1	All	... ...
11-7-10	... Nut, retaining ratchet driver to mainshaft.................	1	All	... ...
12-7-22	... Washer, lock, for retaining nut..................................	1	All	... ...
G-23-1	... Spindle, for kick-starter quadrant.............................	1	All	... ...
G-22-1	... Quadrant, for kick-starter..	1	All	... ...
018340	... Kick-starter quadrant and spindle assembled.............	1	All	... ...
36-8-1	... Spring, return, for kick-starter foot lever..................	1	All	... ...
G-43-2	... Lever, foot, kick-starter, bare...................................	1	16M, 16MS, 18, 18S	...
G-43-3	... Lever, foot, kick-starter, bare...................................	1	16MC, 18C	...
G-43-5	... Lever, foot, kick-starter, bare...................................	1	16MCS, 18CS	...
G-45-1	... Pin, pedal, rigid, for kick-starter lever.......................	1	16M, 16MS, 18, 18S	...
G-45-2	... Pin, pedal, folding, for kick-starter lever...................	1	16MC, 18C, 16MCS, 18CS	...
11-4-5	... Nut, retaining folding pedal pin.................................	1	16MC, 18C, 16MCS, 18CS	...
12-4-3	... Washer, plain, for pin retaining nut...........................	1	16MC, 18C, 16MCS, 18CS	...
12-6-4	... Washer, spring, for pin retaining nut.........................	1	16MC, 18C, 16MCS, 18CS	...
10-4-1	... Bolt, clamping, kick-starter foot lever to spindle.........	1	All	... ...
12-4-1	... Washer, spring, for foot lever clamping bolt...............	1	All	... ...
11-4-1	... Nut, for foot lever clamping bolt...............................	1	All	... ...

FRAME SECTION.

PART NUMBER.	DESCRIPTION.	QTY.	USED ON.	PRICE EACH £ s. d.

FRONT FRAME.

021704	Frame, front portion only, bare	1	16MS, 18S,	...
021703	Frame, front portion only, bare	1	16M, 18	...
021013	Frame, front portion only, bare	1	16MC, 18C	...
022033	Frame, front portion only, bare	1	16MCS, 18CS	
000806	Race, ball, for frame head lug	2	All except 16MC, 18C	...
012594	Race, ball, for frame head, top	1	16MC, 18C	...
012595	Race, ball, for frame head, bottom	1	16MC, 18C	...
000072	Balls, $\frac{3}{16}$ in. diameter, for steering head, per set of 56	56	All	...
000051	Nipple, grease, for frame head lug	1	All	...
021767	Stud, for seat lug (below saddle), $4\frac{1}{8}$ ins. by $\frac{1}{2}$ in. by 26	1	16M, 16MC, 18, 18C	...
021768	Stud, for seat lug (below saddle), $4\frac{7}{16}$ ins. by $\frac{1}{2}$ in. by 26	1	16MS, 16MCS, 18S, 18CS	...
000008	Washer, plain, for seat lug stud	2	All Touring and Scrambles	
000001	Nut for seat lug stud	2	All	...
021084	Stud, uniting front and rear frame, $6\frac{1}{8}$ ins. by $\frac{3}{8}$ in. by 26	1	16M, 16MS, 18, 18S	...
021917	Stud, uniting front and rear frame, $6\frac{3}{8}$ ins. by $\frac{3}{8}$ in. by 26	1	16MC, 16MCS, 18C, 18CS	...
000010	Washer, plain, for frame uniting stud	2	All	...
000003	Nut, for frame uniting stud	2	All	...

REAR FRAME.

021049	Frame, rear portion only	1	16M, 18	...
021050	Frame, rear portion only	1	16MC, 18C	...
017031	Bolt, adjusting rear chain, $2\frac{11}{16}$ ins. by $\frac{1}{4}$ in. by 26	2	16M, 16MC, 18, 18C	...
000005	Nut, lock, for rear chain adjusting bolt	2	ditto	
021665	Rail, frame, right side	1	16MS, 16MCS, 18S, 18CS	...
021664	Rail, frame, left side	1	ditto	
021705	Loop, rear frame	1	16MS, 18S	...
021769	Loop, rear frame	1	16MCS, 18CS	...
021715	Stud, for rear loop at bottom, $10\frac{5}{8}$ ins. by $\frac{7}{16}$ in. by 26 (Also passes through rear fork bridge and both frame rails)	1	16MS, 16MCS, 18S, 18CS	...
000410	Bolt, frame rail end	2	16MS, 16MCS, 18S, 18CS	...
000003	Nut, frame rail end bolt	2	ditto	
000010	Washer, frame rail end bolt	2	ditto	
000002	Nut, for rear loop bottom stud	1	ditto	
000009	Washer, plain, for rear loop bottom stud	2	ditto	
018617	Tube, supporting rear of rear mudguard, right side	1	16MS, 18S	...
018616	Tube, supporting rear of rear mudguard, left side	1	ditto	
000343	Bolt, fixing mudguard to support tube $1\frac{3}{16}$ in. by $\frac{1}{4}$ in. by 26	2	ditto	
000012	Washer, plain, for mudguard support tube bolt	2	ditto	
000191	Washer, spring, for mudguard support tube bolt	2	ditto	
000005	Nut, for mudguard support tube bolt	2	ditto	
015329	Bridge, for rear fork (includes bushes and studs for centre stand spring clip)	1	16MS, 16MCS, 18S, 18CS	...
014672	Bush, for rear fork bridge	2	ditto	
000250	Stud, for rear fork bridge, $\frac{11}{16}$ in. by 2.BA	2	ditto	

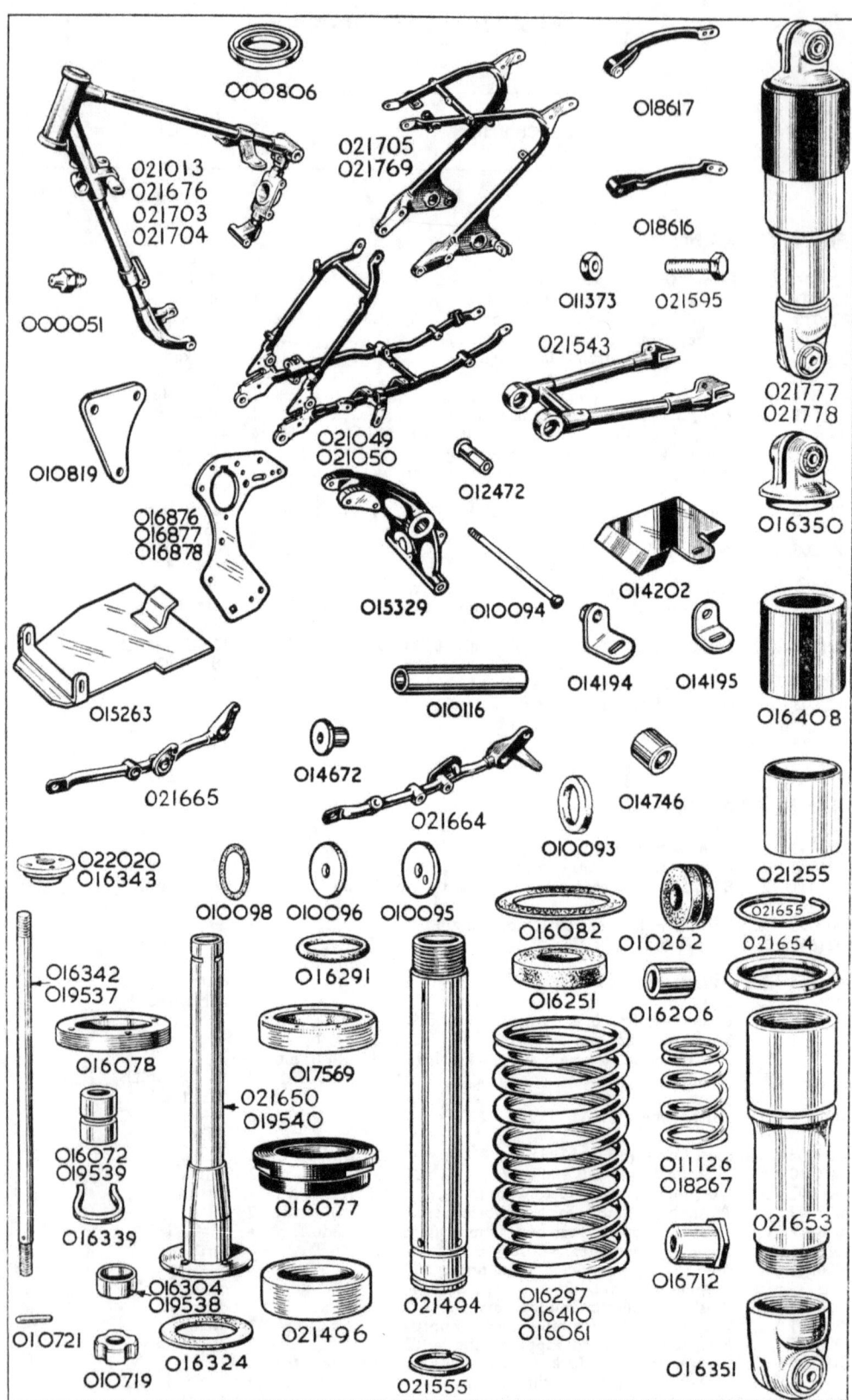

PART NUMBER.	DESCRIPTION.	QTY.	USED ON.	PRICE EACH £ s. d.

ENGINE PLATES AND BOLTS.

Part Number	Description	Qty	Used On	Price
010819	Plate, engine, front	2	All	
010823	Stud, fixing front plate to frame tube, $6\frac{3}{8}$ ins. by $\frac{3}{8}$ in. by 26	1	All	
000010	Washer, plain, for engine front plate stud	2	All	
000003	Nut, for stud fixing engine front plate	2	All	
016876	Plate, engine, rear	2	16M, 16MS, 18, 18S	
016877	Plate, engine, rear	2	16MC, 18C	
016878	Plate, engine, rear	2	16MCS, 18CS	
000303	Stud, for seat tube bottom lug, $4\frac{1}{2}$ ins. by $\frac{3}{8}$ in. by 26	1	16M, 16MC, 18, 18C	
013826	Spacer, $\frac{11}{16}$ in. long, for seat tube bottom stud, left	1	ditto	
013827	Spacer, $\frac{5}{16}$ in. thick, for seat tube bottom stud, right	1	ditto	
000003	Nut, for seat tube bottom lug stud	2	ditto	
000303	Stud, passing through top of engine rear plates, lower end of front frame seat tube and rear fork bridge, $4\frac{1}{2}$ ins. by $\frac{3}{8}$ in. by 26	1	16MS, 16MCS, 18S, 18CS	
000003	Nut, for 000303 stud	2	ditto	
000278	Stud, passing through rear fork bridge, and back ends of engine rear plates, $4\frac{9}{16}$ ins. by $\frac{5}{16}$ in. by 26. (The front chain adjusting eye-bolt block screws on the right-hand end of this stud.)	1	ditto	
000011	Washer, plain, for 000278 stud	1	ditto	
000004	Nut, for 000278 stud	1	ditto	
015263	Shield, for crankcase	1	16MC, 16MCS, 18C, 18CS	
000277	Stud, for engine plate extension, $4\frac{5}{16}$ ins. by $\frac{5}{16}$ in. by 26	1	ditto	
017198	Spacer, $3\frac{7}{16}$ ins. long, for engine plate extension	2	ditto	
000004	Nut, for 000277 studs	3	ditto	
000277	Stud, engine rear plate crosshead, $4\frac{5}{16}$ ins. by $\frac{5}{16}$ in. by 26 (only used if no dynamo fitted)	1	ditto	
014202	Cover, rear engine plate	1	All	
014194	Bracket, long, for horn	1	All	
014195	Bracket, short, for horn	1	All	
000413	Bolt, fixing cover plate and brackets, $\frac{7}{8}$ in. by $\frac{3}{8}$ in. by 26	1	All	
000010	Washer, plain, for cover plate bolt	1	All	

REAR FORK.

Part Number	Description	Qty	Used On	Price
021543	Fork, rear	1	16MS, 16MCS, 18S, 18CS	
021595	Adjuster, rear chain	2	ditto	
011373	Nut, lock, for chain adjuster	2	ditto	
014746	Sleeve, assembly (bushed)	2	ditto	
010116	Tube	1	ditto	
010095	Cap, for rear fork bearing, right side	1	ditto	
010096	Cap, for rear fork bearing, left side	1	ditto	
010093	Washer, felt, for rear fork bearing	2	ditto	
010098	Gasket, for rear fork bearing caps	2	ditto	
010094	Spoke, for rear fork bearing (central tie bolt)	1	ditto	
012472	Nipple, for rear fork bearing spoke	1	ditto	
000485	Screw, plug, for oil, in end cap, $\frac{1}{4}$ in. by $\frac{1}{4}$ in. by 26	1	ditto	
000203	Washer, fibre, for oil plug screw	1	ditto	

PART NUMBER.	DESCRIPTION.	QTY.	USED ON.	PRICE EACH £ s. d.

TELEDRAULIC REAR LEG.

PART NUMBER.	DESCRIPTION.	QTY.	USED ON.
021777	Leg, TELEDRAULIC, rear complete assembly (no fixing bolts, washers and nuts)............................	2	16MS, 18S
021778	Leg, TELEDRAULIC, rear, complete assembly (no fixing bolts, washers and nuts)............................	2	16MCS, 18CS
016350	Pivot, top, assembled (this assembly includes the next three items)...	2	16MS, 16MCS, 18S, 18CS
016059	Pivot, top, bare...	2	ditto
010262	Bush, rubber, for top pivot................................	4	ditto
016206	Spacer, for top pivot rubber bush.....................	4	ditto
016351	Pivot, bottom, assembled (this assembly includes the next five items)...	2	ditto
016060	Pivot, bottom bare...	2	ditto
010262	Bush, rubber, for bottom pivot.........................	4	ditto
016206	Spacer, for bottom pivot rubber bush...............	2	ditto
016712	Sleeve nut, for bottom pivot bolt......................	2	ditto
016873	Washer, plain, for 016712 sleeve nut................	2	ditto
021494	Tube, inner (fits in top pivot recess).................	2	ditto
016291	Ring, sealing inner tube at top.........................	2	ditto
021496	Bush, lower end of inner tube..........................	2	ditto
021555	Circlip, retaining inner tube bush.....................	4	ditto
021653	Tube, outer (screws into bottom pivot).............	2	ditto
016324	Washer, sealing lower end of outer tube...........	4	ditto
016077	Bush, for outer tube..	2	ditto
017569	Oil-seal, between inner and outer tubes............	2	ditto
016078	Collar, retaining oil-seal....................................	2	ditto
021650	Tube, for damper...	2	16MS, 18S
019540	Tube, for damper...	2	16MCS, 18CS
016072	Sleeve, plunger, for damper rod.......................	2	16MS, 18S
019539	Sleeve, plunger, for damper rod.......................	2	16MCS, 18CS
016339	Clip, locating plunger sleeve............................	2	All
016342	Rod, for damper..	2	16MS, 18S
019537	Rod, for damper..	2	16MCS, 18CS
016343	Collar, for top end of damper rod....................	2	16MS, 18S
022020	Collar, for top end of damper rod....................	2	16MCS, 18CS
000074	Nut, locking collar top-end of damper rod.......	2	All
016304	Valve, for damper..	2	16MS, 18S
019538	Valve, for damper..	2	16MCS, 18CS
010721	Pin, stop, for damper valve...............................	2	All
010719	Seat, for damper valve......................................	2	All
000005	Nut, retaining damper seat to damper rod.......	2	All
019555	Buffer spring distance piece.............................	2	16MCS, 18CS
019626	Damper valve assembled (Comprising following 6 items)	2	16MCS, 18CS
019531	Damper valve body..	2	16MCS, 18CS
000072	Damper valve ball..	2	ditto
019535	Damper valve pin...	2	ditto
021280	Damper valve spring..	2	ditto
019534	Damper valve plug...	2	ditto
019532	Damper valve relief plunger..............................	2	ditto
011126	Spring, buffer..	2	16MS, 18S
018267	Spring, buffer..	2	16MCS, 18CS
016297	Spring, main (solo)..	2	16MS, 18S
016061	Spring, main (sidecar).......................................	2	16MS, 18S
016410	Spring, main..	2	16MCS, 18CS
016082	Washer, leather, at both ends of main spring....	4	16MS, 18S, 16MCS, 18CS
016408	Tube, outer, covering top end of main spring...	2	ditto
021255	Tube, outer, covering bottom end of main spring	2	ditto
021654	Collar, retaining bottom outer cover tube........	2	ditto
021655	Circlip, retaining collar....................................	2	ditto
016251	Buffer, for TELEDRAULIC leg........................	2	ditto
018648	Bolt, fixing top pivot, 3⅛ ins. by ⅜ in. by 26....	2	16MS, 18S
014521	Bolt, fixing top pivot (replaces 018648 when carrier is fitted)..	2	ditto
011273	Bolt, fixing top pivot, 2½ ins. by ⅜ in. by 26....	2	16MCS, 18CS
000010	Washer, plain, for top pivot bolt.......................	4	16MS, 18S, 16MCS, 18CS

PART NUMBER.	DESCRIPTION.	QTY.	USED ON.	PRICE EACH £ s. d.

TELEDRAULIC REAR LEG—continued.

016712	Sleeve nut, for top pivot bolt	2	16MS, 18S	
000003	Nut, for top pivot bolt	2	16MCS, 18CS	
016359	Bolt, fixing bottom pivot, 2 1/32 ins. by 3/8 in. by 26	2	All except 16M, 18	
000010	Washer, plain, for bottom pivot bolt	2	ditto	

FORK ASSEMBLIES.

The following fork assemblies are complete and include ball races for the fork crown and top head lug (but not the two frame ball races)

021967	Fork, assembly (TELEDRAULIC Front Fork, Solo)	1	16M, 16MS, 18, 18S	
021968	Fork, assembly (TELEDRAULIC Front Fork, Sidecar)	1	ditto	
021969	Fork assembly (TELEDRAULIC Front Fork, Solo)	1	16MC, 18C	
021970	Fork assembly (TELEDRAULIC Front Fork, Solo)	1	16MCS, 18CS	

For ease of servicing, the inner tube unit and damper unit are listed and supplied as separate assemblies. This enables a complete assembly to be exchanged in minimum time. The Units are listed below.

021971	Front Fork inner tube assembly, Solo	2	16M, 16MS, 18, 18S	
021972	Front Fork inner tube assembly, Sidecar	2	18, 18S	
021973	Front Fork inner tube assembly, Solo	2	16MC, 16MCS, 18C, 18CS	

The above assemblies comprise:—Inner tubes with rubber buffers, bushes and circlips, top bolts with washers and sealing rings, slider extensions with oil seals, fork springs and washers.

021974	Front fork damper assembly	2	16M, 16MS, 16MC, 18, 18S, 18C	
021975	Front fork damper assembly	2	16MCS, 18CS	

The above assemblies comprise:— Rod and two nuts, damper tube with valve, seat and pin, sleeve and clip and bottom fixing bolt with washer.

FRONT FORK.

021927	Crown, assembly, comprising crown, stem and circlip (these parts not sold separately)	1	16M, 16MS, 18, 18S	
021928	Crown, assembly, comprising crown, stem and circlip (these parts not sold separately)	1	16MC, 16MCS, 18C, 18CS	
000805	Race, ball, for fork crown	1	All	
021740	Screw, pinch, for fork crown	2	All except 16MC, 16MCS, 18MC, 18MCS	
021749	Lug, for handlebar and steering head	1	All	
021841	Lug, for handle bar and steering head	1	16MC, 16MCS, 18C, 18CS	
012620	Race, ball, for handlebar lug	1	All	
000051	Nipple, grease, for handlebar lug	1	All	
021741	Nut, adjusting, for fork crown stem	1	All	
021642	Nut, lock (domed), for fork crown stem	1	All	
021652	Tube, fork, inner	2	All	
021911	Buffer, rubber, for fork inner tube	6	All	
021495	Bush, bottom, for fork inner tube	2	All	
021651	Circlip, for fork inner tube bush	2	All	
021830	Bolt, top, for fork inner tube	2	All	
021833	Cap, fork, inner tube top bolt	2	All	
014355	Ring, sealing, for fork inner tube top bolt	2	All	
021831	Washer, plain, for fork inner tube top bolt	2	All	
021399	Slider, fork, with cap, studs and nuts, left and right	2	16MC, 16MCS, 18C, 18CS	
021976	Slider, fork, with cap, studs and nuts, right	1	16M, 16MS, 18, 18S	

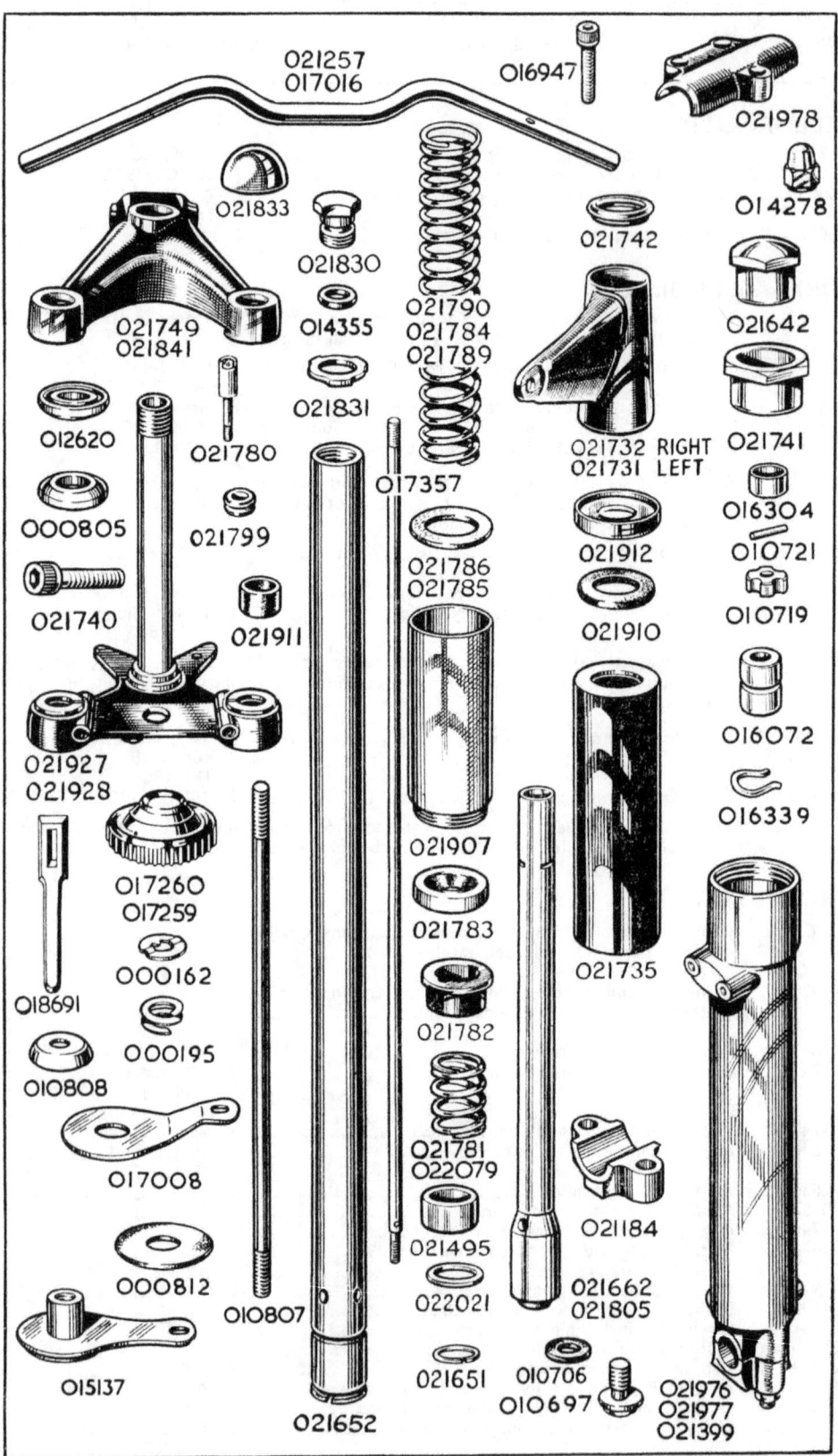

PART NUMBER.	DESCRIPTION.	QTY.	USED ON.	PRICE EACH £ s. d.

FRONT FORK—*continued.*

Part Number	Description	Qty	Used On
021977	Slider, fork, with cap, studs and nuts, left	1	16M, 16MS, 18, 18S
021184	Cap, for fork slider	2	All
010713	Stud, securing fork slider cap, 1$\frac{23}{32}$ in. by $\frac{5}{16}$ in. by 26 and 22	4	All
021780	Fork stop (acts also as pinch bolt)	2	16MC, 16MCS 18C, 18CS,
000003	Fork stop nut	2	ditto
000193	Fork stop nut spring washer	2	ditto
000011	Washer, plain, for fork slider cap stud	4	All
000004	Nut, for fork slider cap stud	4	All
021907	Extension, for fork slider	2	All
021782	Bush, plastic, for fork inner tube	2	All
021783	Oil-seal, for fork inner tube (rubber)	2	All
021784	Spring, main, for front fork, Solo	2	16M, 16MS, 18, 18S,
021790	Spring, main, for front fork, Solo	2	16MCS, 18CS, 18C, 16C
021789	Spring, main, for front fork, Sidecar	2	18, 18S
022079	Spring, buffer, front fork	2	All
022021	Collar, for buffer spring	2	All
021786	Washer, leather, fork spring seating, bottom	2	All
021785	Washer, fork spring seating, top	2	All
021732	Tube, fork cover, top, right, with lamp lug	1	All
021731	Tube, fork cover, top, left, with lamp lug	1	All
021742	Spigot, for top cover tube	2	All
021910	Seat (rubber), for cover tube	2	All
021912	Housing, for top cover tube	2	All
021735	Tube, fork cover, bottom	2	All
000485	Screw, plug, oil drain, for fork slider, $\frac{1}{4}$ in. by $\frac{1}{4}$ in. by 26	2	All
000203	Washer, fibre, for fork slider screw oil plug	2	All
021662	Tube, fork damper	2	16M, 16MS, 16MC, 18, 18S, 18C
021805	Tube, fork damper	2	16MCS, 18CS
010697	Bolt, fixing fork damper tube to slider, $\frac{7}{16}$ in. by $\frac{5}{16}$ in. by 26	2	All
010706	Washer, fibre, for damper tube bolt	2	All
017357	Rod, for fork damper	2	All
000004	Nut, lock, top end of damper rod	2	All
016072	Sleeve, plunger, for fork damper rod	2	All
016339	Clip, retaining damper rod sleeve	2	All
016304	Valve, for fork damper	2	All
010721	Pin, stop, for fork damper valve	2	All
010719	Seat, for fork damper valve	2	All
000005	Nut, lock, for fork damper valve seat	2	All
018691	Steering locking bar (own padlock to be used)	1	All

HANDLEBAR.

Part Number	Description	Qty	Used On
017016	Handlebar, bare	1	16MCS, 18CS
021257	Handlebar, bare	1	All except 16MCS, 18CS
021978	Clip (half only), for handlebar lug	1	All
016947	Screw, for handlebar clip, $\frac{7}{8}$ in. by $\frac{1}{4}$ in. by 26 (socket head)	3	All

---

MAINTENANCE MANUAL 1955 EDITION   PRICE **2/6**
IS THE APPROPRIATE MANUAL FOR THIS SPARES LIST

PART NUMBER.	DESCRIPTION.	QTY.	USED ON.	PRICE EACH £ s. d.

STEERING DAMPER. (This is an optional extra).

022059	Damper, steering, complete set of parts..................	1	All	
017260	Knob, control, for steering damper........................	1	All	
000162	Washer, ratchet, for steering damper knob.............	1	All	
000195	Washer, spring, for steering damper knob..............	1	All	
010808	Cap, for top of steering stem................................	1	All	
010807	Drawbolt, for steering damper...............................	1	All	
015137	Sleeve, assembly, lower end of drawbolt.................	1	All	
000073	Nut, locking sleeve to drawbolt.............................	1	All	
000342	Bolt, fixing sleeve assembly, $1\frac{1}{16}$ in. by $\frac{1}{4}$ in. by 26....	1	All	
000191	Washer, spring, for bolt 000342...........................	1	All	
000012	Washer, plain, for bolt 000342..............................	1	All	
017008	Plate, anchor, top position....................................	1	All	
000070	Bolt, fixing top anchor plate, $\frac{9}{16}$ in. by $\frac{1}{4}$ in. by 26...	1	All	
000191	Washer, spring, for bolt 000070...........................	1	All	
000812	Washer, friction, for steering damper	2	All	
021811	Nut, lock, for fork crown stem (this replaces the domed lock-nut, 021642, when a **steering damper** is fitted)	1	All	

FRONT STAND.

011286	Stand, front, bare..	1	16M, 16MS, 18, 18S	
010694	Bolt, fixing front stand to slider, $1\frac{3}{16}$ in. by $\frac{5}{16}$ in. by 22	2	ditto	
010724	Washer, spring, for stand to slider bolt..................	2	ditto	
000014	Pin, split, for stand to slider bolt..........................	2	ditto	
000342	Bolt, fixing front stand to front mudguard, $1\frac{1}{16}$ in. by $\frac{1}{4}$ in. by 26..	1	ditto	
000012	Washer, plain, for stand to mudguard bolt..............	2	ditto	
000005	Nut, front stand to mudguard bolt........................	1	ditto	
014278	Nut (domed), front stand to mudguard bolt............	1	ditto	

CENTRE STAND.

016340	Stand, centre, bare...	1	16MS, 16MCS, 18S, 18CS,	
014626	Bush, for centre stand, ·7 in. long	2	16MS, 18S	
016435	Bush, for centre stand, $1\frac{3}{16}$ in. long.....................	2	16MCS, 18CS	
014629	Stud, hinge, for centre stand, $8\frac{15}{16}$ ins. by $\frac{7}{16}$ in. by 26	1	16MS, 16MCS, 18S, 18CS	
014630	Spacer, central, for centre stand hinge stud, 4·2 ins. long	1	16MS, 18S	
010924	Spacer, central, for centre stand hinge stud, $3\frac{1}{2}$ ins. long	1	16MCS, 18CS	
014484	Spacer, outside right, for centre stand hinge stud, ·180 in. thick...	1	16MCS, 18CS	
010912	Washer, spigot, for centre stand hinge stud............	2	16MS, 16MCS, 18S, 18CS	
000002	Nut, for centre stand hinge stud	2	ditto	
014627	Spring, return, for centre stand............................	1	ditto	
016399	Spring, stop, for centre stand...............................	1	ditto	
000080	Nut, for centre stand stop spring. (The studs, on which these nuts fit, are listed with the " REAR FORK BRIDGE ")	2	ditto	
000039	Washer, plain, for centre stand stop spring fixing nuts	2	ditto	

PART NUMBER.	DESCRIPTION.	QTY.	USED ON.	PRICE EACH £ s. d.

PROP STAND.

014715	Stand, prop, bare..	1	All	... ...
014713	Bolt, hinge, for prop stand, $2\frac{1}{16}$ ins. by $\frac{7}{16}$ in. by 26......	1	All	... ...
014139	Nut, for prop stand hinge bolt.............................	1	All	... ...
000049	Pin, split, for prop stand hinge bolt........................	1	All	... ...
021261	Spring, return, for prop stand...............................	1	All	... ...

REAR STAND

017107	Stand, rear, bare...	1	16M, 16MC, 18, 18C	...
010788	Bolt, fixing stand to fork end, $1\frac{13}{64}$ in. by $\frac{1}{2}$ in. by 26...	2	ditto	
000008	Washer, plain, rear stand fixing bolt.......................	2	ditto	
000071	Nut, rear stand fixing bolt....................................	2	ditto	
017131	Spring, return, rear stand.....................................	1	ditto	

FRONT MUDGUARD.

021716	Mudguard, front bare..	1	16M, 16MS, 18, 18S	...
013947	Mudguard, front, bare..	1	16MC, 16MCS, 18C, 18CS	...
010795	Bolt, fixing mudguard bridge to right fork slider, $\frac{1}{2}$ in. by $\frac{5}{16}$ in. by 22...	2	All	... ...
000192	Washer, spring, for bridge right fixing bolt..............	2	All	... ...
010624	Stud, fixing mudguard bridge to left fork slider, also retains brake anchor stay and bracket for brake cable adjuster, $1\frac{1}{32}$ in. by $\frac{5}{16}$ in. by 26 and 22	2	All	... ...
014117	Washer, lock, for bridge left fixing stud	2	All	... ...
000004	Nut, for bridge left fixing stud...............................	2	All	... ...
013928	Stay, for front mudguard, forward position.............	1	16MC, 16MCS, 18C, 18CS	...
013929	Stay, for front mudguard, rear position..................	1	ditto	
010795	Bolt, fixing front mudguard stay to fork slider, $\frac{1}{2}$ in. by $\frac{5}{16}$ in. by 22..	4	ditto	
000192	Washer, spring, for stay to fork slider bolt..............	4	ditto	
012565	Bolt, fixing stay to front mudguard, $\frac{1}{2}$ in. by 2.BA.....	8	ditto	
000190	Washer, spring, for stay to front mudguard bolt........	8	ditto	
000039	Washer, plain, for stay to front mudguard bolt.........	8	ditto	
000080	Nut, for stay to front mudguard bolt......................	8	ditto	

BEFORE ORDERING SPARES
PLEASE NOTE THE INFORMATION GIVEN ON PAGES
TWO AND THREE

PART NUMBER.	DESCRIPTION.	QTY.	USED ON.	PRICE EACH £ s. d.

REAR CARRIER.

016418	Carrier, rear, bare...	1	16M, 18	...
014874	Carrier, rear, bare...	1	16MS, 18S	...
000368	Bolt, fixing 016418 carrier at rear........................	2	16M, 18M	...
000364	Bolt, fixing 016418 carrier, right side, at front.....	1	ditto	
000363	Bolt, fixing 016418 carrier, left side, at front.......	1	ditto	
014521	Bolt, fixing carrier at front (replaces 018648 when carrier is fitted)..	2	16MS, 18S	...

Existing nuts and washers are used for above bolts.)

REAR MUDGUARD (16M & 18).

021980	Mudguard, rear, bare (includes both halves and the two binding bolts)..	1	16M, 18	...
021755	Mudguard, rear, forward fixed portion only...............	1	ditto	
021033	Mudguard, rear, rear detachable portion only............	1	ditto	
015117	Bolt, clamping halves of rear mudguard.....................	2	ditto	
000346	Bolt, fixing mudguard to frame bridges, $1\frac{7}{16}$ in. by $\frac{1}{4}$ in. by 26	2	ditto	
000191	Washer, spring, for mudguard bridge bolts...............	2	ditto	
000005	Nut, for mudguard bridge bolts...................................	2	ditto	
016883	Arch, tubular, rear mudguard.......................................	1	ditto	
000270	Stud, in fork end, for tubular arch (also secures lower end of mudguard stay), $1\frac{1}{16}$ in. by $\frac{5}{16}$ in. by 26	2	ditto	
000074	Nut, locking stud in fork end.......................................	2	ditto	
000213	Nut (with collar), locking tubular arch and mudguard stay to fork end stud	2	ditto	
000368	Bolt, fixing mudguard to tubular arch, $1\frac{1}{2}$ in. by $\frac{5}{16}$ in. by 26	2	ditto	
016887	Stay, for rear mudguard, left side................................	1	ditto	
016886	Stay, for rear mudguard, right side.............................	1	ditto	
000363	Bolt, fixing mudguard to stay, $\frac{3}{4}$ in. by $\frac{5}{16}$ in. by 26.....	2	ditto	
000192	Washer, spring, for 000368 and 000363 fixing bolts......	4	ditto	
000004	Nut, for 000368 and 000363 fixing bolts.....................	4	ditto	
000342	Bolt, fixing mudguard to oil tank	1	ditto	
000172	Washer, plain, mudguard to oil tank bolt	2	ditto	
000005	Nut, for mudguard to oil tank bolt............................	1	ditto	

REAR MUDGUARD. (16MS & 18S).

021982	Rear mudguard (both portions with joint bolts)........	1	16MS, 18S	...
021707	Rear mudguard, forward portion only	1	ditto	
021710	Rear mudguard, rear portion only..............................	1	ditto	
021098	Bolt, for mudguard joint..	3	ditto	
021099	Washer, for mudguard joint bolt	3	ditto	
014501	Bracket, for bottom of rear mudguard.......................	2	ditto	
000342	Bolt, fixing bracket to rear mudguard, $\frac{11}{16}$ in. by $\frac{1}{4}$ in. by 26	2	ditto	
000012	Washer, plain, for bracket fixing bolt..........................	4	ditto	
000005	Nut, for bracket fixing bolt...	2	ditto	
000275	Stud, fixing rear mudguard brackets to frame, $3\frac{9}{16}$ ins. by $\frac{5}{16}$ in. by 26..	1	ditto	
000011	Washer, plain, for bracket fixing stud........................	2	ditto	
000004	Nut, for bracket fixing stud..	2	ditto	
000346	Bolt, fixing rear mudguard to frame loop bridge, $1\frac{7}{16}$ in. by $\frac{1}{4}$ in. by 26	1	ditto	
000191	Washer, spring, for bridge fixing bolt........................	1	ditto	
000005	Nut, for bridge fixing bolt...	1	ditto	
000342	Bolt, fixing rear mudguard to oil tank	1	ditto	
000191	Washer, spring, for mudguard to oil tank bolt...........	1	ditto	
000172	Washer, plain, for mudguard to oil tank bolt............	1	**ditto**	
000005	Nut, for mudguard to oil tank bolt............................	1	**ditto**	

PART NUMBER.	DESCRIPTION.	QTY.	USED ON.	PRICE EACH £ s. d.

REAR MUDGUARD. (16MC & 18C).

015167	Mudguard, rear, bare...	1	16MC, 18C	
000345	Bolt, fixing mudguard to frame top bridge, $1\frac{3}{16}$ in. by $\frac{1}{4}$ in. by 26..	1	ditto	
000346	Bolt, fixing mudguard to frame bottom bridge, $1\frac{7}{16}$ in. by $\frac{1}{4}$ in. by 26..	1	ditto	
000191	Washer, spring, for mudguard bridge bolts..................	2	ditto	
000005	Nut, for mudguard bridge bolts..	2	ditto	
000342	Bolt, fixing mudguard to oil tank bracket, $1\frac{1}{16}$ in. by $\frac{1}{4}$ in. by 26..	1	ditto	
000172	Washer, plain, for oil tank bracket bolt........................	1	ditto	
000005	Nut, for oil tank bracket bolt..	1	ditto	
015168	Stay, for rear mudguard, front position........................	1	ditto	
015170	Stay, for rear mudguard, rear position..........................	1	ditto	
000363	Bolt, fixing stays to fork end, $\frac{3}{4}$ in. by $\frac{5}{16}$ in. by 26 ...	2	ditto	
000011	Washer, plain, for stay to fork end bolt......................	2	ditto	
000192	Washer, spring, for stay to fork end bolt..................	2	ditto	
000074	Nut, for stay to fork end bolt...	2	ditto	
012565	Bolt, fixing mudguard to stay $\frac{1}{2}$ in. by 2.BA.............	7	ditto	
000190	Washer, spring, for mudguard to stay bolt..................	7	ditto	
000039	Washer, plain, for mudguard to stay bolt....................	7	ditto	
000080	Nut, for mudguard to stay bolt.......................................	7	ditto	

REAR MUDGUARD. (16MCS & 18CS).

021787	Mudguard, rear, bare...	1	16MCS, 18CS	
016352	Bracket, for bottom of rear mudguard..........................	2	ditto	
000342	Bolt, fixing bracket to rear mudguard, $1\frac{1}{16}$ in. by $\frac{1}{4}$ in. by 26	2	ditto	
000012	Washer, plain, for bracket fixing bolt............................	4	ditto	
000005	Nut, for bracket fixing bolt..	2	ditto	
000275	Stud, fixing rear mudguard brackets to frame, $3\frac{9}{16}$ ins. by $\frac{5}{16}$ in. by 26..	1	ditto	
000011	Washer, plain, for bracket fixing stud............................	2	ditto	
000004	Nut, for bracket fixing stud..	2	ditto	
000345	Bolt, fixing rear mudguard to frame loop bridge, $1\frac{3}{16}$ in. by $\frac{1}{4}$ in. by 26..	1	ditto	
000191	Washer, spring, for bridge fixing bolt............................	1	ditto	
000005	Nut, for bridge fixing bolt..	1	ditto	
015324	Tube, supporting rear mudguard......................................	1	ditto	
000369	Bolt, fixing support tube at front, $1\frac{5}{8}$ in. by $\frac{5}{16}$ in. by 26	2	ditto	
000004	Nut, for support tube bolt..	2	ditto	
012565	Bolt, fixing mudguard to support tube, $\frac{1}{2}$ in. by 2.BA...	6	ditto	
000190	Washer, spring, for mudguard to tube bolt................	6	ditto	
000039	Washer, plain, for mudguard to tube bolt..................	6	ditto	
000080	Nut, for mudguard to tube bolt.......................................	6	ditto	

FRONT NUMBER PLATE.

011835	Plate, number, front...	1	16M, 16MS, 18, 18S	
011698	Plate, number, front...	1	16MC, 16MCS, 18C, 18CS	
011836	Stud, fixing front number plate..	2	All	
000012	Washer, plain, front number plate stud........................	2	All	
000005	Nut, front number plate stud..	2	All	
000861	Screw, fixing front number plate to stud, $\frac{5}{16}$ in. by 2.BA.	2	All	
011889	Fillet, rubber, front number plate....................................	1	16M, 16MS, 18, 18S	

WHEN ORDERING SPARES, IF IN DOUBT REGARDING THE NAMES AND PART NUMBERS OF THE PARTS YOU REQUIRE, PLEASE SEND THE OLD PARTS TO SERVE AS PATTERNS.

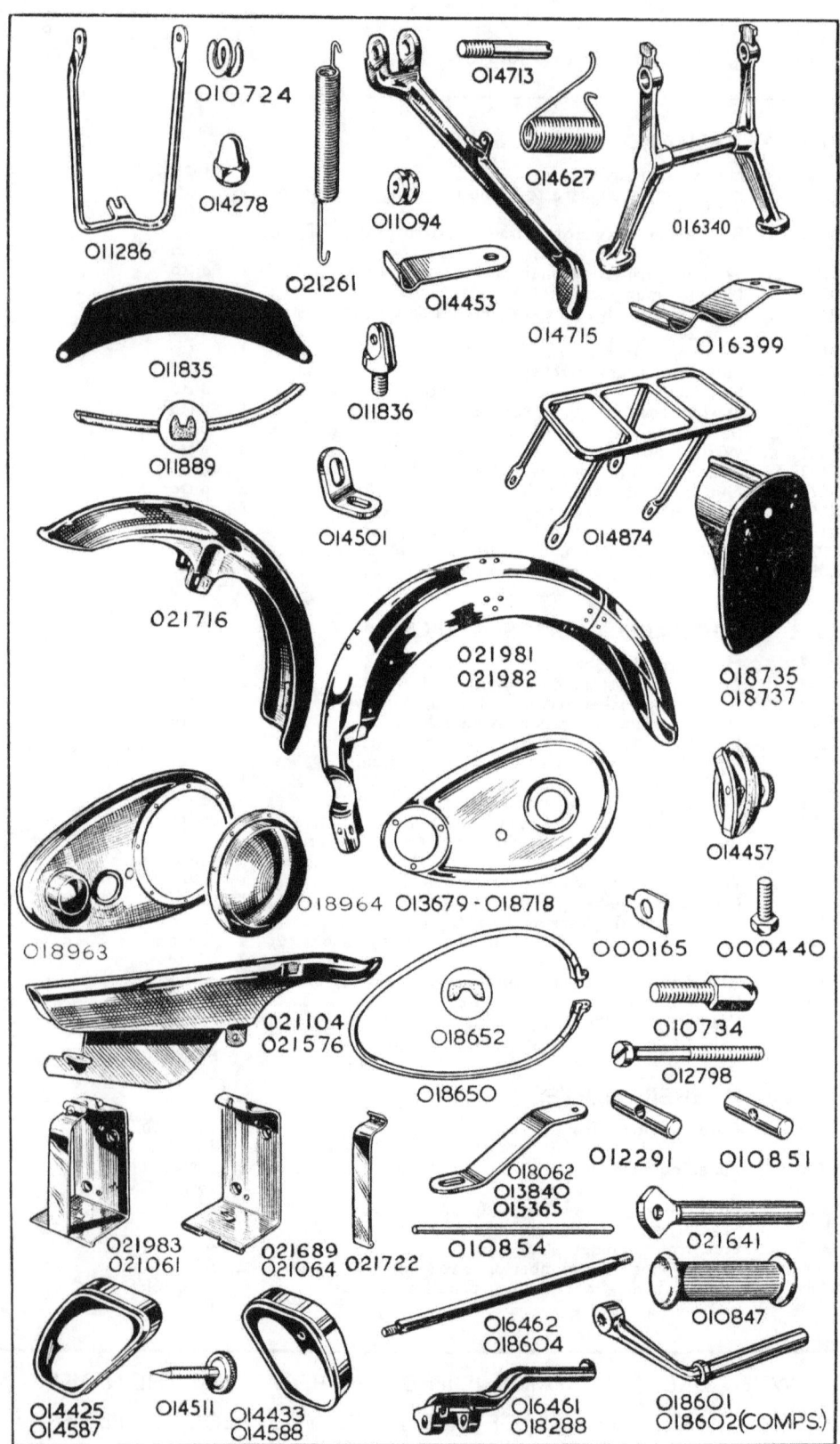

PART NUMBER.	DESCRIPTION.	QTY.	USED ON.	PRICE EACH £ s. d.

REAR NUMBER PLATE.

018735	Plate, number, rear, 8 ins. wide............................	1	16M, 18	...
018737	Plate, number, rear, 8 ins. wide............................	1	16MS, 18S	...
021881	Plate, number, rear, 8 ins. wide............................	1	16MC, 16MCS, 18C, 18CS	
021880	Rear lamp support	1	16MC, 16MCS, 18C, 18CS	
000738	Screw, rear lamp support......................................	2	16MC, 16MCS, 18C, 18CS	
000739	Nut, rear lamp support screw................................	2	16MC, 16MCS, 18C, 18CS	...
000364	Bolt, fixing rear number plate, $1\frac{5}{16}$ in. by $\frac{5}{16}$ in. by 26	2	16M, 18	...
000070	Bolt, fixing rear number plate, $\frac{9}{16}$ in. by $\frac{1}{4}$ in. by 26	2	16MC, 16MCS, 18C, 18CS	
000363	Bolt, fixing rear number plate, $\frac{3}{4}$ in. by $\frac{5}{16}$ in. by 26	2	16MS, 18S	
000192	Washer, spring, rear number plate bolt..................	2	16M, 16MS, 18, 18S	...
000012	Washer, plain, rear number plate bolt....................	4	16MC, 16MCS, 18C, 18CS	...
000005	Nut, rear number plate bolt..................................	2	ditto	
015298	Bracket, for rear number plate..............................	1	ditto	
000363	Bolt, fixing number plate bracket, $\frac{3}{4}$ in. by $\frac{5}{16}$ in. by 26	1	ditto	
000192	Washer, spring, for number plate bracket bolt.........	1	ditto	
000011	Washer, plain, for number plate bracket bolt...........	1	ditto	
000004	Nut, for number plate bracket bolt.........................	1	ditto	

FRONT CHAINCASE.

021374	Chaincase, complete. (Comprises both halves, metal and rubber bands, clamping screw and inspection caps —NO FIXING BOLTS, SPACERS, WASHERS, AND NUTS ARE INCLUDED)....................................	1	All except 16MC, 16MCS, 18C, 18CS	...
021375	Chaincase, complete and sliding seal.......................	1	16MC, 16MCS, 18C, 18CS	...
013679	Chaincase, back half, bare.....................................	1	All except 16MC, 16MCS, 18C, 18CS	...
021036	Chaincase, back half, bare.....................................	1	16MC, 16MCS, 18C, 18CS	
018963	Chaincase, front half, bare....................................	1	All	... ...
018650	Band, metal, for chaincase....................................	1	All	... ...
000453	Screw, clamping chaincase metal band, 1 in. by 2.BA.	1	All	... ...
018652	Band, rubber, for chaincase...................................	1	All	... ...
018964	Domed clutch cover	1	All	... ...
018966	Washer, cork, for clutch cap.................................	1	All	... ...
000450	Screw, $\frac{3}{8}$ in. by 2.BA., round head for clutch cap screw	8	All	... ...
014457	Cap, assembly, chaincase inspection (components not sold as separate spares).....................................	1	All	... ...
000580	Washer, cork, chaincase inspection cap...................	1	All	... ...
000440	Bolt, fixing chaincase to engine, $\frac{1}{2}$ in. by 0.BA........	3	All	... ...
000165	Washer, lock, chaincase engine bolt.......................	3	All	... ...
000316	Stud, fixing centre of chaincase, $7\frac{7}{16}$ ins. by $\frac{7}{16}$ in. by 26 (to be fitted with the longer thread on left side).........	1	All	... ...
010953	Spacer, $1\frac{13}{32}$ in. long, for centre bolt, between chaincase and engine plate..	1	All	... ...
021230	Wide nut, for centre bolt, inside chaincase	1	All	... ...
000166	Washer, plain for chaincase centre bolt behind case ...	1	16MC, 18C	...
000009	Washer, plain, for chaincase centre bolt	2	16MC, 18C	...
000009	Washer, plain for chaincase centre bolt..................	3	16M, 16MS, 18, 18S	...
000002	Nut, for chaincase centre bolt...............................	3	All	... ...
021038	Chaincase sliding seal...	1	16MC, 16MCS, 18C, 18CS	

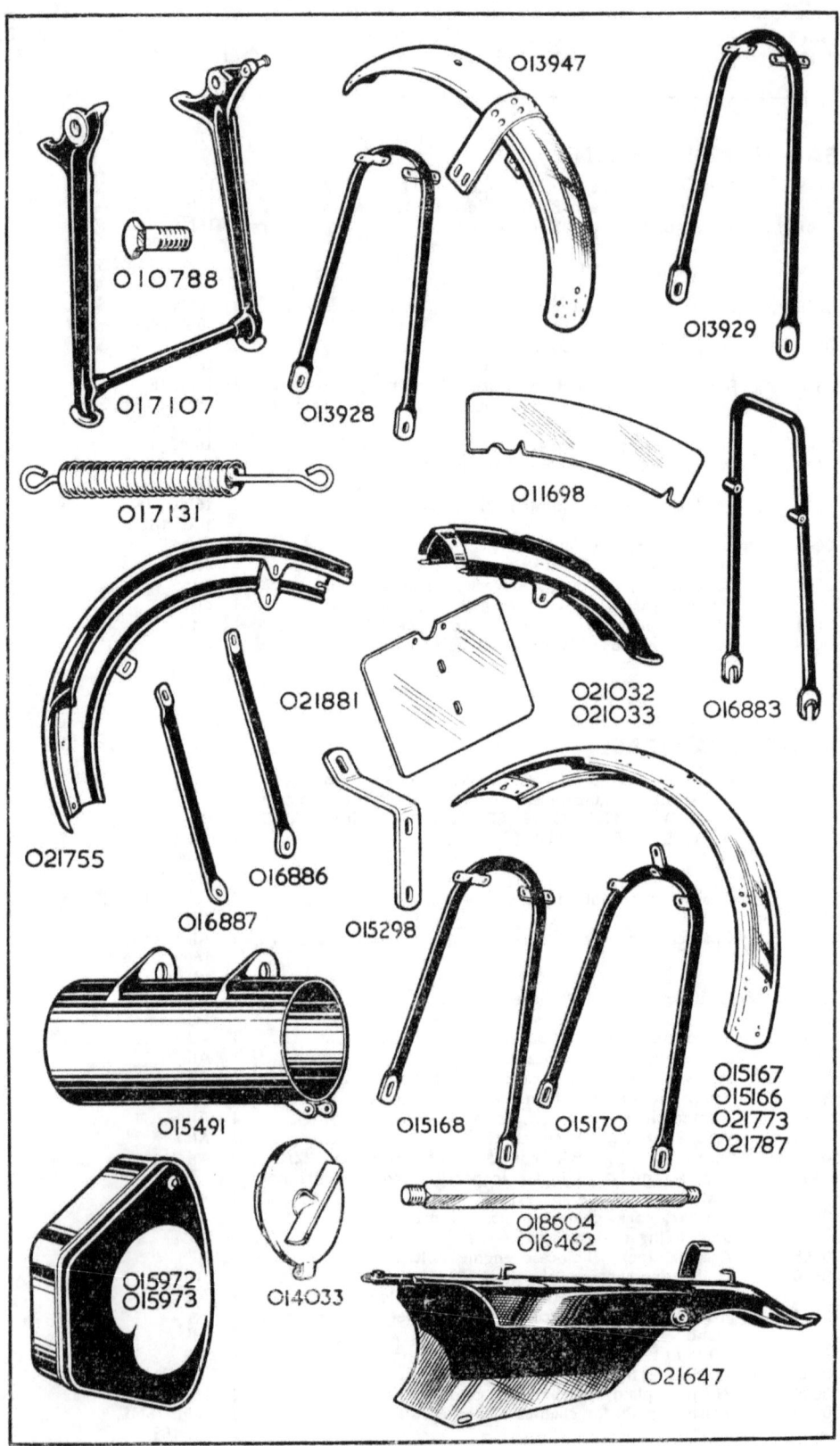

PART NUMBER.	DESCRIPTION.	QTY.	USED ON.	PRICE EACH £ s. d.

REAR CHAINGUARD.

021104	Chainguard, rear, bare...	1	16M, 18	
021576	Chainguard, rear, bare...	1	16MS, 16MCS, 18S, 18CS	
021647	Chainguard, rear, bare...	1	16MC, 18C	
017094	Bolt, fixing top of chainguard in front........................	1	16M, 16MC, 18, 18C	
000350	Bolt, fixing chainguard in front, $2\frac{1}{16}$ ins. by $\frac{1}{4}$ in. by 26	1	16MS, 16MCS, 18S, 18CS	
000070	Bolt, fixing bottom of chainguard, in front, $\frac{9}{16}$ in. by $\frac{1}{4}$ in. by 26	1	16M, 16MC, 18, 18C	
000012	Washer, plain, chainguard, front fixing bolt...............	2	ditto	
000012	Washer, plain, chainguard, front fixing bolt...............	2	16M, 16MCS, 18S, 18CS	
000005	Nut, for chainguard front fixing bolt.........................	1	All	
000362	Bolt, fixing rear of chainguard $\frac{5}{8}$ in. by $\frac{5}{16}$ in. by 26	1	16M, 16MC, 18, 18C	
000349	Bolt, fixing rear of chainguard $1\frac{7}{8}$ ins. by $\frac{1}{4}$ in. by 26 ...	1	16MS, 16MCS, 18S, 18CS	
000011	Washer, plain, for chainguard rear fixing bolt............	1	All	
021579	Washer, spring, for chainguard rear fixing bolt..........	1	16MS, 16MCS, 18S, 18CS	
021578	Spacer, (located inside chainguard), on bolt 000349......	1	ditto	

BATTERY CARRIER.

021983	Carrier, battery, complete	1	16M, 18, 16MS, 16MCS, 18S, 18CS	
021061	Carrier, battery, complete..	1	16MC, 18C	
	The above complete carriers include the binding bolt with its seat and nut.			
021689	Carriers, battery, back portion only..........................	1	16M, 18, 16MS, 16MCS, 18S, 18CS	
021064	Carrier, battery, back portion only...........................	1	16MC, 18C	
021722	Carrier, battery, front portion only...........................	1	All except 16MC, 18C	
012581	Carrier, battery, front portion only	1	16MC, 18C	
010854	Pin, hinge, battery carrier front.................................	1	All	
012798	Bolt, clamping battery carrier, $1\frac{3}{4}$ in. by $\frac{1}{4}$ in. by 26......	1	All	
012291	Seat, battery carrier clamping bolt............................	1	All	
010851	Nut, battery carrier clamping bolt.............................	1	All	
000004	Nut, fixing battery carrier to oil tank stud	2	All	
000174	Washer, plain, for battery carrier and oil tank fixing nut	2	All	
013840	Stay, battery carrier to chaincase...............................	1	16MS, 16MCS, 18S, 18CS	
018062	Stay, battery carrier to chaincase...............................	1	16M, 18,	
015365	Stay, battery carrier to chaincase...............................	1	16MC, 18C	
000040	Screw, fixing stay to battery carrier, $\frac{1}{2}$ in. by 1.BA.	1	All	
000012	Washer, plain, for 000040 bracket screw....................	1	All	
010734	Bolt, fixing battery carrier bracket to chaincase, $\frac{25}{32}$ in. by $\frac{5}{16}$ in. by 26...	1	16MS, 16MCS, 18S, 18CS	
000011	Washer, plain, for 010734 carrier bracket bolt............	2	ditto	
000004	Nut, for 010734 carrier bracket bolt.........................	1	ditto	

PART NUMBER.	DESCRIPTION.	QTY.	USED ON.	PRICE EACH £ s. d.

FOOTRESTS.

018601	... Arm, for footrest..	2	16M, 16MS, 18, 18S	...
018602	... Arm, for footrest..	2	16MC, 18C	...
018288	... Arm, for footrest, right side...................................	1	16MCS, 18CS	...
016461	... Arm, for footrest, left side.....................................	1	ditto	
010847	... Pad, rubber, for footrest arm................................	2	16M, 16MS, 18, 18S	...
018604	... Rod, for footrests, overall length $10\frac{1}{2}$ ins..........	1	16M, 16MS, 16MC, 18, 18S, 18C	...
014380	... Rod, for footrests, overall length 9 ins................	1	16MC, 18C	...
016462	... Rod, for footrests, overall length $10\frac{5}{8}$ ins..........	1	16MCS, 18CS	...
010924	... Spacer, $3\frac{1}{2}$ ins. long, for footrest rod, between engine rear plates...	1	All	...
016169	... Spacer, $3\frac{5}{16}$ ins. long, between engine plates...........	1	16MC, 18C	...
013837	... Spacer, 1 in. long, for footrest rod, outside right plate	1	16M, 16MS, 16MC, 18, 18S, 18C	...
010911	... Spacer, $1\frac{3}{16}$ in. long, for footrest rod, outside left plate	1	16M, 16MS, 16MC, 18, 18S, 18C	...
010911	... Spacer, $1\frac{3}{16}$ in. long, for footrest rod, additional	2	16MC, 18C	...
000009	... Washer, plain, for footrest rod................................	2	16M, 16MS, 16MC, 18, 18S, 18C	...
000009	... Washer, plain, for secondary footrest rod............	2	16MC, 18C	...
010912	... Washer, plain, for footrest rod................................	2	16MCS, 18CS	...
000002	... Nut, for footrest rod..	2	All	...
000002	... Nut, for secondary footrest rod............................	2	16MC, 18C	...

PILLION FOOTRESTS. (This is optional equipment).

021984	... Pair of pillion footrests, complete	1	16MS, 18S	...
011267	... Pair of pillion footrests, complete	1	16M, 18	...
021641	... Spindle, bare, for pillion footrest...........................	2	18MS, 18S	...
011518	... Spindle, bare, for pillion footrest...........................	2	16M, 18	...
011599	... Bolt, hinge, for pillion footrest spindle, $1\frac{3}{16}$ in. by $\frac{3}{8}$ in. by 26...	2	All	...
000073	... Nut, for pillion footrest hinge bolt........................	2	All	...
010847	... Pad, rubber, for pillion footrest spindle................	2	All	...

SADDLE.

013784	... Saddle, complete, with rear springs......................	1	16M, 18	...
021376	... Saddle, complete, with rear springs......................	1	16MC, 18C	...
013873	... Saddle, less springs..	1	16M, 18	...
018998	... Saddle, less springs..	1	16MC, 18C	...
021649	... Saddle, spring...	2	16M, 18	...
014151	... Saddle, spring...	2	16MC, 18C	...
017523	... Cover (or top), for saddle.....................................	1	16M, 18,	...
012880	... Stud, for lower end of spring, $2\frac{1}{4}$ ins. long............	2	16M, 18	...
021349	... Stud, for lower end of spring, 3 ins. long............	2	16MC, 18C	...
000073	... Nut, for spring stud	6	16M, 16MC, 18, 18C	...
000410	... Bolt, for saddle front hinge...................................	1	16M, 18	...
000376	... Bolt, for saddle front hinge...................................	1	16MC, 18C	...
000003	... Nut, for hinge bolt..	1	16M, 18	...
000004	... Nut, for hinge bolt..	1	16MC, 18C	...
000011	... Washer, for hinge bolt	1	ditto	
021214	... Saddle, support channel...	1	ditto	

PART NUMBER.	DESCRIPTION.	QTY.	USED ON.	PRICE EACH £ s. d.

SADDLE—continued.

021217	... Saddle, support spacer	1	ditto	
000372	... Saddle, support/frame bolt	2	ditto	
000004	... Saddle, support/frame bolt nut	2	ditto	
000011	... Saddle, support/frame bolt washer	2	ditto	
021199	... Twin seat	1	18S, 16MS	
021764	... Twin seat	1	16MCS, 18CS	
021219	... Twin seat, grommet for base	2	All	
021208	... Bolt, fixing seat at rear	2	16MS, 18S	
000342	... Bolt, fixing seat at rear	2	16MCS, 18CS	
000012	... Washer, for seat fixing bolt	2	16MS, 18S	
000172	... Washer, for seat fixing bolt	2	16MCS, 18CS	
018160	... Nut, for above	2	16MS, 18S	

PILLION SEAT. (Mudguard Fitting) (This is optional equipment).

011291	... Seat, pillion, with fixing bolts, washers and nuts	1	16M, 18	
000070	... Bolt, fixing pillion seat, $\frac{9}{16}$ in. by $\frac{1}{4}$ in. by 26	4	ditto	
000191	... Washer, spring, for pillion seat bolt	4	ditto	
000012	... Washer, plain, for pillion seat bolt	4	ditto	
000005	... Nut, for pillion seat bolt	4	ditto	

TOOL BOXES.

015973	... Box, tool, bare (with lid but no other fitting)	1	16M, 18	
014425	... Box, tool, bare (with lid but no other fittings), left side	1	16MS, 18S	
014433	... Box, tool, bare (with lid but no other fittings), right side	1	16MS, 16MCS, 18S, 18CS	
015491	... Box, tool, bare (does not include lid)	1	16MC, 18C	
014033	... Lid, for bare, tool box	1	ditto	
013936	... Pin, split, for tool box lid	1	ditto	
014511	... Screw, knurled, for tool box lid	1	16MCS, 18CS	
014511	... Screw, knurled, for tool box lid	2	16MS, 18S	
014511	... Screw, knurled, for tool box lid	1	16M, 18	
000189	... Washer, spring, for tool box lid screw	1	16M, 16MCS, 18, 18CS	
000189	... Washer, spring, for tool box lid screw	2	16MS, 18S	
000005	... Nut, for tool box lid screw	2	16M, 16MCS, 18, 18CS	
000005	... Nut, for tool box lid screw	4	16MS, 18S	
016367	... Plate, tool box fixing	1	16MCS, 18CS	
000070	... Bolt, fixing tool box plate	2	ditto	
000012	... Washer, plain, plate fixing bolt	4	ditto	
000005	... Nut, plate fixing bolt	2	ditto	
000342	... Bolt, long, fixing tool box, $1\frac{1}{16}$ in. by $\frac{1}{4}$ in. by 26	4	16MS, 18S	
000345	... Bolt, long, fixing tool box, $1\frac{3}{16}$ in. by $\frac{1}{4}$ in. by 26	1	16MCS, 18CS	
000070	... Bolt, short, fixing tool box, $\frac{9}{16}$ in. by $\frac{1}{4}$ in. by 26	2	16MCS, 18CS	
014577	... Bolt, short, fixing tool box, $\frac{7}{16}$ in. by $\frac{1}{4}$ in. by 26	2	16MS, 18S	
000639	... Spacer, $\frac{11}{64}$ in. thick, for tool box long fixing bolts	4	16MS, 18S	
016948	... Spacer, $\frac{9}{16}$ in. thick, for tool box fixing bolt	1	16MCS, 18CS	
000012	... Washer, plain, for tool box fixing bolt	12	16MS, 18S	
000012	... Washer, plain, for tool box fixing bolts	6	16MCS, 18CS	
000005	... Nut, for tool box fixing bolts	6	16MS, 18S	
000005	... Nut, for tool box fixing bolts	3	16MCS, 18CS	
000342	... Bolt, fixing tool box at bottom, $1\frac{1}{16}$ in. by $\frac{1}{4}$ in. by 26	2	16M, 18	
000639	... Spacer, $\frac{11}{64}$ in. thick, for tool box bottom fixing bolts	2	ditto	
000012	... Washer, plain, tool box bottom fixing bolts	4	ditto	
000005	... Nut, for tool box bottom fixing bolts	2	ditto	
000361	... Bolt, fixing tool box at top, $\frac{9}{16}$ in. by $\frac{5}{16}$ in. by 26	1	ditto	
000011	... Washer, plain, for tool box, top fixing bolt	1	ditto	
000004	... Nut, for tool box top fixing bolt	1	ditto	

THE PRICES OF SPARES DO NOT INCLUDE THE COST OF CARRIAGE

PART NUMBER.	DESCRIPTION.	QTY.	USED ON.	PRICE EACH £ s. d.

TRANSFERS.

009198	... Transfer, for side of oil tank (top level indicator)......	1	All	... ...
009183	... Transfer, for side of oil tank (low level indicator)......	1	All	... ...
009184	... Transfer, for top of oil tank (service instruction).........	1	All	... ...
009186	... Transfer, for front chaincase (oil level indicator).........	1	All	... ...
009187	... Transfer, for front chaincase (patent).......................	1	All	... ...
009185	... Transfer, for tool box (monogram)...........................	1	16M, 18, 16MCS, 18CS	...
009185	... Transfer for tool box (monogram)...........................	2	16MS, 18S	...
009194	... Transfer, for rear mudguard (" A·J·S ").................	1	All	... ...
009199	... Transfer, for front forks (patent).............................	1	All	... ...
009195	... Transfer, for petrol tank (reserve)............................	1	All	... ...
009200	... Transfer, for forks (" Made in England ")..................	1	All	... ...
009197	... Transfer, for rear fork hinge (patent).......................	1	16MS, 18S, 16MCS, 18CS	...
018495	... Complete set of transfers......................................	1	16M, 18	...
018496	... Complete set of transfers......................................	1	16MS, 18S	...
018497	... Complete set of transfers......................................	1	16MC, 18C	...
018498	... Complete set of transfers......................................	1	16MCS, 18CS	...

CONTROL LEVER AND CABLE SECTION.

PART NUMBER.	DESCRIPTION.	QTY.	USED ON.	PRICE EACH £ s. d.

TWIST GRIP.

16-117	... Twist grip, complete assembly................................	1	All	... ...
16-070	... Grip, rubber, for twist grip....................................	1	All	... ...
16-091	... Rotor, and sleeve, for twist grip (does not include rubber grip)..	1	All	... ...
16-060	... Body, twist grip, top (plain clip).............................	1	All	... ...
16-061	... Body, twist grip, bottom (for friction spring)............	1	All	... ...
11-013	... Screw, long, clamping twist grip body.....................	1	All	... ...
11-014	... Screw, short, clamping twist grip body....................	1	All	... ...
16-008	... Spring, friction, for twist grip................................	1	All	... ...
16-009	... Screw, for twist grip friction spring.........................	1	All	... ...
16-010	... Nut, for twist grip friction spring screw....................	1	All	... ...
16-011	... Stop, for twist grip (throttle) cable.........................	1	All	... ...

DUMMY GRIP.

16-069	... Grip, rubber, dummy..	1	All	... ...

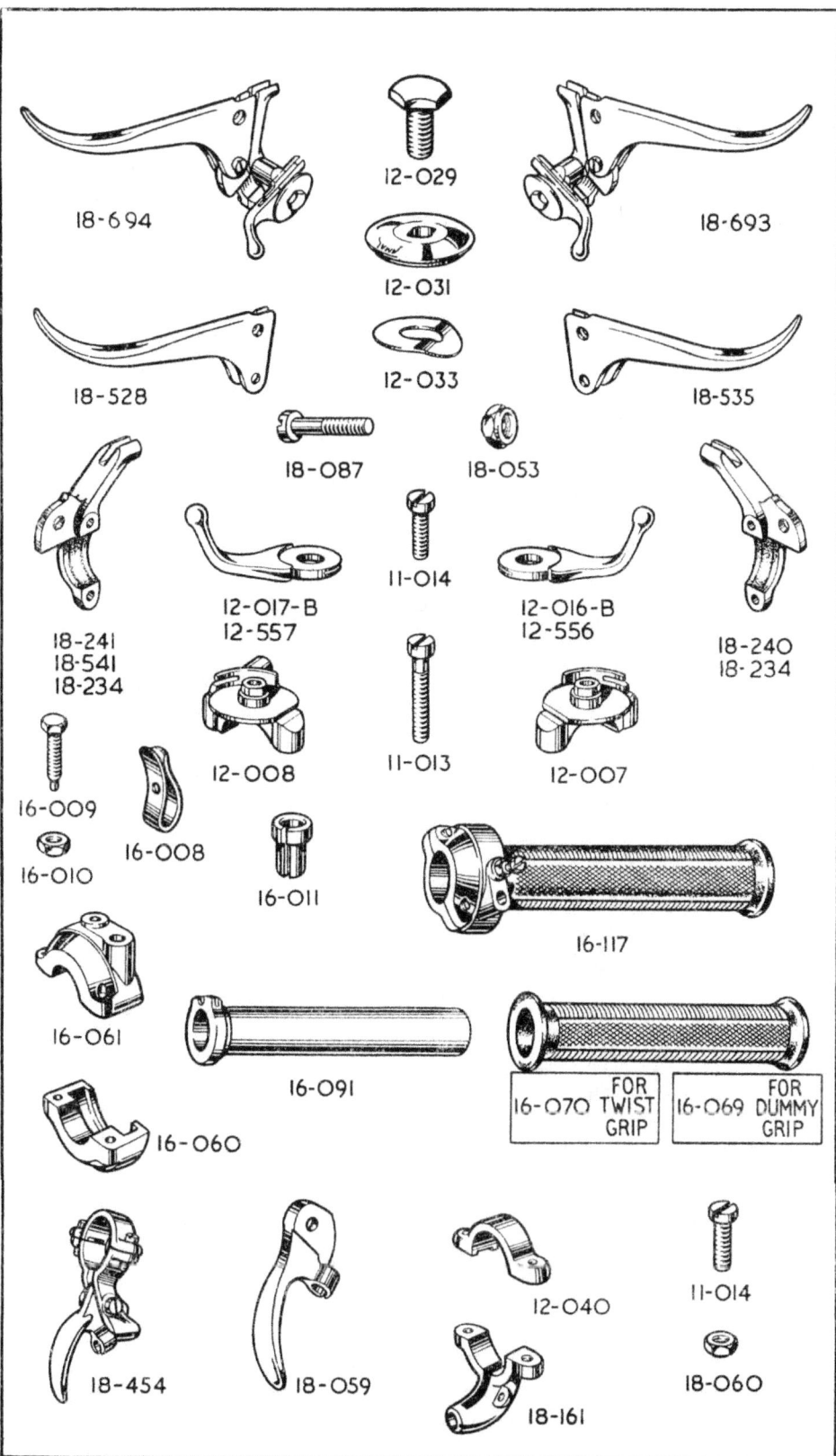

PART NUMBER.	DESCRIPTION.	QTY.	USED ON.	PRICE EACH £ s. d.

BRAKE AND AIR CONTROL LEVERS.

18-693	Lever, assembly, brake and air...............	1	16M, 16MS, 18, 18S	...
18-535	Lever, only, brake...........................	1	ditto	
12-556	Lever, only, air..............................	1	ditto	
18-240	Bracket, for brake lever.....................	1	ditto	
12-007	Bracket, for air lever........................	1	ditto	
11-013	Screw, long, clamping brake and air brackets...........	1	ditto	
11-014	Screw, short, clamping brake and air brackets..........	1	ditto	
18-087	Pin, fulcrum, for brake lever.................	1	ditto	
18-053	Nut, brake lever fulcrum pin.................	1	ditto	
12-029	Bolt, central, for air lever...................	1	ditto	
12-031	Cap, for air lever............................	1	ditto	
12-033	Washer, spring, for air lever.................	1	ditto	

CLUTCH CONTROL LEVER.

18-709	Lever, assembly clutch	1	16M, 16MS, 18, 18S	...
18-696	Lever, assembly clutch	1	16MC, 16MCS 18C, 18CS	...
18-528	Lever, only clutch	1	All	... ...
18-541	Bracket, clutch lever	1	16M, 16MS, 18, 18S	...
18-234	Bracket, clutch lever	1	16MC, 16MCS, 18C, 18CS	...
12-040	Clamp, clutch lever bracket	1	All	... ...
11-014	Screw, clutch lever bracket clamp	2	All	... ...
18-087	Pin, fulcrum, clutch lever	1	All	... ...
18-053	Nut, clutch lever fulcrum pin	1	All	... ...
70-016	Washer, lock clutch lever fulcrum pin nut	1	All	... ...

FRONT BRAKE CONTROL LEVER.

18-695	Lever, assembly, brake........................	1	16MC, 18C, 16MCS, 18CS	...
18-535	Lever, only, brake...........................	1	ditto	
18-234	Bracket, brake lever.........................	1	ditto	
12-040	Clamp, brake lever bracket..................	1	ditto	
11-014	Screw, brake lever bracket clamp............	2	ditto	
18-087	Pin, fulcrum brake lever.....................	1	ditto	
18-053	Nut, brake lever fulcrum pin.................	1	ditto	
70-016	Washer, lock, brake lever fulcrum pin nut.....	1	ditto	

AIR CONTROL LEVER.

12-161	Lever, assembly, air.........................	1	16MC, 18C, 16MCS 18CS	...
12-016-B	Lever, only, air..............................	1	ditto	
12-007	Bracket, air control lever....................	1	ditto	

THE MAINTENANCE MANUAL AND INSTRUCTION BOOK HAS NINETY-TWO PAGES AND THIRTY-EIGHT ILLUSTRATIONS

PART NUMBER.	DESCRIPTION.	QTY.	USED ON.	PRICE EACH £ s. d.

IGNITION CONTROL LEVER.

12-171	... Lever, assembly, ignition..	1	16MC, 18C, 16MCS, 18CS...	
12-017-B	... Lever, only, ignition..	1	ditto	
12-008	... Bracket, ignition control lever.................................	1	ditto	

FITTINGS FOR AIR AND IGNITION CONTROL LEVERS.

12-040	... Clamp, air, or ignition lever bracket......................	2	16MC, 18C, 16MCS, 18CS...	
11-014	... Screw, air or ignition lever bracket clamp............	4	ditto	
12-029	... Bolt, central, air or ignition lever...........................	2	ditto	
12-031	... Cap, air or ignition lever..	2	ditto	
12-033	... Washer, spring, air or ignition lever.......................	2	ditto	

EXHAUST LIFTER CONTROL LEVER.

18-454	... Lever, assembly, exhaust lifter.................................	1	All	... ...
18-059	... Lever, only, exhaust lifter...	1	All	... ...
18-161	... Bracket, exhaust lifter lever....................................	1	All	... ...
12-040	... Clamp, exhaust lifter lever bracket.........................	1	All	... ...
11-014	... Screw, exhaust lifter lever bracket clamp.............	2	All	... ...
11-014	... Pin, fulcrum, exhaust lifter lever.............................	1	All	... ...
18-060	... Nut, exhaust lifter lever fulcrum pin.......................	1	All	... ...

FRONT BRAKE CABLE.

013178	... Cable, complete, assembled, front brake..............	1	All	... ...
000530-40⅞	Wire, inner, front brake, 40⅞ ins. finished length......	1	All	... ...
18-689	... Nipple, brake end, for brake inner wire................	1	All	... ...
18-689	... Nipple, handlebar end, for brake inner wire.........	1	All	... ...
18-690	... Nipple, roller adaptor, handlebar end, for inner wire...	1	All	... ...
000529-26	Casing, outer, front brake, 26 ins. long................	1	All	... ...
000531	... Ferrule, front brake outer casing	2	All	... ...
011348	... Adjuster, front brake cable.....................................	1	All	... ...
017217	... Nut, lock, front brake cable adjuster.....................	1	All	... ...
017049	... End, yoke, front brake cable...................................	1	All	... ...
000736	... Pin, for yoke end, front brake cable.....................	1	All	... ...
000014	... Pin, split, for front brake cable yoke end pin......	1	All	... ...
012478	... Sleeve, rubber, for front brake cable inner wire........	1	All	... ...

CLUTCH CABLE.

021405	... Cable, complete, assembled, clutch, with oil nipple ...	1	All	... ...
000530-43½	Wire, inner, clutch, 43½ ins. finished length............	1	All	... ...
017241	... Nipple, gearbox end, clutch inner wire..................	1	All	... ...
18-689	... Nipple, handlebar end, clutch inner wire..............	1	All	... ...
18-690	... Nipple, roller adaptor, handlebar end, for inner wire ..	1	All	... ...
021406	... Casing, outer, clutch, with adaptor for oil nipple	1	All	... ...
000531	... Ferrule, clutch outer casing.....................................	2	All	... ...
014225	... Adjuster, clutch cable...	1	All	... ...
011373	... Nut, lock, clutch cable adjuster..............................	1	All	... ...
018155	... Cleat, for clutch cable..	1	All	... ...
000051	... Oil nipple...	1	All	... ...

PART NUMBER.	DESCRIPTION.	QTY.	USED ON.	PRICE EACH £ s. d.

VALVE LIFTER CABLE.

014060 ...	Cable, complete, assembled, exhaust lifter...............	1	All	... ...
000530-26	Wire, inner, exhaust lifter, 26 ins. finished length......	1	All	... ...
014061 ...	Nipple, engine end, exhaust lifter inner wire.............	1	All	... ...
017240 ...	Nipple, handlebar end, exhaust lifter inner wire.........	1	All	... ...
000529-21	Casing, outer, exhaust lifter, 21 ins. long................	1	All	... ...
000531 ...	Ferrule, exhaust lifter outer casing, handlebar end......	1	All	... ...
013998 ...	Ferrule, exhaust lifter outer casing, engine end............	1	All	... ...
014225 ...	Adjuster, exhaust lifter cable............................	1	All	... ...
011373 ...	Nut, lock, exhaust lifter cable adjuster...................	1	All	... ...

IGNITION CONTROL CABLE.

022132 ...	Cable, complete assembled ignition	1	16MC, 16MCS 18C, 18CS	...
000527-29¼	Wire, inner, ignition 29¼ ins., finished length	1	ditto	
017266 ...	Nipple, Handlebar end, ignition inner wire	1	ditto	
000526-26	Casing, outer, ignition, 26 ins. finished length	1	ditto	
000528 ...	Ferrule, ignition, outer casing	2	ditto	
022133 ...	Set of control cable parts (Lucas 457117)	1	ditto	

THROTTLE CONTROL CABLE.

022019 ...	Cable, complete, assembled, throttle	1	16M, 16MS, 16MC	...
022134 ...	Cable, complete, assembled, throttle....................	1	18, 18S, 18C	...
018997 ...	Cable, complete, assembled, throttle	1	16MCS, 18CS	
000535-40 1/16	Wire, inner, throttle, 40 1/16 ins. finished length	1	16M, 16MS, 16MC	...
000535-40 3/16	Wire, inner, throttle, 40 3/16 ins. finished length	1	18, 18S, 18C 16MCS, 18CS	
017242 ...	Nipple, carburetter end, throttle inner wire	1	16M, 16MS, 16MC, 18, 18S, 18C	...
018996 ...	Nipple, carburetter end, throttle inner wire	1	16MCS, 18CS	
017266 ...	Nipple, handlebar end, throttle inner wire	1	All	... ...
021408 ...	Casing, outer, throttle, with oil nipple adaptor	1	All	... ...
000528 ...	Ferrule, throttle outer casing	2	All	... ...
000051 ...	Nipple, oil, for casing................................	1	All	... ...

AIR CONTROL CABLE.

022022 ...	Cable, complete, assembled, air	1	16M, 16MS, 16MC	...
022023 ...	Cable, complete, assembled, air	1	18, 18S, 18C	...
021003 ...	Cable, complete, assembled, air	1	16MCS, 18CS	
000527-37⅞	Wire, inner, air, 37⅞ ins. finished length	1	16M, 16MS, 16MC	...
000527-38 3/16	Wire, inner, air, 38 3/16 ins. finished length	1	18, 18S, 18C, 16MCS, 18CS	
017242 ...	Nipple, carburetter end, air, inner wire	1	16M, 16MS, 16MC, 18, 18S, 18C	
018996 ...	Nipple, carburetter end, air, inner wire	1	16MCS, 18CS	
017266 ...	Nipple, handlebar end, air, inner wire	1	All	... ...
000526-32 13/16	Casing, outer air, 32 13/16 ins. finished length	1	All	... ...
000528 ...	Ferrule, air, outer casing	2	All	... ...

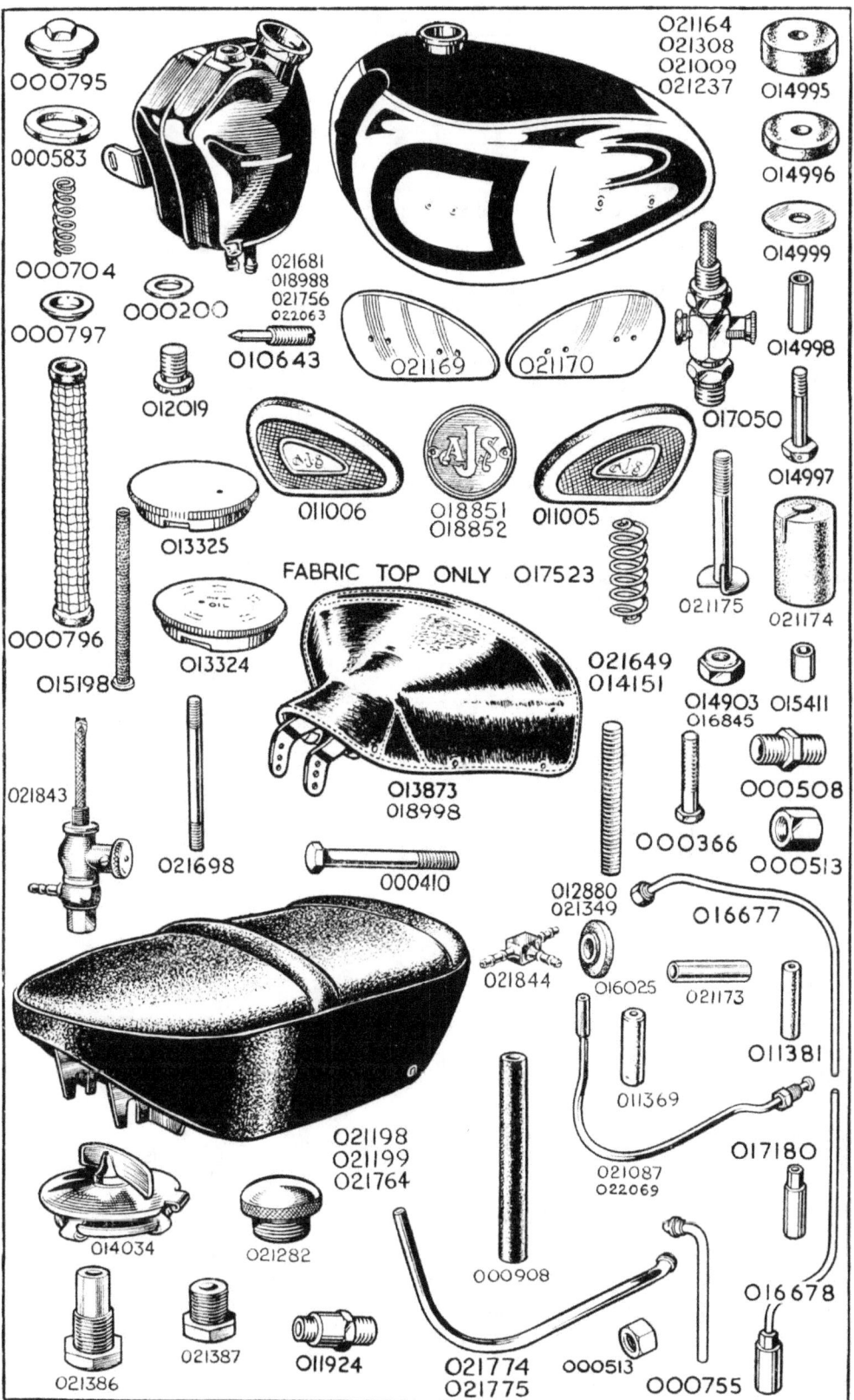

TANK SECTION.

PART NUMBER.	DESCRIPTION.	QTY.	USED ON.	PRICE EACH £ s. d.

PETROL TANK.

021164	Tank, petrol, bare, chrome and panelled	1	16M, 16MS, 18, 18S	
021308	Tank, petrol, bare, enamelled and lined	1	16M, 16MS, 18, 18S	
021009	Tank, petrol, bare, enamelled and lined	1	16MC, 18C	
021237	Tank, petrol, bare, enamelled and lined	1	16MCS, 18CS	
018851	Tank, motif, for enamelled tank (Gilt)	2	16M, 16MS, 18, 18S	
018852	Tank, motif, for plated tank (Silver)	2	ditto	
018853	Tank, motif, seating (rubber)	2	ditto	
000153	Tank, motif, screw for plated tanks (Chrome)	4	All except C and CS	
000152	Tank, motif, screw for enamelled tanks (Bronze)	4	16M, 16MS, 18, 18S	
014997	Bolt, fixing tank, all positions	4	All except C & CS	
014999	Washer, for tank fixing bolt	4	ditto	
014995	Pad, rubber, thick	4	ditto	
014996	Pad, rubber, thin	4	ditto	
014998	Sleeve, metal, for tank fixing bolt	4	ditto	
015411	Sleeve, metal, for tank fixing bolt	2	16MCS, 18CS	
017051	Wire, copper, 5 ft. by 20 S.W.G.	1	All except C and CS	
021175	Bolt, tank, fixing front	2	16MC, 16MCS, 18C, 18CS	
000273	Bolt, tank, fixing rear	1	16MC, 18C	
000365	Bolt, tank, fixing rear	2	16MCS, 18CS	
021174	Rubber, tank, front fixing	2	All C and CS	
014903	Nut, tank, rear fixing	2	16MC, 18C	
016025	Rubber, tank, rear fixing	2	ditto	
021173	Spacer, tank, rear fixing	1	ditto	
000174	Washer, tank, rear fixing	2	All C and CS	
016845	Nut, tank, front fixing bolt	2	ditto	
000010	Washer, tank, front fixing bolt	2	ditto	

PETROL TANK FITTINGS.

014034	Cap, filler	1	16MC, 16MCS, 18C, 18CS	
013325	Cap, filler	1	16M, 16MS, 18, 18S	
013936	Pin, split, for filler cap	1	16MC, 16MCS, 18C, 18CS	
017050	Tap, for petrol feed with filter	2	16MCS, 18CS	
021843	Tap, for petrol feed with filter and banjo	2	16M, 16MS, 16MC, 18, 18S, 18C	
000200	Washer, fibre for petrol taps	2	All	
022110	Banjo, for petrol feed pipe	2	16M, 16MS, 16MC, 18, 18S, 18C	
022111	Nut, dome, retaining banjo	2	ditto	
022056	Washers, fibre for banjo	4	ditto	
022112	Cork, for petrol feed tap	2	ditto	
011006	Grip, knee, left hand side	1	16M, 16MS, 18, 18S	
011005	Grip, knee, right hand side	1	ditto	
021169	Plate, for left hand grip	1	ditto	
021170	Plate for right hand grip	1	ditto	
000348	Bolt, for knee grip plate	4	ditto	
021386	Petrol tap adaptor, long	1	16MC, 16MCS, 18C, 18CS	
021387	Petrol tap adaptor, short	1	ditto	
000183	Washer, petrol tap adaptors	2	ditto	

PART NUMBER.	DESCRIPTION.	QTY.	USED ON.	PRICE EACH £ s. d.

OIL TANK.
022063	Tank, oil, bare	1	16M, 18	
021681	Tank, oil, bare	1	16MS, 18S	
018988	Tank, oil, bare	1	16MC, 18C	
021756	Tank, oil, bare	1	16MCS, 18CS	
013324	Cap, filler, oil tank	1	16M, 16MS, 18, 18S	
021282	Cap, filler, oil tank	1	16MC, 16MCS, 18C, 18CS,	
021698	Stud, oil tank fixing	2	16M, 16MS, 16MCS, 18, 18S, 18CS	
021329	Washer, filler cap	1	16MC, 16MCS, 18C, 18CS	
012019	Plug, drain, for oil tank	1	All	
000200	Washer, fibre, oil tank drain plug	1	All	
000796	Filter, felt, for oil tank	1	All	
000704	Spring, for oil tank felt filter	1	All	
000797	Cap, metal, dished, for oil tank felt filter	1	All	
000795	Cap, screwed, oil tank filter compartment	1	All	
000583	Washer, cork, filter compartment cap	1	All	

PETROL PIPE.
000908-2	Flexible tubing, short, 2 ins.	1	16M, 16MS, 16MC, 18, 18S, 18C	
000908-5⅜	Flexible tubing, long, 5⅜ ins.	2	16M, 16MS, 16MC, 18, 18S, 18C	
013829	Flexible pipe	2	16MCS, 18CS	
021844	Petrol pipe "T" piece	1	16M, 16MS, 16MC, 18, 18S, 18C	

OIL PIPES.
021774	Pipe, oil feed	1	16M, 18	
021775	Pipe, oil feed	1	16MS, 18S, 16MCS, 18CS	
021283	Pipe, oil feed	1	16MC, 18C	
011369	Connection, rubber, for oil feed pipe	1	All	
011924	Union, oil feed pipe (engine end)	1	All	
011925	Nut, union for oil feed pipe	1	All	
015198	Filter, metal gauze, for oil feed pipe	1	All	
015528	Washer, fibre, for engine end oil feed union	1	All	
021087	Pipe, oil, return	1	16M, 16MC, 18, 18C	
022069	Pipe, oil, return	1	16MS, 18S, 16MCS, 18CS	
011369	Connection, rubber, for oil return pipe	1	All	
016677	Pipe, rocker box oil feed, top portion	1	All	
016678	Pipe, rocker box oil feed, bottom portion	1	All	
011381	Connection, rubber, for rocker box oil feed pipe	1	All	
000513	Nut, union, rocker box pipe, top end	1	All	
017180	Nut, union (extended type), rocker box pipe, bottom end	1	All	

OIL VENT PIPES.
000755	Pipe, oil discharge, for release valve	1	All	
000513	Nut, union, oil discharge pipe	1	All	
018742	Extension, for release pipe	1	All Competition	
018743	Rubber, for release pipe extension	1	ditto	
018744	Clip, for release pipe extension	1	ditto	
018188	Pipe, vent (rubber), for oil tank, 12 ins. long	1	16M, 18	
015498	Pipe, vent (rubber), for oil tank, 12 ins. long	1	16MC, 18C	
015119	Pipe, vent (rubber), for oil tank, 8½ ins. long	1	16MCS, 18CS	
015120	Pipe, vent (metal insertion), for oil tank rubber vent pipe	1	ditto	
014936	Pipe, vent (rubber), for oil tank, 5¾ ins. long	1	16MS, 18S	
015138	Pipe, vent (metal), for oil tank	1	ditto	
014584	Clip, for vent pipe	1	16M, 18	
014951	Clip, for vent pipe	1	16MCS, 18CS	

WHEEL AND BRAKE SECTION.

PART NUMBER.	DESCRIPTION.	QTY.	USED ON.	PRICE EACH £ s. d.

FRONT WHEEL.

THE COMPLETE WHEELS LISTED BELOW COMPRISE :—
Rim, spokes, nipples, hub, hub disc, grease nipple, all bearings, and all brake parts including cover plate and expander lever, but does not include the tyre.

021987 ...	Wheel, front, complete with all fittings, chrome rim—black centre..	1	16M, 16MS, 18, 18S ...	
021988 ...	Wheel, front, complete with all fittings, chrome rim ...	1	16MC, 16MCS, 18C, 18CS ...	

THE BARE WHEELS LISTED BELOW COMPRISE :—
Rim, spokes, nipples, and hub.

021990 ...	Wheel, front, bare, less all fittings, chrome rim—black centre	1	16M, 16MS, 18, 18S ...	
021991 ...	Wheel, front, bare, less all fittings, chrome rim ...	1	16MC, 16MCS, 18C, 18CS ...	
012220 ...	Rim, front, 19 ins, by $2\frac{1}{2}$ ins., chrome (AMC 23)—black centre...	1	16M, 16MS, 18, 18S ...	
021151 ...	Rim, front, 21 ins. by $2\frac{1}{4}$ ins., chrome......................	1	16MC, 16MCS, 18C, 18CS ...	
021152 ...	Spoke, front...	40	16M, 16MS, 18, 18S ...	
021153 ...	Spoke, front...	40	16MC, 16MCS, 18C, 18CS ...	
021154 ...	Nipple, front, ·250 in. by 11 G	40	All	
021461 ...	Hub, front wheel, shell only with brake drum	1	All	
000051 ...	Nipple, grease, for front wheel hub........................	1	All	
011090 ...	Tape, for 19 ins. by $2\frac{1}{2}$ ins., rim	1	16M, 16MS, 18, 18S ...	
013693 ...	Tape, for 21 ins. by $2\frac{1}{4}$ ins., rim	1	16MC, 16MCS, 18C, 18CS ...	
011708 ...	Bolt, security, for front wheel	1	ditto	
021464 ...	Disc, for R.H. side of hub..	1	All	
021550 ...	Grommet, rubber for disc.......................................	1	16MC, 16MCS 18C, 18CS ...	

PART NUMBER.	DESCRIPTION.	QTY.	USED ON.	PRICE EACH £ s. d.

FRONT WHEEL BEARINGS.

012825	Spindle, with roller bearings, for front wheel	1	All	
010579	Oil-seal, for front hub bearings	2	All	
017219	Ring, spring, locating front hub bearings	1	All	
018093	Cup, for front hub bearing oil-seal	2	All	
018096	Ring, retaining front hub bearing oil-seals	2	All	
021279	Nut, lock, for front hub bearing adjusting ring	1	All	
021161	Ring, adjusting, for front hub bearing	1	All	
021931	Nut, locating front brake cover plate	1	All	
018071	Nut, outside, securing front brake cover plate	1	All	
000001	Nut, front wheel spindle, left side	1	All	
000008	Washer, plain, front wheel spindle, left side	1	All	

REAR WHEEL.

THE COMPLETE WHEELS LISTED BELOW COMPRISE :—
Rim, spokes, nipples, hub, grease nipple and all bearings assembled, but does **NOT** include the centre solid spindle, washers, spacers, nuts, brake parts, sprocket and brake drum, speedometer drive and tyre.

021995	Wheel, rear, with all fittings, chrome rim—black centre	1	16M, 16MS, 18, 18S	
021997	Wheel, rear, complete, with all fittings, chrome rim	1	16MC, 16MCS, 18C, 18CS	

THE BARE WHEELS LISTED BELOW COMPRISE :—
Rim, spokes, nipples and hub.

021999	Wheel, rear, bare (less fittings) chrome rim—black centre	1	16M, 16MS, 18, 18S	
022001	Wheel, rear, bare, less all fittings, chrome rim	1	16MC, 16MCS, 18C, 18CS	
021814	Rim, rear, chrome rim—black centre (A.M.C. 24)	1	16M, 16MS, 18, 18S	
021817	Rim, rear, 19 ins. by 3 ins., chrome (A.M.C. 25)	1	16MC, 16MCS, 18C, 18CS	
021691	Spoke, rear, left or right, $6\frac{15}{16}$ ins. by 10 G	40	16M, 16MS, 18, 18S	
021692	Spoke, rear, left or right, $6\frac{15}{16}$ ins. by 8 G	40	16MC, 16MCS, 18C, 18CS	
021693	Nipple, rear, left or right, ·250 in. by 10 G	40	16M, 16MS, 18, 18S	
021694	Nipple, rear, left or right, ·300 in. by 8G	40	16MC, 16MCS, 18C, 18CS	
021580	Hub, rear wheel, shell only	1	16M, 16MS, 18, 18S	
021695	Hub, rear wheel, shell only	1	16MC, 16MCS, 18C, 18CS	
021550	Grommet, rubber for disc	1	ditto	
021582	Disc, for right hand side of hub	1	All	
000051	Nipple, grease, for rear wheel hub	1	All	
011090	Tape, for 19 ins. rear rim	1	All	
011707	Bolt, security, for rear wheel	2	16MC, 16MCS, 18C, 18CS	

WHEN IN DOUBT REGARDING THE NAMES AND PART NUMBERS OF THE PARTS YOU REQUIRE, PLEASE SEND THE OLD PARTS TO SERVE AS PATTERNS.

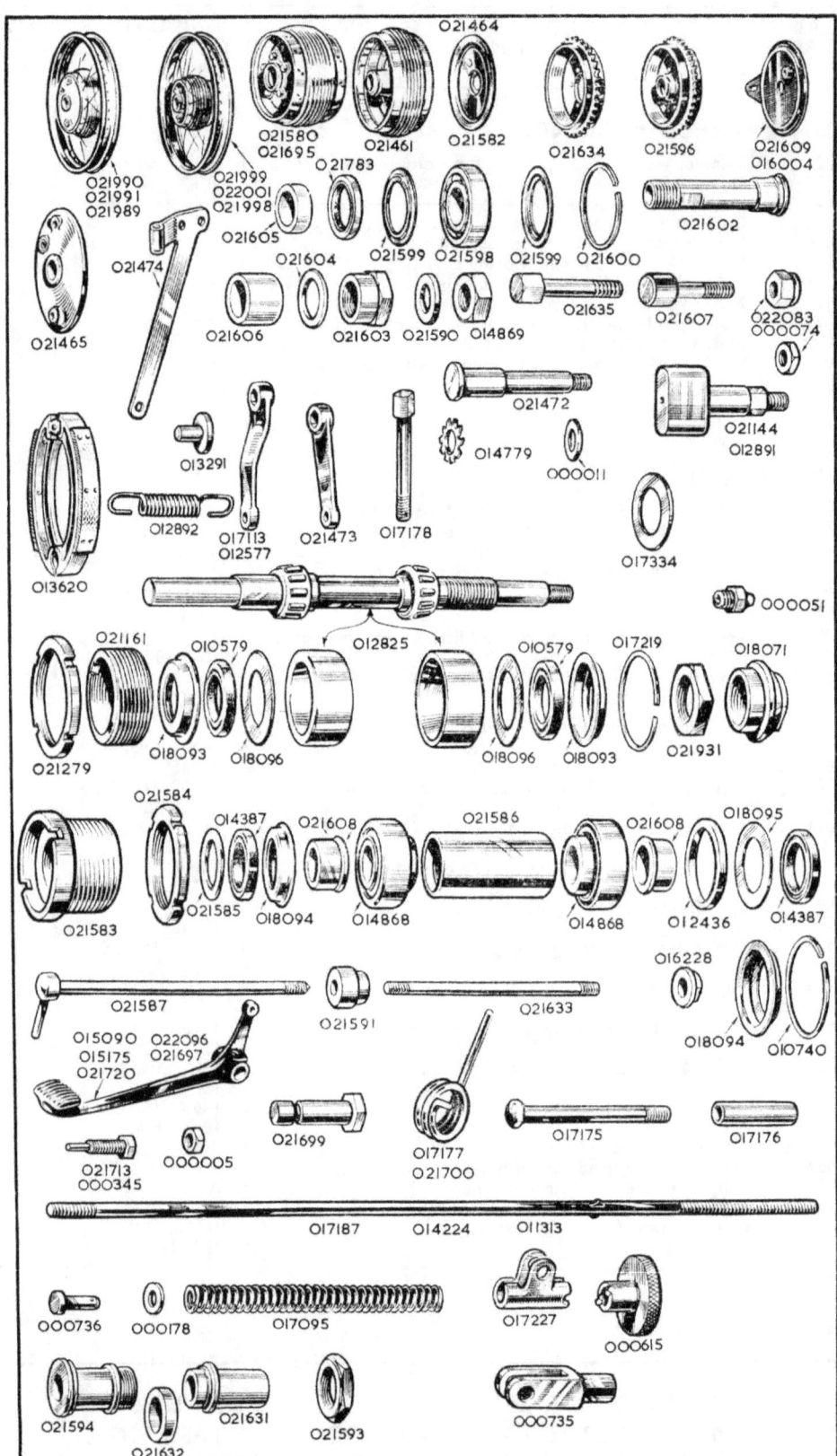

PART NUMBER.	DESCRIPTION.	QTY.	USED ON.	PRICE EACH £ s. d.

REAR WHEEL BEARINGS.

014868	... Bearings, roller, for rear hub (only sold as a complete bearing)	2	All	... ...
014387	... Oil-seal, for rear hub bearings	2	All	... ...
010740	... Ring, spring, locating rear hub bearings	1	All	... ...
018094	... Cup, for rear hub bearing oil-seal	2	All	... ...
021585	... Ring, retaining rear hub bearing oil-seals, small	1	All	... ...
018095	... Ring, retaining rear hub bearing oil-seals, large	2	All	... ...
012436	... Collar, spacing, between bearing and rear hub bearing oil-seal	1	All	... ...
021586	... Spacer, $2\frac{9}{16}$ ins. long between the two bearings of rear hub	1	All	... ...
021583	... Ring, adjusting, for rear hub bearing	1	All	... ...
021584	... Nut, lock, for rear hub bearing adjusting ring	1	All	... ...
021587	... Spindle, centre, solid, for rear wheel	1	16MS, 16MCS, 18S, 18CS	...
021633	... Spindle, centre, solid, for rear wheel	1	16M, 16MC, 18, 18C	...
021608	... Spacer, on spindle, for oil-seals	2	All	... ...
021594	... Spacer, on rear wheel solid spindle, for speedometer gearbox (carries nut)	1	All	... ...
021593	... Nut, locking speedometer gearbox	1	All	... ...
014704	... Sleeve, on rear wheel solid spindle, locating brake cover plate	1	All	... ...
021591	... Spacer, rear wheel solid spindle (abuts against fork end) speedo side	1	16MS, 16MCS, 18S, 18CS	...
016228	... Collar, on rear wheel solid spindle (abuts against fork end)	2	16M, 16MC, 18, 18C	...
014869	... Nut, for rear wheel solid spindle	2	ditto	
014869	... Nut, for rear wheel solid spindle	1	16MS, 16MCS, 18S, 18CS	...
021590	... Washer, for solid spindle	2	16M, 16MC, 18, 18C	...
021590	... Washer, for solid spindle	1	16MS, 16MCS, 18S, 18CS	...

FRONT BRAKE.

021744	... Drum, front brake (must be fitted at works)	1	All	... ...
021766	... Screw, fixing front brake drum to hub shell	5	All	... ...
011846	... Locknut for brake drum screw	5	All	... ...
021465	... Plate, cover, front brake	1	All	... ...
021474	... Stay, front brake cover plate anchor	1	All	... ...
014807	... Bolt, fixing anchor stay to front cover plate, $\frac{5}{8}$ in. by $\frac{3}{8}$ in. by 26	1	All	... ...
014119	... Washer, special, for anchor stay bolt	1	All	... ...
021472	... Pin, fulcrum, for brake shoes	1	All	... ...
000010	... Washer, plain, (inner for pin)	1	All	... ...
000011	... Washer, plain, (outer for pin)	1	All	... ...
000004	... Nut, for brake fulcrum pin	1	All	... ...
013620	... Shoes, pair of, for front brake, with brake linings and thrust pins (only supplied in pairs) per pair	1	All	... ...
013291	... Pin, thrust, brake expander adjusting	2	All	... ...
000174	... Washer, plain, for thrust pin	R	All	... ...
010440	... Linings, brake, per pair of, less rivets	1	All	... ...
000113	... Rivets, for brake linings per set of 12		All	... ...
012892	... Spring, for brake shoes	2	All	... ...
021144	... Expander, for brake shoes	1	All	... ...
017334	... Washer, packing for expander bush	1	All	... ...
021473	... Lever, for front brake shoe expander	1	All	... ...
000051	... Nipple, grease, for brake shoe expander	1	All	... ...
000174	... Washer, plain, for brake shoe expander	1	All	... ...
000004	... Nut, for brake shoe expander	1	All	... ...

PART NUMBER.	DESCRIPTION.	QTY.	USED ON.	PRICE EACH £ s. d.

REAR BRAKE.

021634	... Sprocket, and brake drum, for rear wheel, 42 teeth	1	16M, 16MC, 18, 18C	...
021635	... Bolt, retaining sprocket to rear hub, $\frac{25}{32}$ in. by $\frac{5}{16}$ in. by 26	5	ditto	
000074	... Nut, for rear sprocket retaining bolt..................	5	ditto	
021596	... Sprocket and brake drum, 42 teeth	1	16MS, 16MCS, 18S, 18CS	...
021607	... Pin, driving in hub	5	ditto	
022083	... Nut, for driving pin	5	ditto	
021609	... Plate, cover, rear brake.......................	1	16MS, 16MCS, 18S, 18CS	
016004	... Plate, cover, rear brake.......................	1	16M, 16MC, 18, 18C	
017178	... Bolt, anchor, rear brake cover plate, $1\frac{23}{32}$ ins. by $\frac{3}{8}$ in. by 26, with square head.....................	1	16M, 16MC, 18, 18C	
000003	... Nut, for rear brake cover plate anchor bolt...............	1	ditto	
000006	... Pin, split, for rear brake anchor bolt	1	ditto	
021632	... Spacer, for rear brake cover plate, outer	1	ditto	
021631	... Spacer, for rear brake cover plate, inner	1	ditto	
021606	... Spacer, for brake cover plate, outer	1	16MS, 16MCS, 18S, 18CS	...
021605	... Spacer, for brake cover plate, inner	1	ditto	
021598	... Bearing, ball, for brake drum	1	ditto	
021599	... Washer, for brake drum bearing...................	2	ditto	
021600	... Circlip, for brake drum bearing	1	ditto	
021783	... Oil seal, for brake drum bearing.................	1	ditto	
021602	... Dummy, spindle, for bearing	1	ditto	
021603	... Nut, for dummy spindle	1	ditto	
021604	... Washer, for dummy spindle.....................	1	ditto	
013620	... Shoes, pair of, for rear brake, with brake linings and thrust pins (only supplied in pairs)............per pair	1	All	... ...
013291	... Pin, thrust, brake expander adjusting................	2	All	... ...
000174	... Washer, plain, for thrust pin	R	All	... ...
010440	... Linings, brake, per pair of, less rivets...............	1	All	... ...
000113	... Rivets, for brake linings................per set of	12	All	... ...
012892	... Spring, for brake shoes........................	2	All	... ...
012891	... Expander, for brake shoes.....................	1	All	
017113	... Lever, for rear brake shoe expander...............	1	16MS, 16MCS, 18S, 18CS	...
012577	... Lever, for rear brake shoe expander...............	1	16M, 16MC, 18, 18C	...
000051	... Nipple, grease, for brake shoe expander.............	1	All	... ...
000174	... Washer, plain, for brake shoe expander.............	1	All	... ...
000004	... Nut, for brake shoe expander....................	1	All	... ...

REAR BRAKE OPERATING PARTS.

021720	... Pedal, foot, for rear brake......................	1	16MS, 18S	...
015090	... Pedal, foot, for rear brake......................	1	16M, 18	...
015175	... Pedal, foot, for rear brake......................	1	16MC, 18C	...
022096	... Pedal, foot, for rear brake......................	1	16MCS, 18CS	...
021699	... Fulcrum, for rear brake foot pedal	1	16MS, 16MCS, 18S, 18CS	...
017176	... Bush, for rear brake foot pedal..................	1	16M, 16MC, 18, 18C	...
000051	... Nipple, grease, for rear brake foot pedal............	1	All	... ...
017175	... Spindle, rear brake foot pedal...................	1	16M, 16MC, 18, 18C	...
000009	... Washer, plain, rear brake pedal spindle.............	2	ditto	
000194	... Washer, spring, rear brake pedal spindle............	1	ditto	
000002	... Nut, rear brake pedal spindle....................	1	ditto	
021700	... Spring, return, rear brake foot pedal	1	16MS, 16MCS, 18S, 18CS	...
017177	... Spring, return, rear brake foot pedal	1	16M, 16MC, 18, 18C	...

PART NUMBER.	DESCRIPTION.	QTY.	USED ON.	PRICE EACH £ s. d.

REAR BRAKE OPERATING PARTS—continued.

021713	Bolt, adjusting rear brake foot pedal	1	16MS, 16MCS, 18S, 18CS	
000345	Bolt, adjusting rear brake foot pedal, 1 3/16 in. by 1/4 in. by 26	1	16M, 16MC, 18, 18C	
000005	Nut, for rear brake, foot pedal adjusting bolt	1	All	
011313	Rod, bare, rear brake	1	16M, 16MS, 18, 18S	
017187	Rod, bare, rear brake	1	16MC, 18C	
014224	Rod, bare, rear brake	1	16MCS, 18CS	
000735	End, yoke, for front end of brake rod	1	All	
000736	Pin, for brake rod yoke end	1	All	
000014	Pin, split, for brake rod yoke end pin	1	All	
017095	Spring, for brake rod	1	All	
000178	Collar, for brake rod, spring	1	All	
017227	Clip, adjusting, for rear end of brake rod	1	All	
000736	Pin, for brake rod adjusting clip	1	All	
000014	Pin, split, for brake rod adjusting clip pin	1	All	
000615	Nut, adjusting, for rear brake rod	1	All	

ELECTRICAL SECTION.

PART NUMBER.	DESCRIPTION.	QTY.	USED ON.	PRICE EACH £ s. d.

MAGNETO.

015487	Magneto, type NR-1 (Lucas No. 42179E)	1	16MC, 16MCS, 18C, 18CS	★
021352	Magneto, type SR-1	1	18, 18S, 16M, 16MS	★

For components and service for 015487 magneto apply to nearest LUCAS SERVICE STATION.

458019	Cover, bakelite, for SR-1 magneto	1	16M, 16MS, 18, 18S	
458194	Gasket, for cover	1	ditto	
145220	Screws, fixing cover	3	ditto	
498157	Spring, set, for auto-advance unit	1	16M, 16MS	
498375	Spring, set, for auto-advance unit	1	18, 18S	
015488	Pipe, vent, rubber, for magneto	1	16MC, 16MCS, 18C, 18CS	
021194	Pipe, vent, metal, for magneto	1	ditto	
458053	Contact set for magneto SR-1	1	18, 18S, 16M, 16MS	
021354	Auto-control unit with sprocket	1	18, 18S	★
021680	Auto-control unit with sprocket	1	16M, 16MS	★

MAGNETO FIXING PARTS.

010820	Platform, for magneto	1	All	
000340	Bolt, fixing magneto, left, short, 1/2 in. by 1/4 in. by 20	4	All	
000012	Washer, plain, magneto front fixing bolt	2	All	
010824	Stud, fixing platform at rear, 6 9/32 ins. by 5/16 in. by 26	1	All	
010823	Stud, fixing platform at front, 6 3/8 ins. by 3/8 in. by 26	1	All	
010822	Spacer, 1 9/16 ins. long (5/16 in. internal), platform rear fixing stud	1	All	
010821	Spacer, 1 9/16 ins. long (3/8 in. internal), platform front fixing stud	1	All	
018605	Shield, for magneto	1	16M, 16MS	

★ *Price on application.*

PART NUMBER.	DESCRIPTION.	QTY.	USED ON.	PRICE EACH £ s. d.

DYNAMO.
016599	Dynamo, type E3N-L-O (Lucas No. 20028-A).............	1	All	... ...
200737	Set of brushes, for E3N Dynamo	1	All	... ...
200826	Cover assembly	1	All	... ...

DYNAMO FIXING PARTS.
010962	Strip, dynamo, locating..	1	All	... ...
000044	Screw, fixing locating strip to dynamo, $\frac{3}{8}$ in. by 1 BA....	2	All	... ...
000025	Washer, plain, for locating strip screw......................	2	All	... ...
017197	Strap, clamping dynamo..	1	All	... ...
010963	Pin, hinge, for dynamo clamping strap.....................	1	All	... ...
017145	Sleeve, threaded, for eye of dynamo strap...............	1	All	... ...
018002	Bolt, tightening dynamo strap, $2\frac{1}{2}$ ins. by $\frac{5}{16}$ in. by 26	1	All	... ...
010926	Crossbar, square, for dynamo clamping strap............	1	All	... ...

VOLTAGE REGULATOR.
015070	Regulator, complete unit, type MCR 2 (Lucas No. 37144-A)	1	All	... ...
000342	Bolt, fixing regulator unit, $1\frac{1}{16}$ in. by $\frac{1}{4}$ in. by 26............	2	All except 16M, 18	...
000346	Bolt, fixing regulator unit	2	16M, 18	
000012	Washer, plain, for regulator fixing bolt.....................	4	All	... ...
018160	Nut, for regulator fixing bolt...................................	2	All	... ...
000639	Spacer, for regulator fixing bolt	2	16M, 18	...

BATTERY.
4080157	Battery, with lid, dry and uncharged. This is a battery that has NOT been filled with electrolyte (acid) and is, of course, not charged. It requires no special packing, and can safely be packed with other goods. (Lucas No. PU-7E-9.) (We do not supply charged batteries—for such apply to nearest Lucas Service Station)...	1	All	... ...
4159062	Lid, only, with rubber pads, for battery....................	1	All	... ...

HEAD LAMP.
021802	Lamp, head, with bulb, ammeter, switch, no cable harness (not Europe)...	1	Touring	...
021803	Lamp, head, with bulb, ammeter, switch, no cable harness (Europe, except France)..........................	1	ditto	
021804	Lamp, head, with ammeter, switch, less cable harness and bulb (France only)	1	ditto	
014963	Lamp, head, type MU42, with bulbs, ammeter, switch and socket, no cable harness................................	1	Competition	...
516951	Shell only, top half for head lamp, type....................	1	Touring	...
516952	Shell only, bottom half for head lamp, type.............	1	Touring	...
553248	Rim, bare, for head lamp	1	Touring	
550899	Rim, bare, for head lamp	1	Competition	...
553925	Light unit, reflector and glass (all except Europe)	1	Touring	...
553948	Light unit, reflector and glass (Europe, except France)	1	Touring	...
553940	Light unit, reflector and glass (France only)	1	Touring	...
550875	Glass, only, for headlamp	1	Competition	...
553147	Reflector, only, with bulb holders	1	ditto	
555005	Adaptor (bulb holder) (except France)	1	Touring	...
186131	Screw, fixing panel to head lamp.............................	3	Competition	...
112201	Bolt, fixing lamp to bracket	2	ditto	
137141	Washer, plain, head lamp fixing bolts.......................	2	ditto	
014340	Spacer, for head lamp bracket	2	ditto	

See ELECTRICAL SUNDRIES for Ammeter, Switch, Cable Harness and Bulbs.

PART NUMBER.	DESCRIPTION.	QTY.	USED ON.	PRICE EACH £ s. d.

REAR LAMP COMPETITION.

021879	Lamp, rear, with bulb (Lucas 529)	1	All	
526404	Window cover, red	1	All	
526406	Window cover, White	1	All	
133551	Screws, for red window cover	2	All	
526408	Seat, rubber, for lamp	1	All	
554719	Bulb holder and cable	1	All	
526410	Screw, securing lamp to plate	3	All	
166103	Nut, for securing screw	3	All	
188412	Washer, for nut	3	All	

REAR LAMP TOURING (early models)

018760	Lamp, rear (Lucas 525, No. 53269A)	1	All	
573819	Window cover, red, for rear lamp	1	All	
573814	Rubber gasket, for window cover	1	All	
572072	Screw, retaining lamp window cover	2	All	
166014	Nut, retaining body to rear number plate	2	All	
188330	Spring washer, for body to rear number plate	2	All	
860428	Rear lamp cables with contact disc	1	All	
573825	Rubber cap, covering cable entry	1	All	

REAR LAMP WITH INTEGRAL REFLECTOR, TOURING (later models)

022126	Rear lamp, complete (Lucas L-564)	1	All	
573839	Window cover, red, for rear lamp	1	All	
575200	Window cover, white, for rear lamp	1	All	
575208	Rubber gasket for window cover	1	All	
552928	Screw, retaining window cover	2	All	
575207	Grummet, rubber, for bulb holder	1	All	
575209	Bulb holder	1	All	
860428	Rear lamp wires, with Paxoline washer	1	All	
573825	Rubber cap, covering cable entry	1	All	
166014	Nut, retaining body to rear number plate	2	All	
188330	Spring washer, for fixing nut	2	All	

STOP LIGHT PARTS (Optional Extra)

018854	Complete kit of stop light parts	1	Rigid	
022002	Complete kit of stop light parts	1	Springer	
900269	Snap connector	1	All except competition	
022085	Cable lamp to switch and battery, pair complete	1	All springers	
018866	Cable (6ft.) lamp to switch and battery	1	All rigid	
018720	Stop light switch	1	Rigid frame	
022031	Stop light switch	1	Springer	
018727	Pull off spring for switch	1	All	
018762	Bracket, for switch	1	Rigid frame	
022032	Bracket, for switch	1	Spring frame	
018764	Clip, for pull off spring	1	All except competition	
000738	Screw, securing switch and spring clip	3	ditto	
000739	Nut, for securing switch and spring clip	3	ditto	
000039	Washer, for spring clip screw	2	ditto	
000073	Nut, for securing switch bracket	1	Rigid frame	
000414	Bolt, securing switch bracket	1	Rigid frame	
011907	Rubber cable clip	4	ditto	
018220	Rubber cable clip	1	Springer	
011908	Rubber cable clip	2	ditto	
014453	Metal cable clip	1	All except competition	

SIDE LAMP.

52224	Side lamp complete, type 516	2	All Touring	
516719	Rubber Grummet, for side lamp	2	ditto	
573615	Lens, for side lamp	2	ditto	
573646	Rim and bead, for side lamp	2	ditto	

PART NUMBER.	DESCRIPTION.	QTY.	USED ON.	PRICE EACH £ s. d.

HORN.

015257	Horn, electric, with bracket, type HF.1234 (Lucas No. 70039-A)	1	All	
011569	Horn, bulb	1	Competition	
015245	Bracket, only, for electric horn (Lucas No. 701686)	1	All	
000402	Bolt, securing electric horn, ¾ in. by ⅜ in. by 26	1	All	
015706	Washer, rubber, for horn fixing bolt	2	All	
015707	Washer, plain, for horn fixing bolt, rubber washer	1	All	
000193	Washer, spring, for horn fixing bolt	1	All	
000010	Washer, plain, for horn fixing bolt	1	All	
015705	Nut, sleeve, for horn fixing bolt	1	All	

ELECTRICAL SUNDRIES.

36084	Ammeter, for head lamp panel	1	All	
351551	Switch, main lighting, for head lamp panel	1	All	
351567	Handle, with screw, for main lighting switch	1	All	
380521	Switch, dipping, for handlebar	1	Comp. only	
021301	Switch, dipping, for handlebar	1	All Touring	
380459	Rubber packing, for dip switch	1	ditto	
021299	Screw, securing dip switch	2	ditto	
016427	Switch, horn, for handlebar (Lucas No. 76209)	1	All	
997831	Cable harness, main lighting (no dip switch wire, no horn wire, no regulator wires)	1	Touring	
014964	Cable harness, main, lighting and horn, with socket (Lucas No. 994521)	1	Competition	
858795	Cable harness, triple, for dipping switch	1	All	
860595	Cable harness, for regulator	1	All	
359218	Cable, for horn	1	Touring	
016681	Sheath, for horn cable	1	All	
000543	Cable, high tension, for sparking plug, price per foot	R	All	
809793	Plug, for head lamp	1	Competition	
809795	Socket, for main harness	1	ditto	
000541	Terminal, for high tension cable	1	All	
900269	Connector, snap, for rear lamp cable	1	All	
900269	Connector, snap, for regulator to ammeter cable	1	All	
011094	Bush, rubber, fits in rear mudguard, for rear lamp cable	1	Touring	
312	Bulb, head lamp, main, 6 volt, 30 by 24 watts (not Europe)	1	ditto	
	Plus Purchase Tax	—	—	
988	Bulb, head lamp, pilot, 6 volt, 3 watts	2	ditto	
	Plus Purchase Tax	—	—	
384	Bulb, rear lamp, 6 volt, 18 and 6 watt Double Contact	1	ditto	
	Plus Purchase Tax	—	—	
951	Bulb, rear lamp, 6 volt, 6 watts, S.B.C. Single Contact	1	Competition	
	Plus Purchase Tax	—	—	
200	Bulb, head lamp, pilot, 6 volt, 3 watts, S.B.C. Single Contact	1	ditto	
	Plus Purchase Tax	—	—	
168	Bulb, head lamp main, 6 volt, 24 by 24 watts	1	Competition	
	Plus Purchase Tax	—	—	
015538	Plug, sparking, KLG, type FE-80	1	All	
015399	Cover, waterproof, for sparking plug	1	Competition	
021310	Cover for dyanamo terminals	1	All	

BEFORE ORDERING
PLEASE NOTE THE INFORMATION GIVEN ON PAGES
TWO AND THREE

ACCESSORY SECTION.

PART NUMBER.	DESCRIPTION.	QTY.	USED ON.	PRICE EACH £ s. d.

COMPLETE TOOL KITS.

022026	... Tool kit, complete, with tyre inflator	1	16M, 16MS, 18, 18S	...
022027	... Tool kit, complete, less tyre inflator	1	ditto	
022028	... Tool kit, complete, with tyre inflator	1	16MC, 16MCS, 18C, 18CS	...
022029	... Tool kit, complete, less tyre inflator	1	ditto	

TOOLS.

017253	... Bag, for tools	1	All	... ...
021265	... Screwdriver	1	All	... ...
017248	... Pliers, side cutting	1	All	... ...
011188	... Pliers, for gudgeon pin circlips	1	All	... ...
017246	... Gun, grease	1	All	... ...
017114	... Inflator, tyre	1	All	... ...
017007	... Lever, tyre	2	All	... ...
017052	... Spanner, double end, $\frac{3}{16}$ in. by $\frac{1}{4}$ in.	2	All	... ...
017053	... Spanner, double end, $\frac{5}{16}$ in. by $\frac{3}{8}$ in.	1	All	... ...
018178	... Spanner, double end, 1·010 in. by 1·2 in.	1	All	... ...
017257	... Spanner, double end, $\frac{3}{16}$ in. by ·375 in.	1	All	... ...
017252	... Spanner, box, with tommy, for sparking plug	1	All	... ...
017254	... Spanner, single end, dynamo chain and clutch adjustment	1	All	... ...
017249	... Wrench, adjustable	1	All	... ...
015023	... Spanner, double end, with gauge, for contacts (Lucas No. 415116)	1	16MC, 16MCS, 18C, 18CS	...
021889	... Screwdriver, magneto	1	16M, 16MS, 18, 18S	...
015213	... Spanner, box, $\frac{5}{16}$ in.	1	All	... ...
018153	... Spanner, for petrol taps	1	16MCS, 18CS	...
018055	... Key, for handlebar clip screw	1	16M, 16MS, 18, 18MS	...
018667	... Key, for fork crown pinch screw	1	16M, 16MS, 18, 18S	...
000174	... Brake thrust pin packing washer	8	All	... ...

SPECIAL TOOLS.

017482	... Holder, valve, for valve grinding	1	All	... ...
018276	... Compressor, for valve spring removal	1	All	... ...
022011	... Disc, timing (see Instruction Book)	1	All	... ...

The above tools are NOT INCLUDED in the equipment of a new motor cycle or a " complete " tool kit.

VARIOUS EQUIPMENT.

018691	... Bar, locking, for fork crown	1	All	... ...
016344	... Set of Pannier bags, with frames and fixing bolts, washers and nuts	1	16MS, 18S	...
	Plus Purchase Tax	—	—	
016866	... Set of Pannier bags, with frames and fixing bolts, washers and nuts	1	16M, 18	...
	Plus Purchase Tax	—	—	
011957	... " TEKALL " Rust preventative ½ pint	R	All	... ...
011958	... " TEKALL " Rust preventative 1 pint	R	All	... ...
...	Instruction Manual	R	All	... ...
B-A-H	... Badge, monogram, A·J·S, for button hole	R	All	... ...
B-A-T	... Badge, monogram, A·J·S, for tie	R	All	... ...
B-A-B	... Badge, monogram, A·J·S, for brooch fixing	R	All	... ...

PART NUMBER.	DESCRIPTION.	QTY.	USED ON.	PRICE EACH £ s. d.

SPEEDOMETERS.

022003	Speedometer, trip, 80 M.P.H. complete	1	16M	
022004	Speedometer, trip, 80 M.P.H. complete	1	16MS	
002205	Speedometer, trip, 120 M.P.H. complete	1	18	
022006	Speedometer, trip, 120 M.P.H. complete	1	18S	
022007	Speedometer, trip, 140 K.P.H. complete	1	16M	
022008	Speedometer, trip, 140 K.P.H. complete	1	16MS	
022009	Speedometer, trip, 180 K.P.H. complete	1	18	
022010	Speedometer, trip, 180 K.P.H. complete	1	18S	
021447	Speedometer, trip, 120 M.P.H. complete	1	16MC, 18C	
021448	Speedometer, trip, 120 M.P.H. complete	1	16MCS, 18CS	
021449	Speedometer, trip, 180 K.P.H. complete	1	16MC, 18C	
021450	Speedometer, trip, 180 K.P.H. complete	1	16MCS, 18CS	
021792	Head, only, speedometer, trip, 80 M.P.H.	1	16M, 16MS	
021793	Head, only, speedometer, trip, 120 M.P.H.	1	18, 18S	
021794	Head, only, speedometer, trip, 140 K.P.H.	1	16M, 16MS	
021795	Head, only, speedometer, trip, 180 K.P.H.	1	18, 18S	
491/3	Head, only, speedometer, trip, 120 M.P.H.	1	16MC, 16MCS, 18C, 18CS	
491/7	Head, only, speedometer, trip, 180 K.P.H.	1	ditto	
53279-1	Set of bulb holding parts for head	1	All	
53205	Bulb, 6 volts, 1·8 watts, M.B.C. for head Plus Purchase Tax	1	All	
N-1253	Nut, fixing speedometer head to bracket or lamp	2	All	
000012	Washer, plain, spacing, for head	2	All competition	
W-7216	Washer, spring, speedometer bracket nut	2	All	
53395-1-65	Cable, speedometer drive, complete	1	16M, 16MS, 16MCS, 18, 18S, 18CS	
53395-1-54	Cable, speedometer drive, complete	1	16MC, 18C	
52108-1-65	Cable, speedometer drive, inner only	1	16M, 16MS, 16MCS, 18, 18S, 18C	
52108-1-54	Cable, speedometer drive, inner only	1	16MC, 18C	
53398-1-65	Cable, speedometer drive, outer only	1	16M, 16MS, 16MCS, 18, 18S, 18CS	
53398-1-54	Cable, speedometer drive, outer only	1	16MC, 18C	
52283-5	Gearbox, speedometer, complete	1	All	
016945	Bracket, for speedometer head	1	Competition	
000362	Bolt fixing speedometer bracket to forks, $\frac{5}{8}$ in. by $\frac{5}{16}$ in. by 26	2	Competition	
000011	Washer, plain, speedometer bracket bolt	2	Competition	
000192	Washer, spring, speedometer bracket bolt	1	ditto	
022057	Bracket, retaining speedometer head in headlamp	1	16M, 16MS, 18, 18S	
021798	Gromet, rubber for speedometer head in headlamp	1	ditto	
021454	Washer, outside speedometer gear box	1	All	
021799	Grommet, rubber, for speedometer cable in fork crown	1	All	

CABLE CLIPS.

011907	Clip, rubber, $1\frac{11}{16}$ inch	4	All	
011908	Clip, rubber, $3\frac{1}{4}$ inch	3	All	
018220	Clip, rubber, $4\frac{3}{4}$ inch	5	All	
014453	Clip, metal, holding rear lamp wire inside mudguard	1	All	

PART NUMBER.	DESCRIPTION.	QTY.	USED ON.	PRICE EACH £ s. d.

GASKETS.

Gaskets are supplied as separate spares and in complete sets. Single gaskets are listed in the groups to which they belong. Complete sets are listed below.

018355	... Decarbonising gasket set	1	16M, 16MS, 18, 18S	...
018357	... Decarbonising gasket set........................	1	16MC, 16MCS, 18C, 18CS	...
021384	... Complete gasket set	1	16M, 16MS, 18, 18S	...
021385	... Complete gasket set.............................	1	16MC, 16MCS, 18C, 18CS	...

Each " Decarbonising gasket set " contains :—

1 Cylinder base washer.
1 Compression plate washer (competition sets only).
1 Cylinder head gasket (not in competition sets).
2 Cover tube bottom glands.
2 Cover tube top gaskets.
1 Rocker box side cover rubber fillet.
1 Rocker box gasket.
3 Rocker box cover fibre washers.
1 Carburetter gasket.
1 Carburetter packing piece gasket.

Each " Complete gasket set " contains the above items and :—

1 Timing gear cover washer.
2 Petrol tap fibre washers.
1 Oil tank drain plug fibre washer.
1 Oil tank filter compartment cap washer.
1 Chaincase inspection cap washer.
1 Clutch dome cork gasket.
2 Fork oil drain screw fibre washers.
2 Pump cap paper washers.
1 Oil tank filler cap washer (Comp. and C/S).

SERVICE

The **Service and Repair Department** is situated in **Burrage Grove, Plumstead, London, S.E.18.** **Burrage Grove** is the first turning on the left from Burrage Road when entering Burrage Road from the Plumstead Road. (See final paragraph below.)

The nearest Railway Station is WOOLWICH ARSENAL, SOUTHERN REGION RAILWAY. This Station is five minutes' walk from our Service Depot in Burrage Grove. There is an excellent service of electric trains from Charing Cross, Waterloo, Cannon Street and London Bridge Stations, Southern Region Railway.

Bus routes 53, 54, 163, 99, 122, 122a, 177 and Trolleybus routes, 696 and 698, pass the end of Burrage Road (one minute from the Service Depot).

Bus routes 186, 75 and 161 serve **Beresford Square** which is three minutes' walk from the **Service and Repair Department.**

Visitors from the North can pass into Woolwich via the Free Ferry between North Woolwich and Woolwich. North Woolwich is a British Railways terminus and is also served by Bus and Trolleybus routes 101, 569, 669 and 685. There is also a tunnel under the River Thames at this point for foot passengers. The Free Ferry accommodates all types of motor vehicles and there is a very frequent service. The Southern landing stage is less than a mile from the Service Depot.

Visitors arriving by road, if they are strangers to the locality, should enquire for **Beresford Square, Woolwich.** Upon arrival there, the road skirting the Royal Arsenal should be followed in an Easterly direction for about four hundred yards, and Burrage Road is the second turning on the right after leaving the square. Burrage Grove is then the first turning on the left.

ILLUSTRATIONS

	Page
CARBURETTER	14
CLUTCH AND KICK-STARTER	22
CONTROL LEVERS	43
CRANKCASE AND TIMING GEAR	9
CYLINDERS, HEADS, PISTONS AND VALVES	4
FRAME AND TELEDRAULIC REAR LEG	26
FRONT TELEDRAULIC FORKS AND STEERING DAMPER	30
GEAR BOX SHELLS	18
GEAR BOX, GEARS AND SHAFTS	20
ROCKER BOX AND ROCKERS AND EXHAUST PIPE	12
STANDS, GUARDS, CHAINCASES AND TOOL BOXES	36 and 38
TANKS AND PIPES	47
WHEELS AND BRAKES	52

ALWAYS QUOTE
THE COMPLETE ENGINE NUMBER
(Including all the Letters in it)

THIS ENABLES THE MACHINE TO BE IDENTIFIED

EACH SERIES OF FRAMES IS NUMBERED FROM ZERO UPWARDS. THEREFORE THE QUOTATION OF A FRAME NUMBER ONLY DOES NOT FACILITATE IDENTIFICATION.

VELOCEPRESS MANUALS – MOTORCYCLE BY MAKE

- AJS 1932-1948 SINGLES & TWINS 250cc THRU 1000cc (BOOK OF)
- AJS 1945-1960 SINGLES MODELS 16 & 18 350cc & 500cc (BOOK OF)
- AJS 1948-1956 TWINS MODELS 20 & 30 FACTORY WSM & PARTS
- AJS 1955-1965 SINGLES MODELS 16 & 18 350cc & 500cc (BOOK OF)
- AJS 1957-1966 SINGLES & TWINS (ALL) FACTORY WSM
- AJS 1959-1969 G80CS G85CS & P11 OFF ROAD FACTORY WSM
- AJS 1968-1974 STORMER FACTORY WSM & PARTS LIST
- ARIEL UP TO 1932
- ARIEL 1932-1939 PREWAR MODELS (BOOK OF)
- ARIEL 1933-1951 (WORKSHOP MANUAL)
- ARIEL 1939-1960 4 STROKE SINGLES (BOOK OF)
- ARIEL 1958-1964 LEADER & ARROW FACTORY WSM & PARTS LIST
- ARIEL 1958-1964 LEADER & ARROW (BOOK OF)
- BMW R26 R27 (1956-1967) FACTORY WORKSHOP MANUAL
- BMW R50 R50S R60 R69S (1955-1969) FACTORY WORKSHOP MANUAL
- BMW R50/5 R60/5 R75/5 (1969-1973) FACTORY WORKSHOP MANUAL
- BRIDGESTONE 90 SERIES FACTORY WSM & PARTS CATALOGUE
- BRIDGESTONE 175 SERIES FACTORY WSM & PARTS CATALOGUE
- BRIDGESTONE 350 SERIES FACTORY WSM & PARTS CATALOGUES
- BSA SERVICE SHEETS MASTER CATALOGUE ALL MODELS 1945-1967
- BSA BANTAM D1 TO D7 1948-1966 FACTORY SERVICE SHEETS MANUAL
- BSA BANTAM ALL MODELS FROM 1948 ONWARDS (BOOK OF)
- BSA BANTAM D14 FACTORY SERVICE MANUAL
- BSA DANDY FACTORY WORKSHOP MANUAL (COMPILATION)
- BSA SINGLES & V-TWINS UP TO 1926 inc. 1927 SUPPLEMENT (BOOK OF)
- BSA SINGLES & V-TWINS UP TO 1930 (BOOK OF)
- BSA SINGLES & V-TWINS UP TO 1935 (BOOK OF)
- BSA SINGLES & V-TWINS 1936-1939 (BOOK OF)
- BSA C10, C11 & C12 1945-1958 FACTORY SERVICE SHEETS MANUAL
- BSA OHV & SV SINGLES 250-600cc 1945-1959 (BOOK OF)
- BSA C15 & B40 1958-1967 FACTORY SERVICE SHEETS MANUAL
- BSA OHV & SV SINGLES (ONLY) 1954-1970 (BOOK OF)
- BSA B31, B32, B33 & B34 1945-60 FACTORY SERVICE SHEETS MANUAL
- BSA OHV SINGLES 350 & 500cc 1955-1967 (BOOK OF)
- BSA M20, M21 & M33 1945-1963 FACTORY SERVICE SHEETS MANUAL
- BSA TWINS A7 & A10 1948-1962 FACTORY SERVICE SHEETS MANUAL
- BSA TWINS A7 & A10 1948-1962 (BOOK OF)
- BSA TWINS A50 & A65 1962-1965 FACTORY WORKSHOP MANUAL
- BSA TWINS A50 & A65 1962-1969 (SECOND BOOK OF)
- BULTACO 125cc to 37cc SINGLES 1968-1979 WORKSHOP MANUAL
- CZ 125cc to 380cc SINGLES 1967-1974 WORKSHOP MANUAL
- DOUGLAS 1929-1939 PREWAR ALL MODELS (BOOK OF)
- DOUGLAS 1948-1957 POSTWAR ALL MODELS FACTORY SHOP MANUAL
- DUCATI 160cc, 250cc & 350cc OHC MODELS FACTORY SHOP MANUAL
- HODAKA 90cc,100cc & 125cc SINGLES 1964-1978 WORKSHOP MANUAL
- HONDA 50cc ALL MODELS UP TO 1970 INC MONKEY & TRAIL (BOOK OF)
- HONDA 90cc ALL MODELS UP TO 1966 (BOOK OF)
- HONDA TWINS & SINGLES 50cc THRU 305cc 1960-1966 (BOOK OF)
- HONDA TWINS ALL MODELS 125cc THRU 450cc UP TO 1968 (BOOK OF)
- HONDA C100 50cc SUPER CUB O.H.C. 1959-1962 FACTORY WSM
- HONDA C110 50cc SPORT CUB O.H.C. 1960-1962 FACTORY WSM
- HONDA 50-65-70-90cc O.H.C. SINGLES 1959-1983 WSM
- HONDA 100-125cc SINGLES CB/CD/CL/SL/TL 1970-1984 FACTORY WSM
- HONDA 125-150cc TWINS C/CS/CB/CA 1959-1966 FACTORY WSM
- HONDA 125-160-175-200cc TWINS 1965-1978 WORKSHOP MANUAL
- HONDA 250-305cc TWINS C/CS/CB 1961-1968 FACTORY WSM
- HOHDA 250-350cc TWINS CB/CL/SL 1968-1973 FACTORY WSM
- HONDA 250-360cc TWINS CB/CL/CJ 1974-1977 FACTORY WSM
- HONDA 350F & 400F 4-CYLINDER 1972-1977 FACTORY WSM
- HONDA 450cc TWINS CB/CL 1965-1974 K0 TO K7 WORKSHOP MANUAL
- HONDA 500cc & 550cc 4-CYL 1971-1978 FACTORY WORKSHOP MANUAL
- HONDA 750cc SHOC 4-CYL 1978 K0~K8 WORKSHOP MANUAL
- HUSQVARNA 125cc to 450cc SINGLES 1965-1975 WORKSHOP MANUAL
- INDIAN PONYBIKE, BOY RACER & PAPOOSE ILL PARTS LIST & SALES LIT
- J.A.P. ENGINES 1927-1952 & MOTORCYCLES 1934-1952 (BOOK OF)
- MAICO 250cc to 501cc 1968-1978 WORKSHOP MANUAL
- MATCHLESS 1931-1939 ALL MODELS 250cc THRU 990cc (BOOK OF)
- MATCHLESS 1945-1956 SINGLES G3 & G80 350cc & 500cc (BOOK OF)
- MATCHLESS 1948-1956 TWINS G9 & G11 FACTORY WSM & PARTS
- MATCHLESS 1955-1966 SINGLES G3 & G80 350cc & 500cc (BOOK OF)
- MATCHLESS 1957-1966 SINGLES & TWINS (ALL) FACTORY WSM
- MONTESA 1962-1978 125cc to 360cc ALL MODELS WORKSHOP MANUAL
- NEW IMPERIAL ALL SV & OHV FROM 1935 ONWARDS (BOOK OF)
- NORTON 1932-1939 PREWAR MODELS (BOOK OF)
- NORTON 1932-1947 (BOOK OF)
- NORTON 1938-1956 (BOOK OF)
- NORTON 1945-1963 MODELS 16H, Big4, ES2, 19 & 50 WSM'S & PARTS
- NORTON 1955-1963 MODELS 19, 50 & ES2 (BOOK OF)
- NORTON 1948-1970 DOMINATOR TWINS FACTORY WSM'S & PARTS
- NORTON 1955-1965 DOMINATOR TWINS (BOOK OF)
- NORTON 1960-1970 TWIN CYLINDER FACTORY WORKSHOP MANUAL
- NORTON 1970-1975 COMMANDO 850 & 750cc FACTORY WSM
- NORTON 1975-1978 MK 3 COMMANDO 850 cc FACTORY WSM
- PANTHER 1932-1958 LIGHTWEIGHT MODELS 250 & 350cc (BOOK OF)
- PANTHER 1938-1966 HEAVYWEIGHT MODELS 600 & 650cc (BOOK OF)
- PENTON-KTM-SACHS 1968-1975 100cc & 125cc WORKSHOP MANUAL
- PENTON-KTM 1972-1975 175cc, 250cc & 400cc WSM & PARTS MANUALS
- RALEIGH MOTORCYCLES 1919-1933 (BOOK OF)
- ROYAL ENFIELD 1934-1946 SINGLES & V TWINS (BOOK OF)
- ROYAL ENFIELD 1937-1953 SINGLES & V TWINS (BOOK OF)
- ROYAL ENFIELD 1946-1962 SINGLES (BOOK OF)
- ROYAL ENFIELD 1948-1962 350cc & 500cc PRE-UNIT BULLET WSM
- ROYAL ENFIELD 1948-1963 500cc TWINS FACTORY WORKSHOP MANUAL
- ROYAL ENFIELD 1952-1963 700cc TWINS FACTORY WORKSHOP MANUAL
- ROYAL ENFIELD 1956-1966 250cc CRUSADER & 350cc NEW BULLET WSM
- ROYAL ENFIELD 1958-1966 250cc & 350cc SINGLES (SECOND BOOK OF)
- ROYAL ENFIELD 1962-1970 INTERCEPTOR WSM'S & PARTS (Compilation)
- RUDGE 1933-1939 (BOOK OF)
- SACHS 1968-1975 100cc & 125cc ENGINES WSM & M/CYCLE PARTS LIST
- SUNBEAM 1928-1939 (BOOK OF)
- SUNBEAM 1946-1957 S7 & S8 (BOOK OF)
- SUZUKI 50cc & 80cc UP TO 1966 (BOOK OF)
- SUZUKI T10 1963-1967 FACTORY WORKSHOP MANUAL
- SUZUKI T20 & T200 1965-1969 FACTORY WORKSHOP MANUAL
- SUZUKI TWINS 1962 ONWARDS 125-500cc WORKSHOP MANUAL
- TRIUMPH 1935-1949 SINGLES & TWINS (BOOK OF)
- TRIUMPH 1937-1961 SINGLES SV & OHV 250cc-600cc + TERRIER & CUB
- TRIUMPH 1945-1955 PRE-UNIT 350cc, 500cc & 650cc TWINS WSM No.11
- TRIUMPH 1945-1959 TWINS (BOOK OF)
- TRIUMPH 1956-1969 TWINS (BOOK OF)
- TRIUMPH 1956-1962 PRE-UNIT 500cc & 650cc TWINS WSM No.17
- TRIUMPH 1957-1963 UNIT CONSTRUCTION 350-500cc WSM No.4
- TRIUMPH 1963-1974 UNIT CONSTRUCTION 350-500cc FACTORY WSM
- TRIUMPH 1963-1970 UNIT CONSTRUCTION 650cc FACTORY WSM
- TRIUMPH 1968-1974 TRIDENT T150 & T150V FACTORY WSM
- TRIUMPH 1971-1973 650cc OIL-IN-FRAME FACTORY WSM
- TRIUMPH 1973-1978 750cc BONNEVILLE & TIGER FACTORY WSM
- TRIUMPH 1979-1983 750cc T140, TR7 & TR65 FACTORY WSM
- VELOCETTE 1925-1970 ALL SINGLES & TWINS (BOOK OF)
- VELOCETTE 1933-1952 MOV-MAC-MSS RIGID FRAME FACTORY WSM
- VELOCETTE 1953-1960 MAC SPRING FRAME WSM & ILL PARTS LIST
- VELOCETTE 1954-1971 MSS-VENOM-THRUXTON-VIPER FACTORY WSM
- VILLIERS ENGINE UP TO 1959 INC. 3 WHEELERS (BOOK OF)
- VILLIERS ENGINE UP TO 1969 (BOOK OF)
- VINCENT 1935-1955 (WORKSHOP MANUAL)
- YAMAHA 1961-1967 YA5 & YA6 (WORKSHOP MANUAL & ILL PARTS LIST)
- YAMAHA 1968-1971 DT1 & MX SERIES Inc. GYT WORKSHOP MANUAL
- YAMAHA 1971-1972 JT1 & JT2 (WORKSHOP MANUAL & ILL PARTS LIST)

VELOCEPRESS MANUALS – SCOOTERS BY MAKE

- BSA SUNBEAM SCOOTER WORKSHOP MANUAL 1959-1965
- BSA SUNBEAM SCOOTER 1959-1965 (BOOK OF)
- LAMBRETTA 1947-1957 ALL 125 & 150cc MODELS (BOOK OF)
- LAMBRETTA 1957-1970 LI & TV MODELS (SECOND BOOK OF)
- NSU PRIMA 1956-1964 ALL MODELS (BOOK OF)
- TRIUMPH TIGRESS SCOOTER WORKSHOP MANUAL 1959-1965
- TRIUMPH TIGRESS SCOOTER (BOOK OF)
- VESPA 1951-1961 (BOOK OF)
- VESPA 1955-1963 125 & 150cc & GS MODELS (SECOND BOOK OF)
- VESPA 1955-1968 GS & SS (BOOK OF)
- VESPA 1963-1972 90, 125 & 150cc (THIRD BOOK OF)

VELOCEPRESS MANUALS – MOPEDS & MOTORIZED BICYCLES

- CYCLEMOTOR (BOOK OF)
- NSU QUICKLY 1953-1963 ALL MODELS (BOOK OF)
- PUCH MAXI N & S MAINTENANCE & REPAIR (3 MANUAL COMPILATION)
- RALEIGH MOPEDS 1960-1969 (BOOK OF)

VELOCEPRESS MANUALS - THREE WHEELER'S

- BOND MINICAR THREE WHEELER 1948-1967 (BOOK OF)
- BMW ISETTA FACTORY WORKSHOP MANUAL
- BSA THREE WHEELER (BOOK OF)
- RELIANT REGAL THREE WHEELER 1952-1973 (BOOK OF)
- VINTAGE MORGAN THREE WHEELER (BOOK OF)

VELOCEPRESS TECHNICAL BOOKS – MOTORCYCLE

- 1930'S BRITISH MOTORCYCLE CARBS & ELEC COMPONENTS (BOOK OF)
- 1930'S BRITISH MOTORCYCLE ENGINES (OVERHAUL & MAINTENANCE)
- 1930'S BRITISH MOTORCYCLE GEARBOXES & CLUTCHES (BOOK OF)
- CATALOG OF BRITISH MOTORCYCLES (1951 MODELS)
- LUCAS ELECTRONICS BRITISH M/CYCLES REPAIR & PARTS (1950-1977)
- MOTORCYCLE ENGINEERING (P.E. Irving)
- MOTORCYCLE ROAD TESTS 1949-1953 (Motor Cycle Magazine UK)
- SPEED AND HOW TO OBTAIN IT (Motor Cycle Magazine UK)
- TUNING FOR SPEED (P.E. Irving)
- WIPAC (COMBO) MANUAL NUMBER 3 + M/CYCLE & SCOOTER MANUAL

VELOCEPRESS MANUALS – AUTOMOBILE BY MAKE

ALFA ROMEO GIULIA WORKSHOP MANUAL 1300 TO 2000cc 1962-1975
ALFA ROMEO GIULIA TECH MANUAL CARBURETED CARS FROM 1962
ALFA ROMEO GIULIA TECH MANUAL FUEL INJECTED CARS FROM 1969
ALFA ROMEO GIULIETTA & GIULIA 750 & 101 SERIES 1955-1965 WSM
AUSTIN-HEALEY SPRITE & MG MIDGET WORKSHOP MANUAL 1958-1971
BMW 600 LIMOUSINE FACTORY WORKSHOP MANUAL
BMW 600 LIMOUSINE OWNERS HAND BOOK & SERVICE MANUAL
BMW 2000 & 2002 1966-1976 WORKSHOP MANUAL
BMW 2500, 2800, 3.0 & BARVARIA WORKSHOP MANUAL
CORVAIR 1960-1969 WORKSHOP MANUAL
CORVETTE V8 1955-1962 WORKSHOP MANUAL
FERRARI HANDBOOK ROAD & RACE CARS (SERVICE/SPECS) 1948-1958
FERRARI 250GT SERVICE & MAINTENANCE by JIM RIFF 1956-1965
FERRARI 250GT & 250GTE FACTORY PARTS AND REPAIR MANUALS
FIAT 500 FACTORY WORKSHOP MANUAL 1957-1973
FIAT 600, 600D & MULTIPLA FACTORY WORKSHOP MANUAL 1955-1969
FORD MUSTANG 1965-1973 TRANSMISSION WORKSHOP MANUAL
JAGUAR E-TYPE 3.8 & 4.2 SERIES 1 & 2 WORKSHOP MANUAL
JAGUAR MK 7, 8, 9 & XK120, 140, 150 WORKSHOP MANUAL 1948-1961
MERCEDES-BENZ 230 SERIES 1963-1968
MERCEDES-BENZ 280 SERIES 1968-1972
METROPOLITAN FACTORY WORKSHOP MANUAL
MGA & MGB OWNERS HANDBOOK & WORKSHOP MANUAL
MG MIDGET TC, TD, TF & TF1500 WORKSHOP MANUAL
PORSCHE 356 1948-1965 WORKSHOP MANUAL
PORSCHE 911 2.0, 2.2, 2.4 LITRE 1964-1973 WORKSHOP MANUAL
PORSCHE 911 2.7, 3.0, 3.2 LITRE 1973-1989 WORKSHOP MANUAL
PORSCHE 912 WORKSHOP MANUAL
PORSCHE 914/4 & 914/6 1.7, 1.8, 2.0 LITRE 1970-1976 WSM
TRIUMPH TR2, TR3, TR4 1953-1965 WORKSHOP MANUAL
VOLKSWAGEN TRANSPORTER, TRUCKS & WAGONS 1950-1979 WSM
VOLVO 1944-1968 ALL MODELS WORKSHOP MANUAL

VELOCEPRESS TECHNICAL BOOKS - AUTOMOBILE

HOW TO BUILD A FIBERGLASS CAR
HOW TO BUILD A RACING CAR
HOW TO RESTORE THE MODEL 'A' FORD
MASERATI OWNER'S HANDBOOK
PERFORMANCE TUNING THE SUNBEAM TIGER
SOUPING THE VOLKSWAGEN
SOLEX CARBURETORS (EMPHASIS ON UK & EU AUTOMOBILES)
SU CARBURETORS (EMPHASIS ON UK AUTOMOBILES)
WEBER CARBURETORS (EMPHASIS ON ALFA & FIAT)

VELOCEPRESS BOOKS & GUIDES - AUTOMOBILE

COMPLETE CATALOG OF JAPANESE MOTOR VEHICLES
FERRARI 308 SERIES BUYER'S AND OWNER'S GUIDE
FERRARI BROCHURES AND SALES LITERATURE 1968-1989
FERRARI SERIAL NUMBERS PART I - ODD NUMBERS TO 21399
FERRARI SERIAL NUMBERS PART II - EVEN NUMBERS TO 1050
HENRY'S FABULOUS MODEL "A" FORD
MASERATI BROCHURES AND SALES LITERATURE

VELOCEPRESS BOOKS – AUTO RACING

BOOK OF THE 1950 CARRERA PANAMERICANA - MEXICAN ROAD RACE
DIALED IN - THE JAN OPPERMAN STORY
VEDA ORR'S NEW REVISED HOT ROD PICTORIAL
LIFE OF TED HORN – AMERICAN RACING CHAMPION

www.VelocePress.com